2022 | Volume 6

U.P. READER

Bringing Upper Michigan Literature to the World

A publication of the
Upper Peninsula Publishers and Authors Association (UPPAA)
Marquette, Michigan

UPPAA

U.P. Reader
Volume 1 is still available!

Michigan's Upper Peninsula is blessed with a treasure chest of writers and poets, all seeking to capture the diverse experiences of Yooper Life. Now U.P. Reader offers a rich collection of their voices that embraces the U.P.'s natural beauty and way of life, along with a few surprises.

The twenty-eight works in this first annual volume take readers on a U.P. Road Trip from the Mackinac Bridge to Menominee. Every page is rich with descriptions of the characters and culture that make the Upper Peninsula worth living in and writing about.

Available in paperback, hardcover, and eBook editions!

ISBN 978-1-61599-336-9

www.UPReader.org

U.P. Reader: Bringing Upper Michigan Literature to the World — Volume #6
Copyright © 2022 by Upper Peninsula Publishers and Authors Association (UPPAA). All Rights Reserved.

Cover Photo: by Mikel B. Classen.

Learn more about the UPPAA at www.UPPAA.org

Latest news on *UP Reader* can be found at www.UPReader.org

ISSN: 2572-0961

ISBN 978-1-61599-660-5 paperback
ISBN 978-1-61599-661-2 hardcover
ISBN 978-1-61599-662-9 eBook (PDF, Kindle, ePub)

Edited by- Deborah K. Frontiera and Mikel B. Classen
Production - Victor Volkman
Cover Photo - Mikel B. Classen
Interior Layout - Michal Splho

Distributed by Ingram (USA/CAN/AU), Bertram's Books (UK/EU)

Published by
Modern History Press
5145 Pontiac Trail
Ann Arbor, MI 48105

www.ModernHistoryPress.com
info@ModernHistoryPress.com

CONTENTS

About the Cover
Grand Sable Falls

by Mikel Classen

Grand Sable Falls, as featured on the cover of the book you are holding, is located on the eastern end of Pictured Rocks National Lakeshore. Though it is not the largest waterfall in the park, its beauty makes it one of the park's premier sights. The falls are located a mile west of Grand Marais off County Highway H-58, a well marked parking lot is the trail head. The walk to the falls is short and not difficult. The 168 steps to the bottom provide different views of the falls on the way down and from here can be seen this 75-foot cascade in its entirety. The stream is surrounded by hardwoods of maple and aspen adding to the falls' ever-changing look with the seasons. This is an incredible autumn destination. Look closely during the summer as Trillium and Lady Slippers can be spotted in the forest.

This has always been a special place and marks the beginning of the massive Grand Sable Sand dunes. A small walk from the bottom of the falls to the beach, just a few yards, awaits one of the most spectacular views on all of Lake Superior. Standing there looking up at the immense sand dunes that stretch in an arc to Au Sable Point 15 miles away, is a moment worth walking to. As a suggestion, walk the shore back to Grand Marais from here. It's a great alternative to the stair climb.

The eastern end of Pictured Rocks gets much less traffic than the west end at Mu-nising. Grand Sable Falls is one of the over-looked attractions at the National Park. Missing this is a big mistake. This is a must-see for any trip into Grand Marais.

Special Note: This attraction is located within the National Park. It was announced that the National Park Service (NPS) would be instituting fees or requiring passes for park visitors beginning this year. At this moment it is unclear what that will be and how this will affect visitors to Sable Falls. I advise stopping into the NPS visitor's center first to learn what the requirements are if any. Access has always been free and open before.

Mikel B. Classen has been writing and photographing northern Michigan in newspapers and magazines for over thirty-five years, creating feature articles about the life and culture of Michigan's north country. He is the founder of the *U.P. Reader* and is a member of the Board of Directors for the UP-PAA. In 2020, Mikel won the Historical Society of Michigan's, George Follo Award for Upper Peninsula History. His book *Points North: Discover Hidden Campgrounds, Natural Wonders, and Waterways of the Upper Peninsula* achieved the HSM's highest honor, The State History Award. Learn more at MikelBClassen.com

Problems We Can Solve

by Donna Winters

I usually refrain from expressing my opinion publicly because it generates pushback from those eager to point out the errors in my thinking. Nevertheless, I'm going to propose changes here that I see as beneficial. You may disagree, but if you do, *please don't tell me about it*. Write your own position paper and put it out there for all of us to consider. On the other hand, if you agree, I'd be glad to hear from you!

Missing Persons and Privacy Issues

Have you ever watched a news report of an elderly person with dementia who has walked out of a care facility and is now lost? It's a heart-wrenching problem. And what about a toddler who has wandered off? Or worse yet, been kidnapped? It seems only reasonable that toddlers and those with dementia should be fitted out with GPS trackers. The technology is available, and depending on the type of device, it's quite affordable, with prices as low as $26.95. So why do we leave the most vulnerable members of our society unchipped? Wouldn't chipping be more expedient and economical than sending out a search party?

"What about privacy issues?" you may ask. If your toddler or grandparent is chipped, they lose control over their privacy. Americans are ultra-sensitive to privacy issues thanks to social media data exploiters. Okay, I get it. Really, I do, and I closed my social media accounts with the most irresponsibly run corporations on the planet. Which makes me wonder: If you're concerned about privacy issues, have *you* closed your social media accounts? Missing persons is a problem we can solve. Data exploitation is a problem we can solve. But do we want to?

Football Injuries and Deaths

For some time now, I have been saying that football ought to be outlawed. It's simply the contemporary version of ancient gladiators entertaining stadiums full of eager witnesses to brutal battles. In my opinion, it's uncivilized, disgusting, and phenomenally costly in blood and treasure. But for almost fifty years now, football has been the most popular sport in the US, and with the National Football League raking in $15 billion in annual revenue, it's not going away anytime soon.

Concern over the dangers of football goes back to at least 1905. That year, Teddy Roosevelt held a White House discussion on how to reduce brutality in play. Athletic advisors from Harvard, Yale, and Princeton participated. At least forty-five football players had died from 1900-1905. The cause? Unnecessary roughness. Victims had often been kicked in the head or stomach, causing brain or internal injuries that eventually resulted in death.

More recently, studies have been done on chronic traumatic encephalopathy (CTE), a progressive brain condition that's thought to be caused by repeated blows to the head and repeated episodes of concussion. Through autopsies of 111 brains belonging to players in the National Football League, 110 of them showed CTE—more than 99 percent. An individual with CTE could suffer from a number of symptoms including: memory loss, confusion, impaired judgment, impulse control problems, aggression, depression, anxiety, suicidal ideation, Parkinsonism, and, eventually, progressive dementia.

In September 2021, new position-specific helmets were introduced in the NFL for offensive and defensive linemen. While I'm all in favor of extra padding for the brains of professional football players, I'm more in favor of them walking off the field and preserving their brainpower, or what's left of it, for their retirement years. If enough did that, maybe we could move closer to eliminating the game altogether. Having said all that, does football show up on our TV? Absolutely.

Holidays that Hurt

This is such a touchy subject I almost didn't write about it. But I'm going to go ahead and let you grapple with the concepts I put forward.

Each year on Columbus Day and Thanksgiving Day, a large portion of our population celebrates while a smaller portion goes into mourning. When I first learned about the portion who were suffering, I thought, "What do you mean? This isn't a celebration of the bad things that happened to indigenous peoples; it's a time to go to a Columbus Day sale or gather with the family for some turkey."

As the curators of the Smithsonian's National Museum of the American Indian in Washington, DC have said, "The past never changes, but the way we understand it, learn about it, and know about it changes all the time." For me, change began with knowledge of my ancestry and discovering that, like 35 million others on the planet, I'm a descendant of *Mayflower* passengers. With the recent 400th anniversary of the *Mayflower* landing, a plethora of books about that event were released. I read several of them and learned that the decades following 1620 tell of a horrifying past regarding the indigenous tribes of New England.

At this writing, we have just celebrated/mourned Columbus Day/Indigenous Peoples' Day. Several states (10-14 depending on the source) have made Indigenous Peoples' Day an official holiday. About an equal number of other states celebrate it by proclamation, and more than 100 cities celebrate it. For the first time ever, a US President has declared Columbus Day, which started in 1934, to be Indigenous Peoples' Day. Some groups argue that Columbus Day celebrates Italian American heritage, but their counterparts claim it celebrates genocide, trauma, and colonization. Is it possible to reframe Columbus Day as Indigenous Peoples' Day everywhere in America? I believe so. Its time has come.

Similar controversies have arisen over Thanksgiving Day. While many gather for a family feast of turkey and all its delicious accompaniments, others mark the day with a very different tradition. Since 1970 (the 350th anniversary of the Pilgrim landing), protesters have been gathering on top of Cole's Hill, which overlooks Plymouth Rock, to commemorate a "National Day of Mourning." Comparable events are held in other parts of the country. But would it really be possible to rename and reframe a holiday with roots going back 400 years—a celebration that was officially proclaimed by President Lincoln in 1863 and was signed into law by President Roosevelt in 1941? If we really *could* rename and reframe, what would we call such a day? The National Day of Mourning (currently held in Plymouth, Massachusetts), Unthanksgiving Day (celebrated on Alcatraz Island in San Francisco Bay), National Day of Listening (scheduled for two days after Thanksgiving 2021), Native American Heritage Day (scheduled for the day after Thanksgiving 2021), Restorative Justice Day (since 1996, International Restorative Justice Week has been celebrated for eight days starting on the third Sunday in November), American Family Day (currently celebrated early in August)?

Creating a paradigm shift around Thanksgiving might take a very long time, but it could happen. And, coupled with the changes afoot for Columbus Day, we could eradicate two holidays that hurt from our American calendars. This is a problem we can solve.

Donna Winters has been a published writer since 1985 and is the author of the *Great Lakes Romances*® series. She has over twenty titles in print and has been published by Thomas Nelson Publishers, Zondervan Publishing House, Guideposts, Chalfont House, and Bigwater Publishing LLC. Learn more about her and her books at *amazon.com/author/donnawinters*.

Rain Falls from The Sky as the Stars Bleed Away Their Dreams

by Cheyenne Welsh

Day by day, sunrise to sunset, I'm pushed under the waves of my own subconscious. Emerged within the sea, the bitter cold bites away at all the remaining feelings I have left. My legs become heavy like the anchors attached to a ship, pulling me farther down. At first, I am afraid of the pain drowning would bring, but as I sink farther down, the coldness wears away and everything becomes numb.

With my eyes forced open, water distorting my vision, I watch the sea of life swim by. Everything begins to speed up as my heart slows down. The water that burns my lungs is an acquired taste I long since learn to enjoy.

The loneliness of drowning underneath the waves while the souls around me move on begins to feel like home. A place once feared has become my shelter. And reality has become the starving hunter that stalks me at every turn. It seeks vengeance for my refusal to come back to the surface of the living. It will bait me with shallow promises spit from the mouth of a false god.

But I know what will happen when I emerge from the water: my dreams will fade away as my soul and body are sold off to be just another piece of meat in the market. I'm not anything special. There is no hero coming to save me. I'm on my own, forced to confront every hunter that seeks to hurt me. Forced to relive this cycle until my heart gives out.

So why should I emerge? Why come back to the surface when all that's waiting for me is the cold bite of reality ready to drain me of my dreams. I'd rather drown in the sea of my subconscious, drifting away until reality is something of a dream itself. Until all I know is this other world.

I'd forget everything I've ever known so that I may dream forever. Once I'm ready to stop fighting the inevitable, it will all fade away into a blissful nothing. My brain will devour the last drops of chemicals that fire off, taking me far away to another world, a better world.

I just need to take that first step into the water. The rest will fall into place.

Cheyenne Welsh just recently joined UPPAA when she submitted "Rain Falls From The Sky as the Stars Bleed Away Their Dreams." She hopes to eventually complete and publish a collection of poetry. Cheyenne is a member of the Keweenaw Bay Indian Community and has lived on the reservation in the Upper Peninsula her whole life.

Escanaba · out for a sunday drive

The Freshman

by Victor R. Volkman

September 3rd, 1982, I arrived as a newly minted freshman at Michigan Technological University in Houghton at the tender age of 18 years, 3 months, and 2 days. My love affair with the U.P. began about four years earlier, when I had attended a week-long summer camp at MTU for teenagers, known as the Summer Youth Program (SYP). It was the same year I had learned the barest basics of computer programming in the eighth grade. Although we lived in the suburbs of Detroit, our family was staying with friends in northern Michigan, so it was only another five hours from thereabouts to Houghton. I remember the campus was nearly deserted except for us teenagers and the instructors, often high school teachers from the local area supplementing their summer income.

We were all in the smallest, coziest of dorms, Douglas Houghton Hall, built in 1939 with the traditional communal bathrooms and a dining hall furnished in ancient hardwood. I immersed myself in learning FORTRAN and writing programs on the IBM keypunches in the basement of the Electrical Engineering Resource Center (EERC), a building where I would years later spend many hours in pursuit of a degree in Computer Science. It was the time of my life, freedom to learn and a small modicum of independence. It was heady stuff. The next twelve months, I started a very small paper route with the goal of earning enough to cover next year's week of SYP for tuition, room, and board which I think was in the neighborhood of $250.

The second summer, a week in July 1979, was just as glorious as I got to learn the basics of "machine language", this time on microcomputers the size of an adding machine, instead of the school's massive mainframe. I had no trouble hanging out with the other kids and even made a friend for a week. I remember the R.A. chiding me for spending too much time reading textbooks in my room. Anyway, my fate was sealed by then. I would attend MTU and earn my degree in Computer Science. Everything I did for the next four years was in service of that goal.

Being a kid from a working-class family in a rich person's suburb, it was always clear in high school who had money and who didn't. Those who didn't seemed to have no chance whatsoever with winning a girlfriend, so I can say without reservation that I never even tried to strike up a conversation. I liked my crushes to be silent and, therefore, immune from rejection. I moved through the school with nary a ripple, as the lack of photos in yearbooks will attest.

I only applied to one school—MTU, despite a flurry of letters from other institutions in the Midwest after my PSAT, SAT, and ACT were all said and done. In those days, there was neither online application nor any kind of master application that could be transmitted to dozens of institutions with a single mouse-click. Mice were still years away, much less an Internet. Also, I don't remember ever having a conversation with my parents about what schools they could afford —we never ever talked about money, period. So, I figured a state school was the way to go anyway, the Ivy League was incomprehensible to me and then there was the money thing. So that nine-or-ten-page application was sent along with transcripts and then the eventual acceptance letter came.

Back to September 1982... my first week at college was a whirlwind of activity, immersed in people but in fact overwhelmed by a sense of loneliness I had not even known I could experience. I had great hopes for a college roommate experience, my only real experience being TV shows I had seen where the old roommate was always the crazy best-friend. Although I was back in DHH, my dorm of four years prior, this was nothing like that. Instead, I was "over-assigned"—poor planning by university housing had a hundred of us bunked three to an eleven-foot square room clearly designed for two people. In that tiny space, you couldn't really get more than six feet away from anyone. Worse, it was already occupied by two other kids who had gone to the same high school in another rich suburb, not exactly friends, but they had the easy acquaintance of a shared four-years prior experience.

I was the interloper, simply waiting for another room to open, somewhere, naively assuming that such a thing would magically happen in a few days or perhaps a month. As such, I was mostly the punchline, the butt of jokes, the sexually inexperienced goof who could not even participate in their endless lurid conversations about the practical applications of cunnilingus. Our room was carpeted in lush purple shag Brian H. had brought with him. He and Pete K. conspired to purchase the loft that the prior tenants of room 210 had sold us. A rickety collection of 2 x 4s, bolts, and a homemade ladder that pinned us a mere eight inches from the ceiling, making turning over in bed a chore and not to be taken lightly. They would begin studying around 11pm, just as I was ready to turn in for the night.

It's hard to understate the social isolation of moving 600 miles in an era before a hundred kinds of communication were possible. It would take all day to list what we didn't have: email, cellphones, Internet, WhatsApp, instant messaging, Zoom, Skype, Instagram, FaceBook, TikTok, LinkedIn, chat rooms and on and on. Sending email was still five-plus years away. Long distance charges were horrendous back then, on the order of $20/hour before late night discounts. But I had no one to really talk to. By a weird quirk of fate, all my former friends had been a year or two younger by virtue of the one club I had joined in high school. I knew that to even try to explain my reality would be so far off as to be incomprehensible to them.

People were quick to make their alliances in the dorm, literally within days of moving in. I knew I had to escape the confines of my three-man hell. Luckily, there was a next-door neighbor, Tim Brown, who was easy-going, a natural socializer, and OK with an introverted friend who didn't speak up much. Tim Brown had befriended Amy Brown (no relation), an ebullient and cherubic Yooper from Newberry. I fell for her hard, but didn't want to have my hopes crushed so I never made a definitive move in her direction. The three of us could then sit together at the cafeteria, goof around, and hunt down frat parties without having to worry about romantic encumbrances. Alcohol was the drug of choice in the 1980s, more on that later. They took me shopping to St. Vinnies to get my first set of flannel shirts, a form of attire I had never really considered.

Romantic attachments were never in the cards for me at MTU; I would have better luck at the roulette table putting all my money on double-ought. I had not done my research (nor was there a way to do it) and discovered there were five guys for every girl on campus. They were not lacking for attention in any way, and I had no game. There was worse news: in my major, the representation was far worse. A typical Computer Science class had perhaps three women out of 100 students. In those days, there was no cachet in being the nerd. No one had heard of Bill Gates nor Steve Jobs. True to my nature, I developed a crush on my best friend's girl and of course nothing came of it.

Back to September 1982... there were just a couple days of orientation, and then finally the "first day of class". I guess I was expecting something more like the 1973 film *The Paper Chase* with Sir John Gielgud bemoaning how our "heads were full of mush". Instead, my first ever lecture was by an oldster named Jack who spoke from the stage using plastic slides and an overhead projector for Econ 101. I was underwhelmed. The opposite experience was my Calculus One class taught by a fledgling mechanical engineering grad student named Glenn. It was his first time teaching calculus and our first time learning it. We were ill-suited for each other and his tests bore little resemblance to the curriculum. In fact, I turned in an "F" grade quality test for my first exam. I was mortified—*could my college career really have ended just four weeks into my first semester?* I knew from my degree plan that I must complete four successive calculus classes. It was a heart-stopping moment... Luckily, Glen was mortified too, since the average test score for the class was well below 50%. He stood with the exams poised above the trash can now hoisted to his desk. He merely said, "Any objections?" and you could hear a pin drop as he summarily shitcanned our exams. Another more reasonable exam landed me with a B, I think.

Friday and Saturday nights were always the same, going out in search of a frat within walking distance that had all the beer you could drink for $5. In theory, the goal was to socialize but I drank quickly to numb my loneliness and the music was so loud you couldn't pretend to have a conversation anyway. I had my first blackout within a semester, which scared me enough to cut back to some reasonable level of inebriation. I did manage to graduate without a minor in alcoholism, although in retrospect, it now seems miraculous and was probably aided by the 21-and-over drinking laws at the time which slowed me down a bit.

I made my first real *faux pas* just a few days into the semester. It was K-Day (for Keweenaw Day), when the college would call off classes for a half-day on a randomly chosen day of the second week of school. It was based on the day they thought would have the best weather and festivities were held at McLain State Park on Lake Superior a few

miles out of town. I can't remember but I think there might have been busses back and forth as I was not to own a car until four years later. I was with my tiny little group plus one of Amy's friends. The girls went up to get their beer cups filled at a frat campsite, they were more than welcome to do so but after I stepped up, my glass was grabbed and dumped into the grass. No words were spoken but it was clear that furious fists were coming my way if I didn't clear off in a few seconds. So much for K-Day; I couldn't wait to get back to campus.

The first semester's classes were fully planned out for freshmen except for a single elective P.E. class we could choose from. *What could possibly go wrong?* Well, I had chosen Orienteering because I thought I liked the outdoors, and it would mean some fresh air while wandering the forests outside campus. I soon learned how useless a map was without knowing where you were and how unhelpful a compass was again without any idea where you were. Ostensibly, it was a two-hour class that I expect most students finished in 90 minutes or less. I would always wander back after about three hours, wet and near hypothermia. At one point, I had crossed a river in my blue jeans and sneakers up to my armpits. That was a typical Thursday afternoon for a whole semester. It earned me the nickname "Ranger Vic" for my total outdoor ineptitude.

Travel to and from Michigan Tech was always a leap of faith for anyone who didn't own a vehicle—and I certainly did not have the money to keep a car I would only drive a couple times a year. Again, for lack of technology, the "Ride Board" ruled the day. This was a big corkboard in the Student Union that was a matchmaking service for drivers and riders. Looking back, frankly I'm surprised at how often I got a ride lined up with a single phone call. The local radio station also read them out over-the-air daily. In five years, I was never stranded nor stood up. Typically, it would be 5 guys in a mid-size car for the 10 hour run to Detroit. Only a single stop was allowed by protocol—gas, food, and bladder break in Gaylord, Michigan—the logical halfway point. Sometimes I managed a ride all the way home, but more often my parents would have to drive at least 45 minutes to some pickup location. Oddly, I never bothered to keep the same driver and no drivers ever came looking for me on later trips. Us passengers tried to sleep as much as possible and smalltalk was simply not done. The driver would usually have a cartridge of a dozen cassette pop music tapes and there was no point in picking one tape over another—by the end of trip we would listen to all of them end-to-end. *When was the last time you listened to a whole album in one sitting?* The one time I was allowed to take a driving shift, I landed the car in a snowbank at 3am about 40 miles out of St. Ignace. By a miracle, a guy with a truck and winch showed up and hauled us out of the snow with hardly a word. I emptied out the contents of my wallet—about $15—handed it to him, and apologized that I couldn't do better. I will never forget his kindness or that night.

Only a couple things kept my freshman year from becoming an unmitigated disaster. First was the exodus of the third roommate, Pete, to a frat house. He had become intolerably snobby after rushing the frat and Brian and I quickly grew to despise him. When we were down to two, Brian and I had no trouble getting along, we were both easygoing and his girlfriend Julie kept him busy enough, so we weren't jammed together.

The other piece of my salvation was a grand startup idea called "Michigan Tech Software" that would use legions of student programmers to compete in the commercial market. As we were a spinoff, with no legal ties, apparently, we weren't bound by any type of non-profit corporation rules. Tim Nelson, the president, landed a huge contract for online self-teaching software to be delivered on brand new color graphics terminals from DEC called GiGis. It was a crackpot idea, but it employed more than two dozen of us computer science students of all classes from freshman to senior over the summer semester.

Summer in the Copper Country was as glorious as I had remembered from living there at age 15. I managed to score half-price off-campus housing at the closest available frat house and thus came my introduction to hashish and other wonder drugs. It was huge Victorian monster of a house that probably held 30 people during the school year but there were only six of us for the summer. We had beer bashes on the roof facing US-41 almost every evening it seemed like. Like that famous Beatles concert at Apple Studio, we setup the speakers on the roof and brought down the police at once. Our most audacious act I suppose was shelling the bank across the highway with bottlerockets launched from the aptly named "turret room". One of the guys was an Army ROTC rappelling instructor and he took us out one Saturday for a rappel down Douglas Houghton Falls. To this day, I cannot believe that I suspended myself 50 feet above rocks, but I did so wearing only sweats and an improved rope harness.

We had several other misadventures that summer. We were rounded up by a local farmer to help him bring in his hay harvest, which was three hours of backbreaking work. We didn't actually negotiate for wages in advance so we were "paid" with a home-cooked meal. None of us ever spoke of that Friday evening again. The scariest event was when we took Jim's Edsel over to the public beach in Hancock for some harmless summer fun. Little did we know that his parking brake was dead and the car lurched down toward the beach within minutes of our arrival. A woman was struck by the car but I think she did not get a serious injury. Even so, the townies were massing with pitchforks and torches and were about to teach us stupid tech toots a lesson. We sensed the vibe and managed to escape without a *Deliverance* re-enactment.

The MTU Software crew became my true people and I enjoyed being able to work and earn money for college year-round. I'm still in contact with a couple of them and roomed with some of them in subsequent years off-campus. If I had a couple hours between classes, then I'd do some programming at the Hamar House, an old home landlocked in the middle of campus between DHH and Fisher Hall, so it was never more than a three-minute walk from where my classes were. Without that job and those people, I'm sure I wouldn't have made it the four years. It took me a whole year to "orient" myself (Orienteering not withstanding) but by September 1983, I felt like I belonged, and I could do it, no matter what. We did some cool projects over the years, including a revolutionary standalone interactive kiosk for Uniroyal tire selection that included a LaserDisc player. It was heady stuff for 1985 technology. We were always after the "next big thing" and somehow it was always out of reach.

Taking it a bit slower than other students, due to my never-ending struggle with the capstone Differential Equations class, I graduated with a small class in November 1986, just six months behind schedule. My mom and dad came up for the first and only trip together that they would make in twenty years. They were barely on speaking terms for as long as I could remember, so it boggles my mind that they endured a 20 hour roundtrip to see me. My father passed away a mere 10 years later.

I had already secured a place in the grad school to go on for my Master's in Computer Science. Everything was in the cards for that, except for the fact that MTU Software was to go broke in February of 1987 and took my job with it. I couldn't see myself teaching undergraduate classes; I was much too shy for that and had never had a conversation with an adviser in person. The final nail in my U.P. experience was the return of a medical issue I had just before my freshman year. I sought out a local G.P. finally and he had no idea what I should do about it, so I resigned after one semester complete of grad school, moved back to Detroit, got properly treated, took up a fulltime software development job and that was the end of my U.P. experience.

Victor R. Volkman is a graduate of Michigan Technological University (class of '86) and is the current president of the Upper Michigan Publishers and Authors Association (UPPAA). He is senior editor at Modern History Press, publisher of the *UP Reader*. He knows in his heart that he can never be a yooper because real yoopers are born—not made.

Historical · Mackinac Island man & woman top hat · circa 1880

Up In Michigan

by Edd Tury

"Every man's life ends the same way. It is only the details of how he lived
and how he died that distinguish one man from another."
—Ernest Hemingway

When my grandfather put a bullet in his head it stayed there. Not like Hemingway, who Grandpa greatly admired. No big mess for some poor soul to clean up. Cranial vault intact, but just as dead. He always liked precision. Grandpa, not Hemingway. Well, Hemingway too, at least in his prose. So, when Grandpa decided it was time to check out, he simply put his special cartridge in his deer rifle, sucked the barrel, and pushed the trigger. Clean and dead.

Grandpa sometimes talked about a special cartridge, but I never knew what he meant. Whenever I asked, he'd just say—you know, like I load for deer. A special round for a special job—and I'd say what job and he'd say—you'll find out one day. It's not important now. Remember what I told you about the right tool for the job? A bullet is just a tool. You wouldn't shoot a deer with an elephant gun, now, would you? And I'd just scratch my head and say the deer would sure be dead and Grandpa would say—yeah, but you'd ruin half the meat.

•••

Ever since I was a kid, I had been fascinated by the things my grandpa did and the way he did them. Early on, I knew Grandpa loved deer hunting, deer camp, guns, and some writer named Ernest Hemingway. When I got older, and actually read some Hemingway, I wasn't too impressed; Grandpa and I had some heated discussions about what was good writing and what wasn't.

Grandpa asked, "What was your English teacher's name?"

"What teacher?"

"The one that read the first line of some Hemingway story and made fun of it, telling you what a bunch of dull, macho crap it was." He had me there. It was my eleventh-grade Advanced Lit teacher.

"Mr. Hall. How'd you know?"

"I just know. I had a high school English teacher who called Carl Sandburg *Carl Sandhog* and made fun of every one of his famous poems. He'd read 'the fog comes on little cat feet' in the most smarmy voice and the whole class would laugh. As if we knew what we were laughing at. I hated Sandburg for years until I decided to reread him. For a laugh you know. I found I liked a lot of it. Had I gotten stupider? Or maybe just a little more open minded, a little more willing to trust my instincts and not care what someone else thinks."

So, of course, I went back and reread Hemingway, trying hard to keep an open mind. Except now I had my grandfather's bias to contend with. I guess my old prejudices and the new influence sort of canceled because I found myself reading the stories with the feeling that I was reading them for the first time. I liked much of it; some I loved; some I thought missed the mark. All seemed extremely well crafted and the short, declarative sentences, so maligned by my eleventh-grade teacher, revealed their clarity to my newly unblinded eyes. Grandpa never even said 'I told you so' when we had our first Hemingway discussion after my rereads. He was cool.

I remember one of the first discussions we had was about "The Short Happy Life of Francis McComber." I think it was Grandpa's favorite Hemingway short story, though he never said it. I told him that it was a good story, but I found it a little depressing.

"Depressing?" he asked. "Why is that?"

"Well," I said, "Here's this spineless wimp finally finds his balls and his wife offs him."

"Well, that's true but ol' Frankie doesn't get depressed about it—he's dead. His last moments were his happiest ever. Besides, life's like that. Few happy endings. A good story leaves you thinking. That's what I think."

I knew he was right. I didn't care for stories that were too 'easy', too ready to make you forget them once you were done with them. We discussed a lot of Hemingway's work, but not to the exclusion of other writers. We had lively discussions about Steinbeck's humor and Faulkner's density. Most often we agreed, but not always. I've never known anyone who enjoyed arguing more than Grandpa. He didn't consider them arguments. Debates, he called them. And they were oftentimes heated, with raised voices and table thumping. Occasionally, Mom or Dad would come down to the basement where these debates took place, to make sure everything was all right. It always was—our faces were just redder than usual.

•••

The best times, though, were at deer camp. Grandpa loved to hunt and loved to camp. He always seemed younger there. Even later, when the fire in his debates grew smaller and his voice slowed, he would seem to step back in time a decade or so when the tent was pitched, the fire started, and all that was left to do was to shoot the bull and wait for opening day.

I started hunting when I was fourteen and Grandpa was sixty. For the first ten years we hunted together, I never thought of him as old. He moved through the woods with grace and pleasure—fast if need be; slow as a stalking cat if the situation called for that. He taught me all I know about hunting whitetails. For the most part it was by observation—but if I screwed up, he'd tell me about it that night. In front of the wood stove, when dinner was over and the dishes cleaned up, it would be, "Jesus Christ, what the hell were you thinking out there today? Just because you're bored you don't get up and stroll around. I know I pushed a buck past your blind. But were you in your blind? No, you were screwing around at the swamp edge." My dad would just laugh. He'd been through it all before.

The lessons happened early in my hunting career. I learned fast. Partly because I didn't like Grandpa yelling at me and partly because I really enjoyed deer hunting and studied it. My dad enjoyed it; the hunt and the camp, but it never became a passion for him. It did for me, just as it was for Grandpa. We had twenty good years.

•••

Up until Grandpa was seventy-five years old, he held the camp record for the biggest buck our camp had ever taken. That year I shot a bigger one and Grandpa couldn't stop grinning. It was a huge deer, both body and antlers and, to tell the truth, I really did outsmart the son of a gun.

I had to tell the story a dozen times that night around the wood stove. Dad was happy for me because he understood what it meant. Grandpa rocked back and forth on his camp chair sipping scotch and, when he wasn't asking questions, grinning from ear to ear.

"Fell in his tracks?", he asked.

"Yes sir," I said. "Hit him in the shoulder where you showed me."

"Didn't move?"

"His leg twitched, but that was it," I answered. "Those handloads are the right tool."

Grandpa rocked and grinned some more. Later, when Grandpa crawled into his sleeping bag, he said he was going to sleep in and not to wake him in the morning. In sixteen years, this was the first time he ever did this.

Well, no one in camp got up the next morning; too much celebrating. It was okay, we had a great buck on the buck pole. I think we had breakfast around noon.

We were poking around camp, cleaning up and having a little hair of the dog, when Grandpa asked me if I ever read Baker's biography of Hemingway. I said I had, and he asked if I read all the notes in the back of the book. I said no.

"Well, when old Ernie decided it was time to go, he loaded a shotgun, a twelve-gauge double barrel, stood in the porch of his home, put the barrels in his mouth, and pushed down the triggers. Now, that's a sure way to go and I doubt he suffered much, although he was suffering plenty beforehand. Enough to make it not worth the trouble to go on. Anyway, it explains in Baker's footnotes that he blew out his rear cranial vault which is just fancy talk for splattering your brains all over the wall, taking the back half of your head with it. Pretty disgusting picture don't you think?"

Well, no kidding. I knew he had killed himself that way, but Grandpa made it too vivid, and the image stayed with me awhile. I did think of the people who had to clean up the mess.

"If someone's going to do themselves in, they should have a little respect for those left behind. It doesn't have to be messy. Even if a bullet to the brain is the method of choice."

I let that stand.

•••

After Grandpa turned seventy-six, he seemed to deteriorate. No, deteriorate isn't the right word. Slow down doesn't cut it either. He just flat out got old in a hurry. It was hard to watch, and I tried to deny it, but it was there. Deer camp was still fun, though Grandpa didn't go in the woods near as much. Our 'debates' were still lively but lacked a lot of the table thumping I used to look forward to. Dad helped. When we discussed Grandpa and his 'slowing down' he reminded me that it's a natural thing. No

one gets out alive. Just hope he's happy to the end and doesn't suffer. I was depressed for a week.

Grandpa turned eighty in the spring and buried Grandma. Sixty years of marriage gone in a failed heartbeat. Grandpa started trembling that summer, fingers shaking and hands unsure. It was sad to see.

Grandpa called me down to the basement late that summer and said he needed help. Of course, I was going to do anything I could. He said it was time to test his newest tool, his special load. I said, okay, and how could I help? He said go get five honeydew melons. Huh? Just do it, he said, and I did.

As I drove to the market, it hit me what was going on. The feeling in my gut was almost too much to bear. I pulled over thinking I was going to throw up. That sweaty, clammy feeling lasted a long time before I realized there was nothing I could do but help. What was going to happen was going to happen whether I was there or not. I cried all the way to Grandpa's.

"Do you know what's going on?"

"Yes, sir."

"What do you think?"

"I think you're one tough son-of-a-bitch, like Hemingway. I love you and wish you wouldn't do this. You want to turn me into Kevorkian but I don't want to. Can't you just let things happen?"

My tears wouldn't stop.

"I'm just testing a load. That's all. Besides, someday you'll learn that it isn't the dying that's so scary—it's the losing control; the feeling that things have gotten away. I don't ever want to know that feeling. I refuse to be a burden to anybody."

"Thus, your special round."

"Yeah, well, these shaky hands won't be able to do anything soon. Help me out here. Do what I say."

So, I followed his instructions and we built ten rounds of ammunition, two each of five different loads. A round of ammunition is a simple device. A brass case holds a primer in its rear end and a bullet in its mouth. The body is filled with gunpowder. Different types of ammunition are built to do different jobs. A military round typically carries a bullet with a full metal jacket—designed to maintain its shape while it drills a clean hole through the enemy's flesh. Non-lethal hits, then, don't destroy a lot of tissue and the wounded can be treated and live to be shot another day. It's a Geneva Convention thing.

Hunting bullets, however, are designed to maximize shock and tissue damage. This is achieved by designing bullets that expand when they traverse flesh, then sending them out the barrel at extreme velocities. A seven-millimeter diameter hollow point, expanding bullet traveling at 3000 feet per second will exit a deer's chest, leaving a hole four times that size and a hell of a wound channel. The same bullet traveling half as fast may stay in the animal, perhaps lodged against a far rib. Grandpa loaded his ammo hot. An exit wound leaves a good blood trail in case the deer runs after the hit. The new rounds had half the powder Grandpa normally used and the bullets he selected were light and frangible—something one might use to shoot a coyote.

•••

Out at the gun club, I set out the melons and Grandpa proceeded to shoot each one at very close range. The fourth melon seemed to be the one. The bullet came to rest against the far side husk turning the inside into melon goo. Grandpa put the matching round in his shirt pocket and threw the others into the weeds. I fought off the urge to retch.

I was torn, of course. Grandpa never swore me to secrecy, but in a way he did. We had a bond that needed no words and, as much as I wanted to run to dad and talk, I just couldn't do it. Looking back, I think it's because I didn't believe it was going to happen.

During our last debate, before deer season, I looked Grandpa in the eye and said, "Your special handload has a shelf life of at least twenty years."

"I don't."

"Just promise me this," I said. "Give yourself the benefit of the doubt. You're in good shape. A lot of people love you."

"I know they do, and I know how I feel. It's how I feel at deer camp that matters

to me now. People don't go on forever. Like I said before, no one wants to be a burden. Especially not me. We've had a lot of good years and I really don't care to have my favorite grandson see me rot while I'm breathing."

I couldn't speak.

•••

The tent looked great, as it always did, pitched among the pines. With the opener on a Monday, we had an opportunity to pitch camp a day early and took it. It was an extra day to kick around camp, drink beer, smoke cigars, tell lies and laugh our asses off. Grandpa was in great spirits; he didn't seem to shake so much. During the two days in camp before opening day, I spent a lot of time tending to Grandpa. So much so that he told me to ease up, which stung of course, but I did. He was as happy as I had ever seen him. Even dad commented on Grandpa's spirits and said he thought he'd hunt 'til he's a hundred. My stomach hurt.

Opening morning in deer camp is what keeps hunters hunting. The anticipation is palpable. Breakfast tastes great despite being wolfed down in minutes. Last minute gear checks are done and last-minute visits to the open-air john are cursed and laughed at.

I watched Grandpa as he got ready for the day's hunt. I tried to catch him slipping his special round into his pocket, but of course I knew that it was probably already there.

We were all on post before dawn and the sound of gunfire increased with the eastern light. I had trouble concentrating, waiting for Grandpa's rifle to go off due west of me, but the only one in our group to shoot was my uncle, who killed a dandy eight pointer at eight-thirty in the morning. I relaxed as the day went on, thinking Grandpa had second thoughts.

That night around the campfire, as we toasted my uncle's buck, Grandpa caught me staring at him. He sidled over to where I stood sipping my scotch. "You don't think I'd spoil opening day, do you?" I just whispered, "I guess not."

"Jesus," he said, "Quit thinking about me. My time is past. Your time is now. Have fun. Remember the good times. Hug your dad, hug your uncle, hug me." And I did.

The next few days passed quickly, as camp days do. Dad killed a fat spike. Grandpa said he saw some deer but nothing worth shooting. I can't remember what I saw or when I saw it, if I did, but by the last morning I was convinced I'd hunt another year with Grandpa. Then I heard the pop of Grandpa's reduced load. I lost my breakfast in the snow and fought back tears all the way to his blind.

He was dead. His rifle lay between his knees. I swear he was smiling. There was no blood. The snow was white, and the woods were quiet. No tears. Just feelings of infinite sadness and infinite joy, exploding in a heart expanding to hold them. I knelt on one knee and put my hand on his boot. Then I went for my dad.

Grandpa left a note. It was short with short sentences. It said: "Hemingway was a jerk. He lived a great life. But no better than mine. He really screwed up in the end. Who wants to clean up that kind of mess? Don't cry. I'm feeling less pain than you. Carry me out, burn me up, bring my ashes back next November. Toast me when you spread me around these woods. Love, G."

🧠 🧠 🧠

Edd Tury descended from Hungarian Gypsies. He is a Michigan native and lives in Charlevoix County. He is an electrical engineer and UM alumnus. Edd is an avid transcendentalist and enjoys forest bathing in unpeopled spaces. His writing has appeared in many venues including the *Detroit Metro Times*, *Michigan Out of Doors*, *Michigan Woods 'n Waters* and the *Ann Arbor News*. He is a founding member of Charlevoices Writers Group.

Historical - Cambria arrives in Escanaba

Lucy and Maud

Tyler Tichelaar

When Evan Robinson asked Maud Goldman to go out for a drink at Lyla Hopewell's funeral luncheon, Maud was a little shocked. Not that drinking in the middle of the afternoon was wrong, and not because he asked her at a funeral. It was just that no man had ever asked her out before. What would her mother think?

But then Maud remembered it was the twenty-first century, and her mother had been dead for several years, and it wasn't like she was a teenager anymore. Cripes, she was seventy-eight.

"Well," she told Evan, unsure how to answer, "I don't have a car with me. My cousin Ellen brought me."

"I can drive you home," Evan replied.

Evan seemed so confident. And he was handsome—always had been—even being gray now only made him look distinguished, and he wasn't as overweight as most men his age. But what could such a dapper gentleman possibly see in her?

"All right," she agreed, and then she smiled to make him think she really did want to go.

And she did want to go. But what would Lucy think? She'd have to tell Lucy. In fact, if she went, her sister would wonder why she had taken so long to come home. And, not surprisingly, when Maud went to explain to her cousin Ellen why she wouldn't be leaving with her, Ellen's response was, "What will Lucy say?"

"Could you just call her when you get home and explain for me?" asked Maud. Maud couldn't call—she didn't own a cellphone; after all, she was always home. Lucy had bought a Jitterbug off QVC, but that was six months ago, and it was still unopened in the box.

Ellen sort of wrinkled up the edge of her lip as if considering whether she wanted to get involved.

"Please," said Maud.

"Okay," Ellen gave in.

"Thank you!" said Maud, almost wanting to hug her in front of the few stragglers still at the funeral home.

A few minutes later, Maud was walking across the street to Vango's with Evan Robinson. Whoever would have thought that she, Maud Goldman, an old maid who had always lived with her mother until her mother had died and now lived with her old spinster sister, would be seen in public with the handsome Evan Robinson, son of Matilda Blackmore, whose father had been a wealthy, ne'er-do-well banker? But unlike his grandfather, Evan appeared to be a gentleman.

Maud had been to Vango's countless times, but she had never felt so uncomfortable. She feared that having a drink might entail sitting at the bar or one of those high-top tables. Maud knew she would feel too much on display if she sat at the bar, and she was afraid she might break her ankle trying to get down from one of those high-tops. Why did restaurants even have those stupid chairs? They didn't save space. Maud suspected it was to dissuade old people from dining there so the young, hip crowd could have the place to themselves.

Maud felt relieved when Evan asked the waitress for a booth, and she was even more relieved when they ended up in the very back booth—privacy! No one would need to know now that she had gone out with Evan Robinson. After all, it was the middle of the afternoon, so only a couple of younger people were in the dining room.

Afterward, Maud could barely remember what they talked about. She could scarcely meet Evan's eyes. He told her she had beautiful eyes, but she didn't know how he could tell when she hardly looked at him—perhaps he was just a smooth talker. He'd probably had plenty of girlfriends in his day, though she also knew he had been happily married for many years—his wife had only died a few years ago—Maud didn't know from what; the obituary hadn't said. She didn't think it was the thing you asked on a first date.

Evan ordered them each a glass of red wine. Wine always made Maud feel hot—the last time she'd had a glass was at Ellen's son John's wedding, which had to have been twenty years ago now. She remembered the wine that night had made her a little giggly. She tried extra hard not to be giggly now, but she did giggle when Evan told a joke—that was probably okay—it showed him she was interested. Was she interested? She didn't know, but a man was paying attention to her, and she was going to enjoy it while it lasted.

And then their date was over. The waitress brought the check. Of course, Evan paid it. He helped her on with her coat—he was such a gentleman. He drove her home. She was relieved not to see Lucy staring out the window, watching for her. What if Evan kissed her goodbye?

He didn't, but almost as bad, he asked if she would go out to breakfast with him in the morning. After she said yes, he said he'd pick her up at nine. Then she quickly got out of the car, shut the door, and walked into the house.

Maud half-expected Lucy to greet her at the door with a million questions, but instead, the house was silent other than for the sound of the TV coming from the living room. As Maud walked through the kitchen, she heard her sister's voice. Lucy was on the phone. By the time Maud walked into the living room, skirting her way around piles of unopened boxes from the Home Shopping Network, she realized Lucy was talking to her favorite cable television channel, ordering yet another item she didn't need.

Maud hung up her coat in the front closet and went to the bathroom. When she returned, Lucy was sitting silently, staring at her.

"It was a nice funeral," said Maud, walking toward the sofa. Trying to avoid the crisis to come, she momentarily recalled how her mother had always called the couch a davenport. Couch seemed so common by comparison, but davenport was too old-fashioned now—a word the pre-World War II generation had used. Maud had compromised by calling it a sofa.

"Evan Robinson?" Lucy said.

"Yes," said Maud, standing before her older sister as if on trial.

"I can't believe you said yes to him," said Lucy.

"It was just a drink," Maud replied, and then she sat down on the sofa, picked up a magazine, and tried to act nonchalant.

"He's not in our class," said Lucy.

"No," said Maud, surprised by the remark but casually flipping through the pages of *Woman's World.* "You're right. He has more money than us."

"I mean he's not in our moral class," said Lucy.

"What does that mean?"

"You know."

"No, I don't," said Maud, pretending to be deeply interested in an article about Dr. Oz's latest diet breakthrough.

"You know what those people are," said Lucy.

"What people?" asked Maud, looking up.

"The Blackmores."

"What about them?"

"Really, Maud...."

"Really what?"

"You know Mother told us all about them."

"Told us what?" asked Maud, though she knew quite well what Lucy was getting at.

"Are you living on another planet?" asked Lucy, raising her voice. "Don't you remember Cousin Theodore?"

"Who cares about that?" asked Maud.

"Mother would not be happy to learn you were fooling around with a Blackmore."

"I'm not *fooling around*," said Maud, feeling fire rise in her eyes, "and Evan's last name is Robinson."

"And he's the grandson of a philanderer."

Maud let out a big sigh and set aside the magazine; she might as well get this conversation over with.

"Yes," she said, "and Cousin Theodore was that philanderer's son, but no one disowned him."

"You know Mother wouldn't like it. The secret of Cousin Theodore's birth was an embarrassment to the family."

"That was over a hundred years ago," said Maud. "People aren't so high-strung now, and besides, Evan Robinson isn't illegitimate."

"No, but his mother was Cousin Theodore's half-sister."

"So? We're no relation to her or Evan. And I don't see why the fact that Great-Aunt Sarah got knocked up by Evan's grandfather should decide who I get to date."

"Date?" said Lucy.

"That's what I said," Maud replied, her eyes returning to Dr. Oz.

After a moment, she heard Lucy sigh, and then her sister said, "Well, I just thought you were old enough to know better."

"I'm old enough to know I should do what I want," said Maud. "Anyway, I already told Evan I would go out for breakfast with him tomorrow."

"But tomorrow's Wednesday!" said Lucy.

"So?"

"So, you know we're going to lunch at Big Boy with Ellen and the girls."

"I'm sure I'll be home in time to go to lunch," said Maud.

"Why are you acting like this?" Lucy demanded.

"Acting like what?" asked Maud. "You mean wanting to have a life of my own separate from you?"

"A life of your own?" Lucy repeated.

"Yes, a life that's something more than sitting around here all day listening to how you

feel too sick to go out, but not too sick to be a shopaholic."

"I told you I had a headache today, and besides, I didn't know Lyla Hopewell very well."

"Whatever," said Maud, imitating Maddy Vandelare, Ellen's fourteen-year-old granddaughter.

Before Lucy could reply, Maud stood up and headed for the stairs.

Half an hour later, Lucy knocked on Maud's bedroom door.

"Maud, what do you want for supper?"

"I'm not hungry," Maud replied.

Maud didn't come out of her room again, except to use the bathroom, until a few minutes before nine the next morning.

•••

After so much fussing over a simple drink and going out to breakfast, Maud knew Lucy would not react well when, a few weeks later, she told her Evan had invited her to spend the winter at his Florida condo. "I already said yes," she concluded.

"I'll never speak to you again," Lucy replied.

"That's up to you," said Maud. But in the days that followed, she tried to appease Lucy. She offered to invite Evan over so they could get to know each other; she even suggested Lucy could come visit them in Florida for a week or two. Lucy would have nothing to do with either idea.

Still, Maud convinced Evan to wait until two days after Christmas to leave—she could not be so cruel to Lucy as to leave before the holiday. Not that her thoughtfulness helped to put Lucy in a holly jolly mood.

Maud and Evan had a wonderful time in Florida. They soaked in the sun. Evan bought Maud a bathing suit—she hadn't worn one in fifty years—so they could relax by the pool while they drank fruity alcoholic drinks. They went on a cruise of the Bahamas. They rode the teacups at Disney World. They drank freshly squeezed orange juice for breakfast every morning, and on Valentine's Day, Evan proposed. Maud said yes.

Maud called to tell Lucy. She did not answer. After a few attempts, Maud left the news on the answering machine. Lucy did not call back.

Maud and Evan were married two weeks later at Disney World. Maud felt like Snow White—finally, her prince had come, and he had been worth the wait. Maud sent Lucy a postcard after the ceremony was over. Lucy did not reply until a few weeks later when Governor Whitmer issued a stay-at-home order.

The coronavirus pandemic had reached Michigan. Lucy dug around on the kitchen counter, turning over piles of notepads from St. Jude's Children's Hospital, refrigerator magnets that no longer stuck but she had not thrown away, coupons from Burger King that she would never use since Burger King had moved up the highway and it was too dangerous to drive up there, and countless important pieces of junk mail to find the slip of paper Maud had left with Evan's address and phone number on it. She had thought about writing to Maud, but this was an emergency requiring a phone call.

"I think you better come home before things get worse," Lucy told Maud after Evan had answered the phone, Lucy had asked for Maud without congratulating him on his nuptials, and then Maud had come on.

"We're just fine here," said Maud. "We'll be careful. This is Orlando. It's not like Marquette. We can get our groceries delivered. We don't even need to leave the condo."

"Still," said Lucy, "I would feel better if...."

"You worry about you," said Maud, "and I'll worry about me and Evan."

"Fine," said Lucy, beginning to cry. "I don't know how you can behave like this toward me. What would Mama think?"

"You leave Mother out of this," said Maud. "It's not her fault you became a boring shopaholic homebody."

But they both knew it kind of was Mother's fault. After their father had divorced their mother while Maud and Lucy were still little girls, Eleanor Goldman had held onto her daughters so tightly that they could scarcely breathe, and she had taught Lucy to hold onto Maud that way. Maud, slowly suffocating, had finally broken free. Nothing was going to get her to go back now. Not when she

had a handsome wealthy husband, and a weekly date with Mickey Mouse—or at least she'd had one before the coronavirus shut down the Magic Kingdom.

It also shut down Evan. Maud didn't know it yet when she had spoken to Lucy, but it was already too late. A few days later, she developed coronavirus symptoms. She had chills, a mild fever, and just overall felt kind of crummy, but she told herself it was no worse than the flu. Two days later, Evan began vomiting. His temperature skyrocketed. When he became unconscious, Maud panicked and called 911. A day later, he died in the hospital hooked to a ventilator. He died alone. Maud stayed in the condo and grieved.

Because of the pandemic, no one came to visit her. Because of the pandemic, no one would fly to Florida to comfort her. Evan's adult son, Rolf, called her—unlike Lucy, he'd come to the wedding—and together, they made arrangements to fly Evan's body back to Marquette for burial. Because of the pandemic, Maud was afraid to fly. Because of the pandemic she was trapped.

Months of isolation went by. Finally, Maud could stand it no longer. Summer had arrived and Florida was unbearably hot, even in an air-conditioned condo, for an old lady from Upper Michigan. She called Lucy and told her she was coming home. Lucy didn't like that idea—what if Maud caught the virus a second time on the plane, but Maud convinced her she was immune now.

"You could still give it to me," said Lucy, but when Maud promised to wear her face mask and be careful, Lucy didn't argue.

Ellen's son John picked up Maud at the airport. Lucy had refused to do so since the flight came in at night and she didn't like to drive in the dark—she might hit a deer.

John carried Maud's bags into the house, all the while wearing his face mask to be safe, and then said goodbye to his mother's cousins.

Maud took off her coat, moved boxes of snow globes never opened, Danielle Steel novels never read, and collectible Coke tins collecting dust off the sofa, and sat down.

"I knew you never should have gone to Florida," said Lucy.

"I'm tired," said Maud. "I think I'll go straight to bed."

"I wish you had listened to me," Lucy said.

Maud glared at her sister. She had just flown more than fifteen-hundred miles across country during a pandemic after losing her husband. Couldn't she at least get an, "I'm glad you're home" or, "I'm sorry about Evan" from her sister? "At least I had some fun in my life," she replied.

"At what cost?" asked Lucy.

Maud stood up from the sofa.

"It was more fun," she said, "than sitting around all day like some cloistered nun in a makeshift cathedral of unopened QVC boxes."

Lucy looked startled by her tone.

"Let me tell you something," said Maud, unable to stop herself. "You live like a nun, and nuns get none. Now no one can say that about me."

Maud turned before she could see the shocked look she knew would be on Lucy's face. She grabbed her suitcase by the door and stomped up the stairs. She slammed her bedroom door shut and got ready for bed. Then she turned off the light so Lucy would think she was asleep when she came upstairs. Maud just couldn't deal with her sister anymore tonight.

But Maud knew that in the morning they'd be back to their old routine. They'd have breakfast, though at home; going out to eat wasn't safe, even if the restaurants had re-opened with limited capacity. Then Lucy would shop on TV. After lunch, they'd go for a ride around Presque Isle Park and get home in time to watch *Dr. Phil* and read the mail. Then they might both take a nap before they had supper, followed by watching more TV until bedtime. It wasn't an exciting life, but after those isolated months in Florida, Maud was glad to have a home—and a sister—to return to. She knew most widows ended up alone. She wouldn't. But she didn't regret her brief romance. And in the morning, she would move all those QVC boxes off the kitchen table, whether Lucy liked it or not.

Tyler R. Tichelaar is the author of twenty-one books including *When Teddy Came to Town*, *Haunted Marquette*, *Kawbawgam: The Chief, The Legend, The Man*, and *The Marquette Trilogy*. Tyler is also a professional editor and the owner of Superior Book Productions. Visit him at www.MarquetteFiction.com.

Historical Au Train - Lake Camp

The Ospreys
by Brandy Thomas

I stand on a cliff overlooking the lake
A great inland sea

The insistent wind tugs and pulls at me.
Cold fingers lingering beneath my collar and cuffs,
Around my shirt hem
Lifting my hair and sliding down my spine.

Tugging, pulling, pushing

'Till I give in and step off the cliff edge.
As I fall toward that bitter cold water and those sharp rocks
I wonder if this time I will be dashed and broken against
the shore.

But no.

I break apart into a flock of Ospreys.

Soaring on that cold wind
Some of me flying as high and far as I can,
Other parts playing on the wind close to shore.

Finally, the flock of me comes together and
Reforms into a woman upon the cliff.

But…
Not all of me has returned.
I feel the loss.
But am not sure which part is gone.
Something missing,
Incomplete

I will continue to come to the cliff
And maybe next time my stray Osprey will find me again.

Or maybe a little more of myself will fly away,
'Till nothing is left.

Autumn Jewel Box
by Brandy Thomas

Every fall I find
Myself nestled in the
Heart of a jewel box.

Maples provide the
Ruby Red.

Aspen and Birch
A Golden Hue.

Hints of Silver
Peek through,
Birch branches glow throughout

The verdant needles
Of firs and spruce
Glow an Emerald Green
A dark depth that
Makes the lighter shades
Shine brighter still.

As the Autumn wanes
Those forest jewels
Are spent
Providing nutrients for
The future riot of
Color that is spring.

Brandy Thomas is a professional freelance editor who lives and works in Marquette, Michigan. She edits across the publishing spectrum, but she specializes in science fiction and fantasy as well as children's books. In addition to editing the written word, she is also an audiobook narrator and editor. For more information about Brandy, visit www.ThomasEditing.com

The First Time

by Ninie Gaspariani Syarikin

The first time
I heard your heartbeat,
I cried.
I covered my face with
the two palms of my hands.
I, then, wiped my tears of joy in disbelief.
"You are alive."
You do exist, though unseen.
Your heart was beating in my womb,
hard and strong, loud and clear.
Duk duk duk, duk duk duk, duk duk
Like knocking on the door of my soul.
"Let me in, Ummi, let me in!"
And I answered: "You are in, Baby."

I can't deny you, even in my fear.
I couldn't give you up, even in uncertainty.
I shan't abandon you, even in my poverty.
I shouldn't surrender you, even in my despair.
And I won't leave you, even in my imperfection
I just wouldn't.
I might hesitate but may not falter.

Suddenly,
the lioness in me surfaced, overwhelmed me.
And I made this pledge:
I will protect you
feed you
love you
nurture you
And I am going to take you wherever I go
'Till the time arrives for me to bear you,
and hear you, and see you, then hold you.

The first time I heard your heartbeat,
I fell in love, without seeing you.

Copper Country Crochet

by Ninie Gaspariani Syarikin

The Keweenaw Art Fair in Houghton High School Gym and the bazaar at the Copper Country Mall were simultaneous events I never wanted to miss from year to year in November. And this year was last Saturday, the 13th. It was an opportunity to go out with my good friend Stacey and enjoy the flamboyant arts and crafts welcoming the holiday season and new year. But this year's fair was even more memorable because I met a new friend from my old country region.

Houghton, as remote and isolated location as it is in the Upper Peninsula of Michigan, is actually quite cosmopolitan thanks to the Michigan Technological University, which recruits from all over the world. But a majority of international students live on campus and mostly interact among themselves, so it doesn't really feel like they are well-integrated with the American society at large or Houghton and Hancock communities specifically. Imagine how delighted I was when I heard this vendor mention that her daughter-in-law was from Malaysia!

"Welcome to my booth!" a middle-aged Caucasian lady greeted me cheerfully among her so many vibrant products. She was a tall and big woman with a large forehead and plump cheeks. When she spoke, both of her brows were lifted, her eyes shining with friendliness, with a grin from ear-to-ear that never left her lips, showing her well-maintained teeth. As if that was not enough, she offered me a bowl of choco-

lates to pick from, which I took a piece to reciprocate to her gracious gesture. "Thank you," I said.

In her booth, a pile of aprons here, a stack of dishcloths there, a row of cute kitchen napkins hanging, and a spread of coasters, potholders, squares, and rounds were nicely arranged on top of each other, not to mention jars of potpourri and aromatic candles, etc, etc. The good smells, though, could not defeat my sight where I noticed a small finger map of the Keweenaw Peninsula with a descriptive paragraph, as follows:

Legend has it that during the Copper Rush in the 19th century in the Keweenaw Peninsula of Lake Superior, the largest of the Great Lakes, local ladies feverishly crocheted colorful coasters to welcome their men at the end of each-and-every day from working in the mines. Husbands, fathers, and sons, as well as sons-in-law. As soon as their beloveds arrived before sunset, according to storytellers, those wonderful women, wearing their jolly smiles, would serve a cup of tea, ginger tea, hibiscus tea, or peach tea, or coffee on a beautiful coaster with a plate of delicious pasties.

To this day, the tradition of crocheting in the Copper Country continues on and alive. So, treat yourself now to a pretty coaster or potholder, and have extra for your loved ones!

Kaarina Heikkinen, Sole Proprietor
Copper Country Crochet
Website: www.CopperCountryCro-
chet.com
Contact: info@CopperCountryCro-
chet.com

My mind was immediately imagining the hectic scene in the paragraph when I heard supposedly Kaarina asking me: "Are you from Malaysia?"

"Not quite," I replied rather surprisedly at her almost close guessing. "From Indonesia, its neighboring country," I added.

"Oh, my daughter-in-law Aminah is from Kuala Lumpur (she pronounced the name of the Malaysian capital with difficulty, yet funny). She's coming in one hour to help me. I noticed that you are wearing a headcover like her."

The vendor was referring to my hijab, a headscarf usually worn by Muslim women. Here, in this bazaar, I noticed a few Amish women were wearing their hair kapps or bonnets, manning their booth selling jams, bread, fruit cakes, sugar cookies, and children's toys. Well, we had something in common, I thought.

"Oh? I'd like very much to meet your daughter," I responded spontaneously, emphasizing NOT to mention 'in-law' as a sign of respect and affinity to her, since in Malay culture, in order to promote a strong familial bond, parents make efforts to treat their children's spouses as their own.

"Although there are many Asian students and professors at Tech," I quipped, "I don't often meet Malaysians or Indonesians here. Mostly Chinese, Indian or Arab students or faculty."

"Yes, I want her to meet you, too. Ami, as I call her, sometimes expressed sighs of loneliness, not able to speak her tongue," the kind woman rendered. I felt she was very observant. I promised Kaarina that Stacey and I would drop by again to her booth before leaving the bazaar.

Stacey and I made our merry rounds both at the Houghton High School and at the Copper Country Mall. We visited the new romance writer Emorie Cole who exhibited her debut novel and two others. She is quite a young author, to whom I asked: "Are you a member of UPPAA?" to which she answered: "Not, yet, but I am thinking of it." Not only did I admire her creativity but also her spirit of entrepreneurship and her love of her hometown, as all her romances are based in the UP. Our other significant visits were an art photographer who documented the Northern Lights occurrences in the UP as well as a seamstress who made keepsakes for her customers from the used clothes of their dead relatives in the effort to hold onto the good memories.

When we finally dropped by at the booth "Copper Country Crochet," Kaarina and Aminah were already waiting for us. In her early 30s, she was quite a charming young woman. Her turquoise headscarf complemented her teal attire. Instantly, we conveyed our Islamic greetings to each other: "Assalamu'alaikum" and "Wa'alaikum assalaam," which means "Peace be upon you" and "And upon you, peace." From our Arabic salutation, we immediately switched to our common language, Malay. And I could see relief and happiness on Kaarina's face. She understood; what an extraordinary mother-in-law she was.

"How did you end up in the UP?" I questioned her, like the same query often directed to me.

"I am doing my doctorate in civil engineering, Makcik," she addressed me respectfully as "Aunty" in our Malay tongue. "How long have you been living here?" her turn to ask me.

"Visit me soon at my house, Aminah," I dodged her question. "I'll tell you then, but just so you know, my oldest son could be your age, and all my three sons were born in the US. So, you are like my daughter."

At the end of our conversation, we exchanged our contact information. I invited both Kaarina and Aminah for a luncheon or dinner at my home at their convenience.

"Ami did crochet some of those coasters and potholders, Ninie," Kaarina interrupted quickly our line of chatting. "And, surprisingly, she is quite good at that."

All the while saying those words, I could tell that Kaarina's eyebrows and eyeballs were dancing.

"Oh, that I can assure you," I countered. "Most Malay girls learn cooking, sewing, crocheting, even embroidering, no matter how later on in their life they turn to be an engineer, a doctor or a lawyer."

"Richard became a better son to me. But, you know, Ninie, I don't understand this," Kaarina looked a little perplexed as if wanting to confide something but at the same time joking. "Ami is a Heikkinen now, but she refused to change her last name. She remains Aminah Abdullah."

Aminah and I looked at each other for a few seconds, then understood the cultural significance. I soon explained lightly to Kaarina: "Don't you worry about that, Kaarina. Ami will be your daughter; it's just that in our custom, wives have the right to keep their own family name."

We all parted this past weekend with joy. As Stacey dropped me in front of my house, she asked jokingly if we would plan to see the Keweenaw Art Fair together again next year.

"Are you kidding me?" I retorted.

"Who knows? You got a new friend now," she quipped.

"Nah... I still prefer to go out just the two of us, we are about the same age."

Ninie Gaspariani Syarikin works as a writer, translator/interpreter, and researcher. Her working languages are English, Indonesian, Malay, and Javanese. Passionate about travel, she has visited all continents but Antarctica. Ninie is a life member of the National Coalition of Independent Scholars, the Fulbright Association, and the American Translators Association. She lives in Houghton, Michigan, and welcomes correspondence at: ngsyarikin@ncis.org

Historical Au Train - Women Fishing

My Surprising Encounter With a Baby Raccoon

by David Swindell

One day last spring, a chance encounter took place that both startled and delighted me. Before my eyes was setting a creature all furry and small, with black ringlets around its eyes and a tail so long and slender. This magnificent creature came right up to my door, looking delighted to meet the occupant of the house. Gently scratching on the screen door, this rascal wanted in. If my surprise visitor had the ability to speak, the conversation may have sounded like this. "Hi, Daddy, I am home, let me in to play." So, to commemorate this encounter with a creature from the wild, I have composed these special poems for you to hold in your hearts.

The Animals Sing Their Songs to You

The Gull

The gull sweetly sang out an enchanting call,
soaring high above the white covered cliffs.
The white caps on the lake below,
magnificently unfurled themselves,
as nature's asserted supremacy over the
    water and the wind.

The roaring waves beneath mean nothing.
For in that moment, this bird of the air flew
    towards the sun,
experiencing a freedom and exhilaration as
    he went higher and higher.

As the ascent continued,
the gull became one with the sky that
    embraced his earthly presence.
Reaching into his very depths this creature
    climbed toward the stars in the heavens,
as he touched the very essence of the light
    from above.

The Bear

Upon emerging from his cave,
this massive creature gave thanks for his
    home, the forest.

He was so glad to have survived another winter.
Now the glories of spring were beckoning our friend,
offering him an edible array of plentiful bounty.
The grass and flowers called out as well,
showing this creature of the woodlands a beauty that warmed his heart.
All the sights and smells in spring gave new hope to the noblest of creatures.

Speaking through his heart, the bear went on to make these profound statements.
We are all fellow travelers in the journey of life.
Come share with me the forest that is so lovely and rare.
Watch as the seasons cascade into an array of colors that heighten your senses.
Come into my home and see the glories that await you here.
Follow your soul to an extraordinary place and lay down your burdens and cares.

The Raccoon Family

The raccoon family greeted visitors along the trail.
Their playful manner and curiosity spoke a gentle welcome to everyone passing their way.
These mischievous creatures will call out to you if you give them a chance.
Their message is telling; their message is true.
Now let us explore what they may say to you.
The call of the seasons brings change to all who dwell on the land.
So, my friends take time to play.
Take time to enjoy.
And, my friends,
Discover a new meaning for life along the way.

The Red Fox

This land has a special calling to you.
Come see the wonders that nature unfolds before you.
The majesty of the land unfolds its incredible magnificence before your eyes.
So, spend some time, relax, and reflect in its presence.
Enjoy the coolness of a mountain stream that winds and rushes below.
And know that you're always welcome,
respecting the earth,
preserving its presence for future generations to grow.

The Sleepy Little Opossum

The opossum emerged from his hollowed-out log near the path.
He stuck his little head out as travelers passed on their way.
Wasting no time this proud creature of the forest,
looked upon his visitors with purpose and devotion.
He spoke to those entering his world through kindly eyes,
penetrating even the most distant observer.
His message is revealed through a sincereness,
even penetrates the most distracted among us.

In the forest, time is marked by the season and the setting and rising of the sun.
This glorious abode we call home,
is not governed by noisy mechanical machines,
or by inhabitants needlessly rushing about.
Instead, we honor the ancient tradition of letting time dictate to us in its own accord.
We let the brilliance of color and light that filters down through the trees,

serve as symbols of freedom and purpose to
the greatest of these.
Instead of letting ambitions and passions
govern our lives,
we turn instead to something that is more
profoundly wise.
We let the light of day guide our actions,
and only take what is needed for our
survival.
We never destroy the forest for gain or
profit.
We, instead, only seek to give honor to the
mystery that marks these
lands so incredibly conceived.

The Coyote Foretells the Future of our Planet

◆❖◆

My friends, pay close attention to the saga
that is unfolding before you today,
because your choices matter and affect our
planet in this way.
The key to the future rests squarely in your
hands.
So do what is right for both animal and
man.

The forests of the world are being depleted
and used in the name of progress,
but little thought is given to their loss and
redemption.
More is taken than given back to our home,
the land.
So, an imbalance is progressing that
threatens all,
no matter which side of this issue you
stand.

As creatures of intellect and promise, you
have the capacity to do great good or
destroy the
very existence you hold.
Therefore, you must choose wisely to
preserve all life and the balance you hold.
It is time to choose rightly, it is time to do
more.
All our destinies depend on you keeping
and preserving the earth once more.

David Swindell's endeavors have included a
diverse number of jobs and employment opportunities over the span of fifty some years,.
Through the years, his passion has always
been centered towards public service. While
attending college late in life, the art of writing became a priority that has taken him to
new heights.

historical Manistique - A German band

Joe Linder: Hockey Legend from Hancock, Michigan

by Bill Sproule and John Haeussler

Joseph Charles "Joe" Linder distinguished himself as an amateur star in two communities during hockey's formative era. He was a standout at Hancock Central High School and local leagues in Michigan's Copper Country in the 1900s, and then captained a team representing the Duluth Curling Club to prominence in the 1910s. Sportswriters have often acclaimed Linder as "the first great American hockey player."

Linder was born on August 12, 1884, to Charles and Caroline Linder; however, there is conflicting information regarding his birth year and the confusion may have been an attempt to obfuscate the fact that he was born less than six months after his parents were wed. He was baptized on October 19, 1884, at St. Anne's Catholic Church in Hancock and the family soon welcomed three siblings—a brother George in 1885, a sister Caroline in 1887, and another sister Cecilia in 1888. Charles and his brother operated a barber shop in Hancock and later Charles became the proprietor of Hancock's premier rooming house, the Northwestern Hotel. Tragedy struck the family in July 1895 when Charles died at the age of thirty-six during a transatlantic voyage to Germany and was buried at sea. Joe became the man of the household at age eleven.

Ice hockey was introduced in the Copper Country in the late 1890s and within a few years, new arenas opened, and several hockey teams and leagues formed. A note in the November 17, 1898, edition of the Houghton *Daily Mining Gazette* newspaper reflected the area's excitement for hockey—"Hockey will soon be the fashion. If you want to keep up the times, play hockey."

The first major indoor arena was the Palace Ice Rink. It opened in 1899 in a building that was originally built as a smelter in the early 1890s by the Lake Superior Smelting Company and was converted to a natural ice rink for skating and hockey. The Palace had seating for over 1,000 spectators, but as the popularity of hockey grew, many had to be turned away for the best games and then in the summer of 1902, local entrepreneurs under the leadership of James Dee began planning a new indoor arena in Houghton on the Portage Lake waterfront. Construction began in the fall and the arena opened in late December with seating for 2,500 hockey fans and room for an additional 600 standees. The first game in the new arena, named the Amphidrome, was played on December 29, 1902, between Portage Lake and the University of Toronto. The local newspaper reported that over 5,000 attended the opening game as Portage Lake defeated the team from Toronto 13-2. The Portage Lake team was led by Canadian-born dentist, Jack "Doc" Gibson. It was a good team that went undefeated for the season and all of their games, except for the final two, were played at the Amphidrome as it was seen as the best hockey venue in the Midwest, and everyone wanted to play in this new facility. Portage Lake played sixteen games that season against teams from Detroit, Duluth, St. Louis, St. Paul, and Pittsburgh and they defeated the Pittsburgh Bankers for the United States Championship. The hockey season also saw the beginning of a high school hockey league in the Copper Country; as freshman Joe Linder played left wing and was the captain of Hancock Central High School (HCH). The team defeated Houghton High School for the league's first championship.

In the fall of 1903, the management of the Amphidrome purchased a silver cup to be awarded to the best high school hockey team in the Copper Country. Should any school win the cup for three consecutive years, it would retain permanent possession of the trophy. Hancock Central High School defeated Houghton again in 1904 to win the league's championship and the inaugural Amphidrome Cup. Linder was captain and led the HCH team as its rover. Joe's younger brother, George, played left wing and their teammates included John Tamblyn and Albert Black. A few years later Tamblyn earned a medical degree from the University of Michigan and Albert Black is believed to be the first black high school hockey player in the United States.

1904 Hancock Central High School Hockey Team
(Houghton County Historical Society)
Standing, left to right: E.A. Meyers (manager), Will Waara (forward), **Joe Linder** (rover and captain), James Corrigan (point) Seated, left to right: John Steinbeck (forward), John Tamblyn (cover point), Albert Black (spare), Ed Reid (goal) In foreground, left to right: George Linder (forward), Earl Guibault (spare) with Amphidrome Cup

In the fall, Dee and Gibson made a momentous hockey decision when they decided to recruit the best players from Canada and openly pay them to play for the Portage Lake hockey team. The team won the 1904 U.S. Championship and defeated a team from

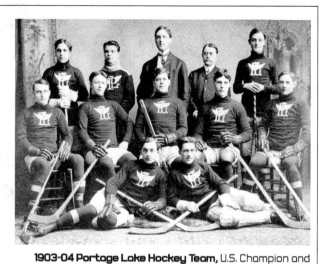

1903-04 Portage Lake Hockey Team, U.S. Champion and World Champion (Michigan Technological University Archives and Copper Country Historical Collections) Standing left to right: Fred Westcott (spare), James Duggan (trainer), Charles Webb (manager), James Dee (president), **Joe Linder** (spare) Seated left to right: Bert Morrison (rover), "Cooney" Shields (forward), "Doc" Gibson (point and captain), Hod Stuart (cover point), Bruce Stuart (forward) In foreground: Ernie Westcott (forward), Riley Hern (goal)

Montreal for what was billed as the World's Championship. During the season, Gibson recruited Joe Linder, then a high school sophomore, as a substitute defenseman for three games with the Portage Lake team and although Linder only played sparingly, he appeared in the annual team photo. At the time, Gibson was quoted, "He has all the tools you look for in a hockey player. He's a fast skater and a tough player."

Following the successful season, Gibson and Dee began promoting the idea of a professional hockey league and in December 1904, play began in the International Hockey League (IHL). The league had five teams—Calumet, Pittsburgh, Portage Lake, Sault Ste. Marie, Michigan, and Sault Ste. Marie, Ontario—and although the league lasted only three seasons it was the start of professional hockey.

The 1904-05 HCH team was captained by Ed Reid as Joe played point and George Linder was the team's center. Despite losing to Houghton twice during the regular season, Hancock swept Houghton in a two-game championship series to retain the Amphidrome Cup. The Hancock team was excited to start the 1905-06 season with the opportunity to claim permanent ownership of the Amphidrome Cup, but Joe was ruled ineligible because of a four-year rule. He began playing high school baseball and football while in the eighth grade, so when he reached the close of his junior year it was discovered that he had played four years and was ineligible for further high school athletics. Unable to play in his senior year, Linder coached the Hancock high school baseball, football, and hockey teams, and played for the Portage Lake junior hockey team. The HCH hockey team was again successful in winning the Amphidrome Cup by defeating Houghton in a five-game championship series. George Linder was the team's center and John Tamblyn was team captain. It was also during this 1905-06 season that Linder dressed one game as a substitute for the Calumet team in the International Hockey League.

In the 1906 edition of HCH's yearbook *Ingot*, it was noted that since few high schools in Michigan had hockey teams, and the best teams in the state were arguably in the Copper Country, Hancock was also the state champion. The yearbook also claimed that Michigan was the only state in the country in which hockey was played by high school teams to any great extent, so they concluded that it would be safe in claiming the U.S. national championship too.

Joe graduated in 1906 and he would have been twenty-two, so it is suspected that he may have taken time off from school to earn money for the family following his father's death. After graduation, Linder remained in the Copper Country, played on several local amateur hockey and baseball teams, and was always a consensus selection to league all-star teams in both hockey and baseball.

In December 1912, Linder was recruited to captain a new Duluth Curling Club hockey team and work as a lathe operator for the National Iron Company. In announcing his arrival, the Duluth *News Tribune* described Joe as "probably the best hockey player in the country." Hockey in Duluth started as an outgrowth of ice polo in the late 1890s,

and early hockey games were played on outdoor rinks or at an old curling club until the Duluth Curling Club opened a new two-story facility for curling and hockey in 1913. Curling was on the ground level with 12 sheets of ice and at the time, it was considered to be the finest curling facility in the United States. Hockey was played on a natural ice surface on the second level with seating for 2,000 spectators and as captain, Linder was responsible for putting together a team and arranging games. In the first year, the team played an independent schedule against American opposition and teams from Winnipeg, Fort William, and Port Arthur (now Thunder Bay).

The Duluth Curling Club (Northeast Minnesota Historical Center)

Joe returned to the Copper Country and married Alma Barkell in Hubbell, Michigan, on January 4, 1913, but in addition to the nuptials, it was also a recruiting trip and Joe convinced Alma's brothers, Russell and Jack, and former Hancock high school teammates, Will Bogan and John "Doc" Tamblyn, to join him in Duluth. Joe also made a tempting offer to a third Hancock teammate, goalie Ed Reid, but he turned him down. The team had some success and faced Portage Lake in a critical four-game series in early March to determine the best team in the West. The first two games were played at the Amphidrome in Houghton followed by two home games at the Duluth Curling Club and, as the series approached, excitement built in both communities. Extra trains were added, and it was reported that a local theatre was negotiating with a moving picture company to film the Houghton games. It would have been the first attempt to make moving pictures of a hockey game, but unfortunately the arrangements could not be finalized. Portage Lake won every game and went on to defeat a Cleveland team for the 1913 U.S. Amateur Championship. The Portage Lake team included Elmer Sicotte and Carlos "Cub" Haug, both who later became coaches of the Michigan College of Mines (Michigan Tech) varsity hockey team.

In the fall of 1913, a new league was established that included Duluth, Calumet, Portage Lake (Houghton), Sault Michigan, and Sault Ontario. It was the Western Division of the AAHA (American Amateur Hockey Association). Linder added a few more players from the Copper Country, including his cousin Frank "Nick" Kahler from Dollar Bay. In early December, James MacNaughton, general manager of the Calumet and Helca Mining Company, donated a trophy to the AAHA to be presented to the best amateur hockey team in the United States. The trophy has become known as the MacNaughton Cup and is now awarded to the season champion of the Central Collegiate Hockey Association (CCHA).

The Sault Michigan team defeated Sault Ontario in the last game of the season to win the league's inaugural championship and went on to face the Eastern champion, Cleveland Athletic Club, for the U.S. Amateur Championship. The Cleveland team defeated Sault Michigan to become the first winner (1914) of the MacNaughton Cup, but Sault Michigan would gain revenge against Cleveland to win the Cup in 1915. Sault Michigan-born "Muzz" Murray was the captain and played defense and forward for the Sault team during this era. He went on to play for the Seattle Metropolitans and was a member of the team when the 1919 Stanley Cup series was cancelled due to the Spanish flu. Murray was inducted in the United States Hockey Hall of Fame in 1987.

Joe Linder in Duluth Curling Club uniform (Michigan Technological University Archives and Copper Country Historical Collection)

In a 1914 post-season challenge, Duluth played the Winnipeg Victorias in Duluth and defeated the Victorias 5-4 as Russ Barkell scored four times for the Duluth team. This was a major victory for Duluth and U.S. hockey at the time, as the Victorias were considered to be one of top amateur teams in Canada. A Winnipeg sports reporter wrote that, "Captain Linder played like a veritable demon. On offense and defense Linder stood out as one of the greatest men I have ever seen on ice."

After one season with Duluth, Kahler accepted an offer to captain and coach the St. Paul Athletic Club for the 1914-15 season and when Duluth and Sault Ontario suspended operations for the 1915-16 season, St. Paul joined the AAHA. In their first season in the league, St. Paul defeated Sault Michigan in the league playoffs to win the 1916 MacNaughton Cup, but following the season much of senior amateur hockey was suspended due to World War I and the MacNaughton Cup went into storage for three seasons. Kahler went on to play for many years with the Minneapolis Millers and was inducted into United States Hockey Hall of Fame in 1980.

In August 1915, Linder was laid off and returned to the Copper Country where he was employed as a machinist for the Calumet and Hecla Mining Company, a position that he would hold for more than five years. It was also during this time that Alma and Joe welcomed the birth of two sons. Linder joined the Calumet AAHA hockey team for the 1915-16 season with Fort William-born Jack Adams, a future NHL player and Detroit Red Wings coach and general manager, and several former Duluth players including Russ Barkell. Barkell led the team in scoring, but Calumet finished last in the four-team league behind St. Paul, Sault Michigan, and Portage Lake. Following the season, Barkell moved back to Duluth and served in World War I while Linder remained in the Copper Country.

After the war, Russ Barkell returned to Duluth and bought back several former Duluth stars to play in a challenge series in March 1919 against the St. Paul Athletic Club at the Duluth Curling Club. The Duluth team won the series, and the local press wrote, "Of all the Duluthians to come in for applause none outshone Joe Linder... 'Joe, Joe,' was all one could hear when Linder played the puck." In November 1920, the Linder family moved to Superior, Wisconsin, where Joe and Russ Barkell opened a grocery store, and although Joe retired as a hockey player, he continued to be active in the local business and the sports community. He later served as a Douglas County supervisor and coached the Superior State Teachers College (now the University of Wisconsin -Superior) hockey team for two seasons in the 1930s. Linder's two sons, Charles and George, played on the team.

Barkell continued his hockey career and spent two outstanding seasons playing at the University of Michigan and he has been described as Michigan's first hockey star. Russ then coached the men's hockey team at Williams College in Massachusetts for one season before moving to Texas and Louisiana. Barkell's father became Joe's business partner and then Russ's brother, Jack, became a partner after his father died. The store operated in Superior for over twenty-five years.

In February 1941, an article in *Esquire* magazine noted that any list of the thirty best hockey players in the world has to include American born Joe Linder. Linder later suffered from a critical heart ailment which forced him to give up many of his business and sports interests and in his later years he was a custodian at the local Court House. He died on June 28, 1948, about six weeks shy of his 64th birthday. In recognition of his outstanding playing career in Michigan's Copper Country and Duluth, and his role in developing hockey in both communities, Joe Linder was inducted into the United States Hockey Hall of Fame in 1975.

•••

References

Bacon, John U. *Blue Ice: The Story of Michigan Hockey.* The University of Michigan Press: Ann Arbor, MI, 2001.

Godin, Roger. *Beyond the Stars: Early Major League Hockey and the St. Paul Athletic Club Team.* Minnesota Historical Society Press: St. Paul, MN, 2004.

Sproule, William J. *Houghton: The Birthplace of Professional Hockey.* Self-Published: Houghton, MI, 2019.

Newspapers: *Calumet News, Copper Country Evening News, Daily Mining Gazette (Houghton), Duluth News Tribune, Minneapolis-St. Paul Star Tribune*

Bill Sproule is a Professor Emeritus, Michigan Technological University, Houghton, where he taught transportation engineering, public transit, airport design, and hockey history. He is the author of three local history books—*Images of Rail: Copper Country Streetcars, Houghton: The Birthplace of Professional Hockey,* and *Michigan Tech Hockey: 100 Years of Memories.*

John Haeussler is a former Hancock mayor and has written extensively on Hancock history including *Images of America: Hancock* and *Hidden Gems and Towering Tales: A Hancock, Michigan Anthology.*

poet's dream odyssey
by T. Kilgore Splake

waking early hour
star lights dancing
bedroom wall rorschachs
low whisper calling
"come visit cliffs"
tranny tripping north
climbing trail upward
trekking forest shadows
as first dawn
passes into morning
quiet joy in stillness
soft gentle breeze
pine needles humming
reaching granite summit
view from rocky overlook
knowing i am home

cliffs magic
by T. Kilgore Splake

standing in forest shadows
sun rising above horizon
lighting tree tops
small birds in puckerbrush
singing morning melodies
deer jumping across trail
feeling something larger
influencing body and soul
nature's cleansing power
stronger than alcohol or drugs
sustaining lost person
through troubled times

T. Kilgore Splake ("the cliffs dancer") lives in a tamarack location old mining row house in the copper mining village of Calumet in Michigan's Upper Peninsula. splake has become a legend in the small press literary circles for his writing and photography. His just-published biography entitled *The Road to Splake* by Robert Zoschke, contains a collection of splake poems and photographs.

The Beaver
by Christine Saari

The beaver comes out from under the
  waters
at nine in the evening and criss-crosses
  the river.
Loud splashes from his powerful tail
tell us we are not wanted here.
The Whitefish is his territory. We are
  intruders.

Only once he let us come close.
We canoed toward the falls
where the river becomes dark and
  narrows,
where dead cedars hang into the water
like giant porcupines.

As we drifted past the hollowed-out bank
we saw his eyes gleam.
Holding still, we looked him in the eye.
He looked back, without alarm.
Then he quietly slid into the river.

Christine Saari, writer and visual artist of
Austrian descent, has lived in Marquette,
Michigan, since 1971. Her 2011 memoir *Love
and War at Stag Farm: The Story of Hirschen-
gut, an Austrian Mountain Farm 1938-1948*
covers the formative years of her childhood
during WWII. Her poetry book *Blossoms
in the Dark of Winter* was released in 2018.
*Her poems have appeared in the UP Reader,
Maiden Voyage, Water Music and Me as a
Child Poetry Series)*

Abandoned Dreams
by Christine Saari

A new roof keeps out
wind and rain,
but not the vandals.
The back door is broken in half,
the refrigerator overturned.
They bashed in windows,
rammed a four-by-four
through the most sacred
place in a woman's body
painted on a bedroom wall.
Broken keys still vibrate sound
on a water-logged piano.
The cook stove was already
stolen before this latest assault.
No one has taken the books
left in what was the library:
Travel guides to Cuba and Spain,
a tome on herbal remedies.
Instructions for birthing a child.

Not long ago a family lived here.
The husband transformed driftwood
into tables and chairs.
The wife painted goddesses
and fairytale gnomes on the walls.
Altars and cozy corners
nurtured their creative spirits.
Their child looked like an elf.
In the end deep winter snows,
isolation and poverty drove them
to give up their wilderness life
and seek another.

Today, grape vines climb a trellis,
faithfully bearing fruit.
Bright purple lavender peeks out
from under dark green ferns.
No one will harvest these treasures.

Superiority Complex

by Cyndi Perkins

It is our water. We will fight.

The Remington feels strange in my hands, but also comforting. I used to believe in gun control. Now I'm fighting control with guns. The irony of this makes me smile, more a grimace, really, as I survey Copper Harbor from the Crow's Nest, a Bed and Breakfast converted to watchtower with a wide-open view of the entrance channel. The red-and-white striped bell buoy that marks it clangs merrily.

I scan the horizon, gut fluttering, a bad actor in an old Movie of the Week. Nothing in my sights except a thirty-nine-year-old bartender going gray around the temples doing a poor imitation of trying to look tough. At least that's what the mirror over the bathroom sink shows when I strike my best commando pose.

Some of the resistors in our Keweenaw network can surveil from the lighthouses that dot the points of our horn-shaped peninsula. But here in the Harbor, it's important to be in shooting distance of where the troops are likely to land equipment.

Not local troops, mind you. Nobody up here is fighting on the other side. The right-wing nutters, religious extremists, lefties, white supremacists, the hermits, the artists, the academics, the idealists, and other fools— we're all on the same side now. That's a first.

It took another first to pull us together.

Montgomery Mussell came from outside the Beltway. He wasn't like any leader who had come before. Zero respect for the establishment, contempt for rules, and a dedica-tion to saying whatever he thinks whenever he wants—nobody'd seen that before. Lots of folks thought it was refreshing. That's why the self-proclaimed Biggest-Mouth-In-Texas won the presidency. At least that's what the pundits said.

But in the end, Ol' Monty was no different than the others.

He promised to "drain the swamp." Instead, he came for our water. Even the climate change deniers couldn't deny he'd gone too far.

"A pipeline to restore our power, our self-determination, our worldwide reputation," he intoned in the first of several prime-time TV specials on national infrastructure, tossing back his unnaturally cobalt fetlock like a wild stallion. One almost expected him to paw the ground then mount a mare. "And it won't be a tiny little pipe, like a pipe cleaner," he went on. "It'll be the biggest pipeline ever constructed, delivering millions of gallons per minute, billions per day." Dramatic pause as the hand-picked ralliers behind him nod in appreciation, Nancy Reagan eyes shining adoringly upon their oracle.

"Running from the great northern wilderness to the fields of Texas, Arizona, New Mexico, California, and beyond, the American Promise Pipeline will revitalize the Western Frontier!"

"Fuck that noise." It takes a minute to register the expletive to Gabe, one of my quieter regulars, who usually sits on the dark end of the bar, nearly under the overhead TV. A conservative fifty-something in the inevitable plaid flannel shirt-jack, chook, jeans, and steel-toed work boots, he drinks a couple of Labatt Blues a couple of nights a week after work. There's usually two, three people tops in the bar when he comes in. The rowdy retirees have already consumed as many KBC $2 tap brews as they can handle for one night and the night owls haven't gotten off their own shifts in the other bars and restaurants yet. The Harbor is all tourism. That's our industry. The dark sky and the clear water, the mountain, and the trails, are our four-season stock in trade and our reason for living here. You don't pass through the Harbor on the way to anywhere. It's at the terminus of US Highway 41. The sign will tell you: Miami, Florida, the other end of 41, is just 1,990 miles away.

I work my way down to Gabe's stool, tracing overlapping circles on the shiny mahogany with a clean bar rag.

"Do you think he's serious?"

"Doesn't matter," Gabe says. "Ol' Monty's about to find out what happens when you mess with Keweenaw."

"Fuckin' A right!" Jeannie likes to sit next to the taps, where the light shows her curves and the whole look to perfection. I've never seen her pick anybody up during my shifts, but you have to give her snaps for style and effort. Sequins are a fine thing in a far north tavern. The world could use more sequins in general, if you ask me.

The declaration establishing the American Promise Pipeline was issued a few weeks before the people of Keweenaw faced the fight of our lives—for the water that gives us life. What else could we do? In less than a month, we mobilized. We took up arms. We mined the mines, wiring explosives for detonation. We activated the old Calumet Air Base. Surprising, the amount of equipment left behind after decommissioning. We were up and running in no time.

One thing people forget is Keweenaw's high concentration of folks who served in the armed forces. Over all the wars, we sent more per capita to the battlefields than any other counties in Michigan, from World Wars I and II, to Korea, to 'Nam and Desert Storm, and on to Afghanistan. Navy seals,

special ops, heavy equipment battalions, all based out of the Calumet Armory. The Keweenaw Liberation Front hadn't been active in years, but they all hung out in the same pubs, bought their drugs of choice from the same dealers, and rode with the same bike clubs. They'd brought things back to the states that weren't legal. Grenades. Machine guns. Machetes. Weaponry that would have horrified law enforcement. Except now the cops were fighting for Keweenaw, too. And the University contingent. Many of the cybersecurity, engineering, ecology, and environmental experts have lived here long enough to know Keweenaw is worth defending. The scientists were on board; the military science department was especially helpful. Army and Air Force ROTC were in their glory. The Old Guard had to rein them in.

"Friggin' brats! This ain't a run up the ski hill." Reggie, a 'Nam vet, liked to stop in for a blackberry brandy with a Pabst chaser on the daily. He cut back during the build-up, but his eyes twinkled more than they'd ever done on a "jingle" as we call an extended bout of partying in these parts, while he regaled the bar with the story of how he got the college kids to fall in line.

About fourteen days after Mussell's proclamation, we were, as they say, armed to the teeth and loaded for bear. Humans always need time to process. But when you talk about taking Lake Superior water, it doesn't take long to get down to brass tacks. Oh, there were the usual outraged letters to the editor in *The Daily Mining Gazette*, public hand wringing, and assignment of blame. A little more whiskey drinking at the bar.

But Keweenaw walks the walk. We weren't kidding when we backed a 51st state and we're not joking now.

American flags came down. Monty's trademark disappeared from the landscape, including the big box franchises south of the Portage Lake Lift Bridge who pride themselves on flying the largest Old Glories possible.

All state and federal regulations moot, all regional divisions meaningless, there is no national Law of the Land left in Keweenaw.

We will rule our water. We are the sentries and stewards, standing fast.

I scan the horizon. The lighthouse blinks. Darkness falling. Shipping season will be over in a couple of weeks. If we can hold on, the waves, snow, and ice will be our strongest ally.

Lake Michigan is already gone. We had no choice but to surrender the portion of Upper Peninsula shoreline 295 miles over on the opposite shore because the lower peninsula gave up easy. Can't count on the trolls for squat. Let the feds right over the Mackinac Bridge. Those wimps didn't give the privilege and responsibility of living in the Great Lakes State a second thought. Maybe because they're used to invaders, from chemical factories and nuke plants to Pacific salmon.

We plan to send reinforcements to patrol the east end of the peninsula. But there's no one to spare now. We rely on the groups we know are actively sabotaging attempts to come ashore at St. Ignace. They guard our flank. They can prevail. They are, after all, Yoopers.

Wisconsin had one lake to defend and barely put up a fight. No surprise there. Their eel-spined lamprey of a governor has been sucking the blood out of environmental regs for years, like his predecessor before him. The ass-kissing mirrors the hungry political alewives out West, puckering up to Ol' Monty, endorsing everything the sharp-tongued hothead says almost before it comes out of his ill-informed mouth. In desperate need of his help to steal our water. Motherfuckers.

There's a rumor that the Cheeseheads fell in line thanks to something Big Brother put in their beer. Probably just bar talk.

We used to watch Monty's game show, *Money Talks,* in the bar. The major network broadcast featured minor celebrities debasing themselves by performing fund-raising stunts later judged by Monty in his boardroom. This is the MO for the Mussell presidency.

Mussell's chief Congressional sidekick, whose name is beyond mention (just looking at that thick-lipped, fat-tongued round goby face makes me want to puke) made sure the ruling party's agenda to siphon off Great Lakes water was rammed through as speedily as it stacked the Supreme Court.

If they don't respect the wishes of the people, we can't respect the laws they make.

"Don't mess with Texas? Yeah, right." Gabe swigs his Labatt. "Whoever said that never met anybody from Keweenaw."

Damn skippy.

The wind has picked up, four-to-six-footers shattering against the barely visible shoals of the narrow Harbor entrance channel, dramatic, shiny, malevolent, and permanent bergs waiting beneath the surface to bash and destroy. The bell buoy bongs frantically.

Maybe we'll get lucky, and whoever tries to drive into this port will be unaware of how meticulously you must line up with the range light and where to turn sharply to starboard, just so, before you run out of water.

I lift the binoculars, eyeing the rectangular line of man-made matter on the horizon, stack belching, four miles out in the shipping lanes. Duluth-bound most likely. Freighter or warship? Friend or foe? I make a note in the log for Cory, who's on the next shift in twenty minutes. It's time to get ready for work. Supplies have been choked at the Mackinac Bridge, but as long as there's booze in the tavern stockroom, I have a job.

The running lights on the bow are now visible. The bulk carrier appears to be altering course. It steams toward the harbor. My breastbone beneath my tee is damp with sweat. I inhale, blow out through my mouth. Raise the Remmy.

Seeds Well Planted: Healing Balm from a Keweenaw Garden

by Cyndi Perkins

For thirty-five growing seasons, I posed as a casual gin-and-tonic gardener (a phrase coined by author Janice Wells) tending my cottage-style beds of perennial herbs and flowers with *joie de vivre* and complete indifference to order. The parsley, sage, rosemary, and thyme intermingled like a Simon and Garfunkel harmony. Rampant Sweet Peas invaded the Sweet Williams and twined through the Lavender. Plants without borders roamed freely over Lake Superior driftwood, North Atlantic seashells, broken mirrors, and found objects. The plastic flamingo flock free-ranged among Jacobsville sandstone, impertinent Daylilies, and nodding Poppies, as carefree as agate-picking Keweenaw beachcombers on July vacation. Solar butterflies and hummingbirds blinked on at dusk like faerie lights.

The gardens looked effortless in their imperfection. Truth be told: there was a tight-lipped martinet directing everything behind

the scenes. A stentorian weed tamer who secretly craved flawlessly clipped hedges and symmetrical rows—a 1950's *Better Homes and Gardens* kind of gardener who was never satisfied.

Meet Control Freak.

Control Freak shoved the gin-and-tonic gardener out of the way quite often, obsessively dead-heading petunias while ripping out riotous bursts of vining wild morning glories, battling insistent Jerusalem artichokes, stubborn Queen Anne's Lace, and prolific, unstoppable profusions of forget-me-nots. Attacking the Tansy and Horsetails with a vengeance.

You can't get around it. Gardens are messy. Daisies *will* spread. Iris fall over. Dahlias need staking. Mint marches on. Whatever dream garden you saw in the magazine or on Pinterest might be achievable—if that's all you do.

The gin-and-tonic gardener never minded all the little details (oh, the stories we tell ourselves!). She was only able to maintain the delusion because Control Freak was able to stay on top of the squatting, lugging, pulling, and hefting. Until the back attacked.

It was no more than a two-second crackle in the low spine, followed by a slight twang where right fanny cheek meets upper thigh. It felt like a hamstring pull. *Slow down! You know better,* Control Freak admonished. I've been practicing yoga for twenty years. I'm naturally limber and can still do the splits I learned as a gymnast and cheerleader. But I have a long way to go when it comes to mindfulness.

When I blew out my back, I *was* being mindful. Mindful of how neatly and quickly I was dumping twenty-five-pound bags of organic potting soil into one of several giant terra cotta pots. The remedy seemed clear. A sweat in my backyard barrel sauna, a YouTube stretch class, and an Epsom salts bath would set things to rights. I dumped the rest of the dirt into the wheelbarrow and began potting the fragrant Alyssum and pungent Rosemary I'd just purchased. Company was coming. Control Freak needed the yard to look beautiful. *Don't forget to stretch later,* I reminded myself. It was the last planter I filled for two years.

As yogis know, most aches and pains are easily handled over time, gently, with breath and the right movements. For the next three weeks, my nagging right hamstring was always there, singing (more like moaning) up my leg. *Can you feel me? Feel me now? Huh?*

I was confused about what my body was telling me. Then came the morning I could not walk. The hamstring was not the problem. I'd seriously pissed off my sciatic nerve, the longest and biggest nerve in the body, which runs from the base of the spine down the legs. Do you know the pain? I think some of you must. Sciatica is common. But it was new to me.

A herd of Charlie horses galloped up my right leg, radiating from second joint of my tingling fourth toe (the terminus of the nerve) and bottom of the heel. The meat of my right calf spasmodically clenched as the horses rumbled through, searing sharp, hot, wiry sensations into my right buttock. As is often the case with sciatic injury, my sacrum and lower back didn't hurt. Later, in the physical therapist's treatment room, I saw the intricate branches of the main nerve and its associates and understood how from one tiny root such widespread pain could bloom.

It hurt to stand, and it hurt to sit. It hurt to live.

As weeks went by, the dirt in the wheelbarrow turned to black soup. Every plan I'd made for my debut novel and summer adventures dissolved. When you can't wipe your butt without wincing, it's hard to celebrate dreams come true. Tear-blind, I hobbled out to the back garden, where the cardboard and old blankets thrown over winter ground would not be removed this year. There was a small patch of exposed black soil. I cast my Calendula seeds.

It was a beautiful summer. My husband, a veggie guy, took over our warped old back deck with white pickle buckets full of Early Girls and cherry tomatoes.

I inhaled that sharp tomato-leaf aroma redolent of everything that's right about summer and watched my untended garden grow from the vantage of an old quilt thrown on the lawn. I carried that quilt everywhere for months. Dubbed "the floor blanket," I'd drop to rest upon its purple, yellow, pale green and turquoise flower patchwork as needed—at the Walmart service counter, at work when I could finally return, in the checkout line at the grocery store—wherever I was. Lying down on my left side, the right knee hiked up as close to my chest as I could get it, was the only comfortable position. Ice bag down my pants to chill my sacrum, I aced the lesson: care less about what people think.

When I could stand upright for longer periods, I tried a little weeding in the front flowerbed. The grass was having a field day. It was as if the roots knew they could resist. That I didn't have the strength to pull without my own nerve roots screaming. I tried not to take it personally. Nature is always just doing what she does. Maybe it should have felt liberating. But I was a sad gardener. A limited gardener.

Until I let my garden tend me.

From the floor blanket, I watched sprigs of oregano spiral upward in passionate, spicy-scented profusion. Volunteer petunias sprouted in a planter from the year before. For the first time in two decades, a dormant rosebush bloomed. Unclipped herbs blossomed. "Riders of the Purple Sage," I quipped, thrilled that wielding scissors was painless.

The bristly-leaved comfrey in the back bed demanded my attention. It was forming the tiny drooping bells of its pale-periwinkle flowers. In the midst of my suffering, I'd forgotten the healing properties of this native perennial, which soothes everything from deep muscle aches to bruises. It's important to harvest comfrey before full flowering. *Herbalist, heal thyself.* Simply clipping the leaves is enough effort: it's ready for dropping in the bath or drying to use in balms and oils. Not long after comfrey pinged me, my smelly friend valerian showed its white umbels, the delicate splay of blossoms reminding me that the herb does more than promote rest; it also eases muscle spasms. As I laid on my belly on another spot on the lawn, I spotted my tender old friend plantain, which is not the southern hemisphere banana leaf you might be thinking of, but grows wild and tough underfoot here in the north country. For years I'd been making and sharing healing herbal balms with friends. Now these balms could heal me.

In this summer of limping and limits, the primroses, seeds from Grand Rapids, Michigan, stood tall when I could not. Their dainty yellow blossoms were easily plucked. But before I picked them, I kissed them. I kissed the Calendula, too. The seed sown wild grew obligingly, asking only to be deadheaded from time to time to reassure it that it was still a good time to grow. I thanked the Lavender smelling up the place.

That year, the Upper Peninsula experienced a golden autumn. The garden flourished well past the wild rice season and the harvest moon. Control Freak noted that the harvest was about the same, if not better, than it ever was.

The healing continued. Time is a friend to both the perennial garden and the human intent on personal growth. We can still do the things we love for our whole lives. They are done differently. Waist-high planters protect the back. Helpful tools and people assist with the heavy lifting. Consistent self-care, including acupuncture, chiropractic, exercise, massage therapy, and physical therapy are vital.

Control Freak yields, truly, to the gin-and-tonic gardener. Although when Life gives you so much mint, you sometimes swap out the G&Ts for mojitos and juleps.

Make Your Own Balm

My base recipe for soothing, gentle balms is by no means original. You'll find variations of it all over the internet. My original source is the Wellness Mama blog founded by Katie Wells (wellnessmama.com). She has a journalism background, which means she does her research and writes clearly.

My variation on the recipe has been fine-tuned over the years, created with home-grown and Keweenaw-harvested plants that I know have not been exposed to pesticides or commercial fertilizers. I cultivate, harvest, dry, steep, and formulate my balms with loving intention. That's what'll make your balms special, too.

Cyndi's Abundant Unguent Ingredients

Cultivated plants: Calendula, comfrey, Lavender, rosemary, and thyme

Gathered plants: Plantain, yarrow, and wild rose petals

The plant parts with the most useful properties vary depending on plant composition. For example, I harvest Calendula and rose petals, whole comfrey leaves, and Lavender and rosemary sprigs throughout the growing season. You can learn more about the best times to harvest your plants and which parts to harvest, but essentially, it's on dry days when the sun is strongest and the oils are rising into the plant parts.

Dry the plants out of direct sun where air circulates (I use paper grocery bags and am not at all picky about meticulously separating stems from leaves). I shake the bags periodically and check to ensure they're not too crowded because mold can ruin your harvest.

The dried plant material goes into wide-mouthed glass jars completely covered with cold-pressed virgin olive oil and left to steep for six to eight weeks (occasionally shake the jars and don't forget to label them).

When you're ready to make balm, strain the oil out through cheesecloth. I use glass bowls with a spout that makes it easy to pour the oil into Mason jars. That way you don't have to do everything at once, and you can reserve some oil to use in the bath or rub directly on your skin.

The Basic Recipe
½ to ¾ cup of your plant oil
½ cup organic beeswax (you can buy pellets, or blocks to grate)

Heat the oil in a heavy-bottomed saucepan on medium to low, gradually dropping in beeswax shavings or pellets until fully dissolved. Remove from heat. If you like, add 8-10 drops of vitamin e oil, to help preserve. Pour into containers (check your health-food store, local co-op or online sources for the kind you want). Leave uncovered until mixture sets.

Tips and Cautions
Please note by way of disclaimer that I'm not a doctor, this recipe should not be considered medical advice, and it's important to consult with your physician, especially if you have skin allergies.

Research the shortcuts if you want balm faster or don't have easy access to herbs. For example, you can buy dried herbs from wellness companies or local farms. You can cut down on oil-steeping time by using a crockpot.

Stick balms in the fridge to firm up; they tend to get melty in high heat. But don't freeze your balm. It will thaw as a liquid, which can be messy!

Apply with care. The formula has an olive oil base that may stain clothing.

Don't eat the balm. Sure, it's natural, but for external use only.

Long-time Keweenaw resident **Cyndi Perkins** is the author of *More Than You Think You Know* (Beating Windward Press). The former Houghton *Daily Mining Gazette* managing editor, whose work has appeared in numerous regional and national publications, is senior content specialist at Michigan Technological University, writing and editing for digital and print publications. Read her latest work on mtu.edu/news and connect on social media @cyndiperkins.

Astrid the Lighthouse Keeper

by Nikki Mitchell

"Turning, she looked across the bay, and there, sure enough, coming regularly across the waves first two quick strokes and then one long steady stroke, was the light of the Lighthouse. It had been lit."
—from "To the Lighthouse" by Virginia Woolf

Most fairytales come equipped with roaring seas and enchanted forests, but I'm here to tell you of one that has neither of those. You see, they aren't the only pieces of the earth that contain magic. Come with me to the shores of Lake Superior before the hustle and bustle of people drove away the lighthouse fairies.

•••

The fairies were gathered around a large stone table filled with acorn cups and blooming flowers. It was the fall gathering, and they were preparing for Lake Superior's great storms.

"Do we have enough sea glass?" a fairy wearing a buttercup tutu asked. Her name was Astrid, and she was the youngest lighthouse fairy in the room.

"Yes. Some of the glass must be replaced, but that isn't the problem," Queen Maryn said, carefully setting her cup onto its saucer.

"Then what's the problem?" an old male fairy demanded. "We have five days until the waves start coming over those rocks and we need to get the ships through safely."

"We don't have enough glowing pebbles. We can fix the glass all we want, but the lighthouses won't glow without them."

"What happened to the ones we stored from last year? There's no way we could have gone through all of those," Astrid said.

Queen Maryn sighed in defeat.

"The wind season was much longer last year, completely depleting our reserve," she said.

The old fairy slammed his fist on the table, causing the acorn cups to bounce. "Then we will just go collect more. Put in a mandatory work order for all lighthouse fairies. Let's get to work."

He stood up, bowed to the queen and was about to leave when she spoke up.

"I'm afraid that there may not be enough on the shores."

"Is there a way that the Ontario fairies can help?" Astrid asked. "They may have extra that we can use. We all have the same goal in mind."

With that, a burst of conversation filled the table, all the fairies trying to talk over one another. Queen Maryn let it go on for a few minutes before silencing everyone.

"That was my thought as well, Astrid," she said. "Break into groups and visit each of the Great Lake fairies. We can pay in sea glass, which is a rare find in some of the places you'll be traveling. We have five days, so you need to leave first thing in the morning."

Without hesitation, Astrid began breaking the fairies into groups and assigning them to each one of the Great Lakes—Superior, Ontario, Huron, Michigan, and Erie. She had the hardest time finding fairies to agree to Erie, since rumors of ghosts had recently started. Astrid sent everyone out to prepare, and once the room was cleared of the bumbling fairies, she collapsed in a chair and sipped her honey tea.

She had tasked herself with the most dangerous search for the glowing pebbles—the cave of the blackened rocks. Her wings trembled at just the thought of it.

Long ago, a giant ship had crashed into a cliff, causing the black rocks to crumble, leaving behind a giant cave filled with whatever Lake Superior decided to wash up at any given time. Treasure hunting fairies frequented the area and had the skills to do so without getting caught up in the mighty currents.

She had never been to the cave but had heard stories in the fairy village about how it glows at night. Astrid was sure there would be several of the pebbles there—pebbles they needed for a successful wind season.

•••

The very next morning, Astrid made her way to the map keeper and asked for a detailed map to the cave of the blackened rocks. He peered over his winged glasses and raised his eyebrows.

"And what business do you have of that place? Why would a lighthouse fairy have any interest in a looter's cave?" he asked.

Astrid knew that her duty as a lighthouse fairy was to not raise an alarm, especially since the last time the lighthouse glow went out, the entire fairy village was smashed to pieces by a small boat lost at sea.

"Please, no questions today. The queen has allowed it, I assure you," she lied.

"You know, not many fairies make it back from there," he said, sliding the map across the counter.

She handed over a couple of snail shells for payment and left with the map. "Thanks," she yelled over her shoulder before the door closed behind her.

Astrid looked the map over before dropping it into her bag, and she flew off in the direction of the cave.

She breathed in the sunshine and crisp air as she crossed over the lake. This was her favorite type of day and feeling the spray of the water on her as she flew was refreshing. For a moment, she had forgotten that she was headed to the most dangerous spot on the lake, and she needed to find as many of the glowing pebbles as possible.

Astrid paused for a moment in a tree on an island and pulled out the map. She was halfway there. If she was successful today, she would have enough time to help one of the other groups find rocks as well.

Her parents had been lighthouse fairies too, and the queen had bestowed that honor onto Astrid at the time of her birth. Her older brothers had been given healer occupations and had succeeded at creating many new tinctures for the village. Astrid had been in their shadows for a long time and wanted this to show that she was dedicated to the village and skilled at being a lighthouse keeper. The queen did not know where Astrid was headed; she would have never allowed it. But Astrid knew the importance of these pebbles.

The wind picked up as she flew toward the blackened rocks, and the lake had gotten angrier. She pulled her hood up over her head and tucked her wings as flat as she could while still allowing her to fly.

She knew the danger of getting too close to the water when the waves were strong. Lake Superior had washed up many fairies that way. Treasure hunting fairies wore guards on their wings, which prevented them from getting wet and bogged down. Astrid wished that she had asked to borrow a pair.

"There," she whispered to herself, as the cave of the blackened rocks came into view. A sudden wave of panic came over her once she saw the height of the waves beating the rocks at its entrance.

•••

Astrid got closer to the lake and the wind bounced her about, causing her to crash into a rock.

"Ouch!" she said, grabbing her arm. Her shirt had a small tear in it, but it hadn't cut into the skin.

The wind was too strong for her to just to fly into the cave entrance. She knew she needed to be smart about this. Astrid found a taller rock a few feet from the hole and sat for a moment. Astrid could see the floor of the cave glowing—blue, purple, and even a fiery orange. Even the collection of the lighted pebbles in storage weren't as pretty. The cliffs were huge and didn't allow sunlight into the cove, casting an eerie feeling over the entire place.

Astrid shook it off and found a rock path to follow into the cave. Very carefully, she hopped from one rock to another, almost losing her balance a few times.

With one more hop, she was able make it into the cave. She hadn't noticed until landing that the lake continued into the mouth. The glowing water came up just past her ankles and sent a chill through her spine. Even in the latest part of the sun season, areas of Lake Superior were still freezing cold.

Astrid set her eyes on the glowing pebbles—pebbles that only the lighthouse fairies could see. To everyone else, they looked like normal rocks. She took out her satchel and filled it with as many of the pebbles as possible. There seemed to be a million of them. Astrid wished she had brought another fairy or two to help bring these pebbles home, but she knew the risk was too great.

Once her satchel was full, she was about to fly off, when writing on the cave wall caught her eye. She set her bag down for a minute and looked around. The drawings told of epic adventures and looting the treasure-finding fairies had left to tell others of their travels.

The last image, however, was of the largest lighthouse Astrid had ever seen in her life. They had used a glowing paint, most likely made from the pebbles, and made the whole lighthouse glow. The lighthouse in the painting was surrounded by the same rocks that covered the cave floor.

"What is this?" she said to herself.

The other drawings had been done by treasure fairies, but this one was different. This one had been drawn by a lighthouse fairy. Astrid followed the rocks down to a small set of initials under the painting.

"R.S," she read aloud. "Grandpa?"

Astrid looked to the cave ceiling and let out a gasp when she saw what she was looking at. This wasn't an actual cave she was standing in. It was inside the base of a lighthouse. The ship hadn't crashed into a cliff—it had crashed into a lighthouse.

"I have to tell the village about this!" Astrid said.

But just as she threw her satchel around her shoulder, a loud crash of thunder was followed by a streak of lightning that caused the entire entrance to be covered in fallen rock.

"Oh no!" Astrid screamed, trying to push the rock to the side and find a way through. If she didn't make it home in five days' time, there wouldn't be enough rocks to light the lighthouse and all hope would be lost.

She hoped that the other fairies were having some type of luck because she was not.

Defeated, she leaned against the wall. Her legs ached from the chilly water, and she knew this was it. Nobody knew she had come here other than the map keeper, but she had told him the Queen knew where she was headed.

After a while, Astrid's whole body began to shiver. She knew she had to find somewhere drier than where she was right now.

She walked deeper into the lighthouse, hoping for a dry spot. Instead, she found a staircase. It had rotted out, and she was thankful that she had wings. She flew up into the dark abyss and used one of the rocks to light her way. She reached the main control room of the lighthouse and was surprised to see it was still in working order. She would look more later—first she needed to sleep. Sleep allowed fairies to heal from exhaustion and extreme weather conditions. She found a bench and rested her head on her bag full of pebbles.

•••

Four days had passed, and the fairies returned to the village with little success. The fairies of Lake Michigan had shared what they could, but the other lakes were preparing for a wind season like the one before and couldn't risk their own lighthouses going out.

Queen Maryn called a lighthouse fairy meeting once again to discuss what they would do now and tally up what was collected from their own shores.

"We only have enough to light two lighthouses, and we must hope for a short wind season, because strong waves and dark skies will deplete these pebbles quickly," she explained.

The meeting was almost over when she noticed a certain fairy had not piped up with a suggestion like she had in every meeting since coming of age to sit in on one.

She quickly scanned the room.

"Has anyone seen Astrid?" she asked.

"No, she was supposed to come with us to our beaches, but never showed up," one fairy said.

"We need to look for her. Search the village. Ask everyone you know," Queen Maryn said.

Just then, the map keeper flew through the doors. "What of the fairy that went to the cave of the blackened rocks?" he asked. "She has not returned my map."

"Cave of the blackened rocks?" Queen Maryn asked. "We didn't send a fairy—oh, Astrid."

"Yes! That was her name. She came four days ago for a map to the cave. I warned her, but she said you had allowed it."

"I did no such thing. I don't know why she would go there alone. With the storm we had last night, there is no way she made it."

•••

Astrid woke suddenly and looked around to figure out her surroundings. She was no longer freezing, but panic came over her as she remembered what happened.

How long have I been asleep? she thought.

She knew there was no time to waste, and the entrance had been sealed with rocks. She looked around at the control room, searching for a way out. The controls caught her eye. They were still in working order. The bin for the glowing pebbles was empty; all of the levers looked fine except one. She flew up to the light room and looked at the damage the ship had made. There were a few busted glass panels, but the mesh formed around the glass was still intact. Relief filled Astrid's mind when she saw the bulb was whole, even after all these years.

I can fix this, she thought. Excitement filled her and her wings couldn't help but flutter a bit.

A lighthouse this big and powerful would light the whole area. Astrid understood now why they had built the lighthouse here so long ago. Lake Superior's waves washed in so many of the pebbles, there was almost an endless supply. No hunting, no restocking. If Astrid fixed this lighthouse, it would be a game changer for the lighthouse keepers.

She flew back down to the base of the lighthouse, in search of sea glass. She knew once she had the lantern room repaired, all that was left to do was fix the lever, refill the bin, and hope for the best.

Not only would the light help the ships come wind season, but it was also her only hope for rescue. Astrid pushed that thought out of her mind and began to work.

Astrid buzzed around for hours, bringing the lighthouse back to life. She was surprised the treasure hunting fairies had never mentioned the lighthouse before, although she knew they were only interested in things they could sell. Plus, shipwrecks were the best to loot, and lighthouses prevented those.

After fitting the last piece of green glass into the surrounding, she stepped back to admire her work. A bit of light came through the hodgepodge of colored sea glass. Each lighthouse had a unique pattern, and it was one of Astrid's favorite things.

She flew back down to the base several times collecting rocks until the bin in the control room was full.

Astrid examined the broken lever. She tried to pull up on it, causing the whole thing to come loose and send Astrid flying onto her back.

She brushed herself off and looked at the lever in her hand. Without allowing her mind to accept defeat, Astrid flew back down to the base and searched for something that could be a makeshift lever. It didn't have to hold long, just long enough for her to get the signal across the lake.

After a few minutes of digging through piles of rubbish, she found a flat piece of metal that she was sure would work.

She thanked her grandpa for showing her how to work the lighthouse controls as a young fairy. She knew exactly what to do. The levers were set on a timer and controlled when and how much of the pebbles were harvested. From there, the glowing fluid filled the tubes and fed the bulb. Once the bulb was full, anyone in the lantern room could hear the hum of the magic from the pebbles, and a ray of light would shoot out across the lake.

Astrid managed to secure the new lever and set the levers at the times according to the chart on the wall. She quickly flew to the lantern room and waited for the hum from the bulb. At first, nothing happened, and Astrid's heart sank. The new lever must not have worked.

But then it happened—a loud hum filled the air and Astrid did a few loops in the air in celebration. The winds howled outside, and she knew she had done it just in time. The wind season was here—and Astrid had fixed the biggest lighthouse in the land.

Now she just had to wait to be rescued.

•••

Argument erupted in the room filled with lighthouse fairies. Nobody could agree on what to do about the lighthouses. Astrid was gone, they didn't have enough pebbles, and the wind season was upon them.

The Queen was about to send everyone home when the map keeper busted through the doors again.

"She's alive!" he shouted.

"What? How do you know?" Queen Maryn asked.

"She lit a lighthouse."

"That's impossible. There are no lighthouses that far out. Plus, it's daylight. There's no lighthouse bright enough to cut through sun."

"Well, she found one! And it's the brightest I have ever seen!" He looped through the air.

The fairies all looked to the queen with questions on their faces.

"Could it be?" the old male fairy asked.

"Be what?" Queen Maryn asked, raising her hand to the rest of the fairies in a way to command silence.

"The fabled lighthouse of the blackened rocks," he said. "There have been tales of it that date back to the beginning of the light-house fairies, but it was never found. A lighthouse fairy a few generations back said he had found it in a cave, but nobody believed him. The whole thing was a child's imagination. The legends say that it is the only lighthouse needed and once it is lit, no ships will be lost at sea again."

"I remember that fairy—it was Astrid's grandfather."

"Looks like he wasn't wrong after all," the old fairy said.

"Let's go!" the map keeper shouted.

Everyone rushed out to see the light that the map keeper had rushed in about and stood in awe at the light beaming across the lake—even in daylight!

Queen Maryn looked to the map keeper.

"Send the treasure seekers to bring her home safe and prepare a feast," she said. "Tonight, we are celebrating the true treasure of our village—Astrid the lighthouse keeper."

Nikki Mitchell is an Upper Michigan native and lives with her husband and two kids, three cats and a rabbit in Iron River, Mich. She is a 2011 graduate of Northern Michigan University and spends her days daydreaming of fairytale lands. She is the author of *Eleanor Mason's Literary Adventures*, a middle-grade fairytale series and *How to Write a Book with a Kid on Your Lap*.

Driving a Hole for Dynamite circa 1860

Dinner for Two

by Becky Ross Michael

Built at the advent of the twentieth century, the proud house on Tamarack Street keeps watch over the neighborhood. With a facelift of white paint and new porches, the home embraces the whispers, laughter, and tears of those who came before. Tulips and daffodils reappear like clockwork each spring, and perennial flower beds rebloom every summer. Each autumn, the maple leaves let go of life and flutter to the ground. And the inevitable snows blanket the dormant lawn and insulate the foundation every winter.

Within the walls, modern updates conceal remnants of faded papers in floral prints and musty wooden lath. Residues of past colognes and stale cooking aromas occasionally escape into the air to puzzle the present-day residents.

•••

In the kitchen, snowflakes swirl beyond the windows as the man carefully constructs a multi-layered vegetable dish. No meat or dairy, as a nod to her favored eating trends. Together, they learned to cook by trying new recipes and ingredients in their remodeled kitchen.

A snowplow churns past the corner, throwing a wall of white.

He places the pan into the oven and sets a timer for one hour. *Surely, she'll come. It's her birthday, after all.* Taking a sip of white wine from his glass, he glances at the bottle of red set aside for the occasion. *I hope she's careful driving on these roads.*

While cutting and chopping vegetables for a colorful salad, he thinks back to other birthdays. One year, he hired a string quartet to accompany their meal. For another, the two dressed in Victorian garb for the memorable occasion. The man chuckles aloud, thinking of a time early in their story. The beef Wellington had refused to bake beyond an overly rare pink. *Maybe that led to her dislike of meat?*

He checks the timer and savors the lovely smells filling the kitchen. *Now to set the dining room table.* He has purchased roses, not easy to find in the North during long winter months. *I'll wait to light the candles.* While choosing some of their favorite music, the man rests on the sofa near the fireplace, enjoying the ghostly reflection of flames dancing on the surrounding tiles. With escalating winds outside, the old house creaks and sighs.

The sound of the timer startles him, and he moves back to the kitchen, switching the oven from bake to warm. As he reaches for the wineglass, the man notices the quickening beat of his heart and admits to feeling nervous after all these years. Things have been rocky between them, as of late, with more time spent apart than together. *Hopefully, this evening will be a step in the right direction.*

Seated at a small bistro table near the stove, he finally opens the saved bottle of red wine, noting her still-empty glass. The sky is now dark. Through the frosty window above the sink, he sees the revolving white lights of a snowplow as it cycles through the neighborhood. He peers at the clock and is at first surprised to admit she is late, worrying that dinner will turn dry.

The furnace clicks on, disrupting the stillness in the room and breathing a soft puff of air upon his neck. Suddenly, a new dread grabs hold of his mind. *What if she's hurt and needs me?*

When he jumps to his feet, the man's shoe catches on wrought iron. The chair topples on its side with a clatter and jars his senses. Only then does he remember that she is gone. There will be no more shared birthday dinners or plans for a renewed future. The rooms will remain silent and lonely. They had already said their final goodbyes without realizing the truth at the time. This life is the "empty after" he has always feared.

With tears of regret burning his eyes, he leaves the warmth behind and heads out for a cold winter's walk. After the door is closed and latched, the house heaves a long moan of sorrow.

Becky Ross Michael grew up in Michigan, where she raised a family and taught in the Calumet-Laurium-Keweenaw and Sault Ste. Marie schools. She now gardens and works on her sunny balcony in North Texas. Writing for adults and youngsters, Becky's pieces appear in magazines, anthologies, and children's readers. In addition, she enjoys the challenge of working as a freelance editor. Visit Becky at platformnumber4.com

Historical Manistique - Logging camp

Doe Season

by Robert McEvilla

If anything, the whole episode made me wonder: maybe it isn't always that the fittest survive. That doe wasn't the fittest deer in the woods. She had a serious disability, but she carried on for three years against the odds. Was it luck?

Every spring since I've been retired, I travel from Florida to spend my summer in the Upper Peninsula. I stay at a hunting cabin that's been in the family for three generations and going on four. My brother, Hank, refers to it as the "camp." I call it my summer home.

Hank usually gives me a hand to open the place every spring. The first thing I do is spread some corn out for the deer. Hank always shakes his head at this and says I'm wasting my money. But I like to keep the deer around so my grandchildren can see them when they come up to visit.

It was Hank who saw it first as we stood on the porch that morning. "If that ain't the craziest thing," he said. "Look at that." He pointed to a half dozen deer munching on the corn I had put out. The biggest doe in the herd had its front leg extended straight out in front of her. It had to be at almost a ninety-degree-angle and parallel to the ground. I assumed she would lower the leg any second when I saw that she couldn't. An arrow was stuck in her just below the shoulder. The arrowhead must've cut just enough nerve and muscle that prevented her from lowering the leg.

"The poor thing, you have to feel sorry for it," I said.

"Yeah, well maybe, but I feel sorry for the bow hunter. Not only did he lose his quarry, he lost an arrow to boot. Those aluminum arrows aren't cheap."

•••

Leave it to my brother the old woodsman to say that. He stayed in the UP all his life while I left for college and never returned until I retired, with the exception of a few funerals and an occasional wedding.

"Maybe we should call the DNR. They might be able to—"

"No," Hank interrupted. "Don't get them involved. There's nothing much they can do. Besides, it's just a deer, not some endangered animal." He paused, then as an afterthought he said, "The thing will be out of its misery soon enough. It can't survive long on three legs. It'll either starve, get hit by a car, or the wolves will get to her."

"Yeah," I said. "You probably got something there, but hell, it has survived this long. Who knows how long it still has to suffer?"

Hank pushed back the bill of his cap. "You can always put it out of its misery. The Winchester is in the cabin. It's an easy shot from here."

"I suppose that's the best thing. I'll go get it."

The old lever action .30-30 Winchester was more of a decoration than a practical deer rifle. Every spring, I'd bring it up north and hang it over the fireplace. After I took it off the wall, I tried to remember where I kept the shells. I was still searching when Hank came into the cabin.

"Forget it," he said. "The deer just finished the corn and left. They're all gone."

The next day I found a box of cartridges. I loaded the rifle, so I'd be ready when the deer returned to feed. I knew they'd be back. For most of the spring, the deer have always appeared outside the cabin right after dawn. They would wait and watch me go to the shed and come out with a bucket of shelled corn. They appeared like clockwork until June approached and then their pattern changed, and you wouldn't see much of them until the waning days of August when they would trickle by again. By Labor Day, they would reestablish the routine they had in the spring. There was one exception. For the last few years, a lone doe would show herself about thirty feet from the cabin a couple times a week and I'd always give her a handout. She wasn't skittish. I could get within a couple of feet next to her before I spread the corn.

Sure enough, the next morning a herd of does and yearlings waited outside my window. As I walked toward them with the bucket of corn, they did what they always did and bolted away a few yards; all except the one with the arrow wound. It's difficult for me to identify one doe from another, but sometimes I can recognize and single out one doe by their actions. The doe with the arrow stood her ground and allowed me to get up close. I now knew she was the

same one that always came around in the summer. I studied her while she ate. A large knot had formed over the wound that held the arrowhead. As soon as I walked away, the rest of the herd joined her.

•••

I was certain I was doing the right thing when I loaded the rifle. The doe had to be living in misery. How could it not? With the .30 .30 propped up on the arm of a chair, I took aim. I decided to wait and let the poor thing finish her last meal. Soon three more does joined the feed. There would be a fight over the remaining corn; there usually was.

One mature doe kicked a yearling away. The aggressor turned on my intended target and reared up to land a blow. It wouldn't be much of a challenge to push away the three-legged competition. It was a mistake. To her surprise and my disbelief, the wounded doe bolted forward and poked the intruder in the neck with her permanently extended leg, like a running back stiff-arms a would-be tackler. That was all it took for the bully to retreat. The crippled deer finished the corn in peace. I put the rifle away.

She continued to wait for me each morning, sometimes twice a day. I always obliged with my offer of grain. One day a spike horn tried to move in on her and he got the same treatment any deer got that tried to muscle in on her corn. A stiff poke from that rigged leg kept them all at bay. I began to call her Lancer.

Hank paid me a visit one evening and brought beer. He asked if I had shot the deer with the arrow wound. I told him I hadn't seen it since the time he first saw it.

"Well," he said, "I didn't think it would last long."

I acted in bad faith because I knew what he would say, and I wasn't in the mood to listen to it. If I had been truthful all I would hear would be: "If you do see it again, make sure you shoot it. The best thing that can happen to a deer is to get shot. That's the compassionate thing to do. It's either that or getting hit by a car, starving to death in the winter, or get eaten by wolves."

Lancer continued to accept my handouts along with a few other does and yearlings. It was my regular morning routine until a few days before hunting season. Camps were beginning to open up for the hunt. There was more traffic in the area. The deer tell you rifle season is about to begin by the way they change their pattern.

I didn't see Lancer again that year. After I closed up the cabin for the winter, I had Thanksgiving dinner at Hank's before I made my way back to Florida. Would that disabled deer make through another Michigan winter?

•••

There was still a half foot of snow on the ground when I got back north the next April. Hank had to plow the road up to the cabin so we could open it up. As soon as Hank left, I cleared away the snow where I always spread the corn. There were no takers until the next morning. Six deer were feeding with Lancer jabbing them away if they got too close to her. She had survived the winter.

For the next month the feeding routine was reestablished before the pattern began to break apart. Three or four yearlings would show up in the morning but there was no sign of Lancer. By the end of May the deer stayed away. That was their normal habit; nothing new about that, but I did miss seeing Lancer. I went for a walk one evening around the end of June. On my return to the cabin, I saw a figure ahead of me. It was her. You couldn't miss that doe with the front leg sticking straight out. She stood and watched me as I turned down the path that led to the cabin. She followed me with her surprise behind her. It was her fawn. She waited until I threw some corn in the usual place. She ate while the fawn suckled.

She continued to visit once or twice a week with her fawn for the rest of the summer. Near the beginning of fall, she was joined by a various herd of does, yearlings, and an occasional spike horn. They would hassle each other over the corn but kept their distance from Lancer. One morning I noticed the arrow in her shoulder was slightly bent. I never knew if that was a recent development or if it was always that way.

I had to leave for Florida just a few days before hunting season. I dumped over fifty pounds of corn before I left to give the deer something before winter. There was already snow on the ground.

The next spring Hank had to plow the road so I could get into the cabin; nothing unusual about that. Once I was settled in, a herd of nine deer stood outside my cabin. I didn't have any corn left. They had to settle for birdseed and were glad to get it.

After a few days, the snow was gone except for some spots in the woods. I went for a walk. On the side of an old logging road, I spotted the remains of a deer. The head and legs were missing which is typical of a wolf kill. The only thing different about this carcass was the bent arrow beside it. I knew what Hank would say.

Robert Mcevilla is a retired engineer who lives in the woods near Channing, Michigan. His latest novel is *Fender Head*, released in June of 2021, about a German soldier who escapes from a POW camp in Michigan's Upper Peninsula.

Historical Marquette - JW Spear Rolling Mill Store

Woodpecker

by Raymond Luczak

in English and American Sign Language (ASL) gloss

the holes	tree
left behind	{dot}
in the bark	{dot-down}
are messages	{dot-down}
once tap-	inform-inform
drummed	{middle-finger-stuck-out-heart-throb}
out in	inform-inform
telegrams	{tweet-off-index-finger-tweet-off-index-finger}
echoing	woods-all-around
across the web	hear what
of forests	sing-sing
now forlorn	{flat-rhythm-over-heart}
with songs	lonely-lonely
for the lovelorn	{one-one} stand-far-apart

When I started noticing the tiny holes up and down the trunk of a birch tree, I initially thought they had been made by nails and then pulled out. Then I began seeing such holes everywhere. No one could possibly bother to make so many holes all over the woods! I've seen a great many birds in the U.P., but strangely enough I've yet to see a live woodpecker. But oh, what mysterious messages they leave behind!

Solivagant

by Raymond Luczak

I felt ashamed of my slim passport
with only its first two pages stamped. I
   couldn't claim

to possess a bottomless font spouting funny
stories gleaned from days and weeks traversing

this planet from one border to another.
I was an inveterate armchair traveler,

zipping along the rails of YouTubed trains,
sipping in the champagne sights of first-class
   seats

on overnight flights between New York and
   Singapore,
and learning new hacks to squeeze every
   centimeter

out of a backpack to outfit clothing essentials,
avoiding those ghastly baggage check-in fees.

I prowled the aisles at Midwest Mountaineer-
   ing,
where hikers, obsessed with the overall yoke

of their backpacks, stood with their hands
gauging the weight between a collapsible sili-
   cone bowl

and a sturdy bowl made of titanium.
I tried on one backpack after another.

Did it feel right on my back, and not too high
above my hips? The shoulder straps not too
   thin?

Compression straps? Waterproof? YKK zip-
   pers?
Padding for the laptop? A water bottle pocket?

The legendary properties of merino wool arose
in the mountains of my mind. How it could
   keep

me warm in cool weather, and cool in warm
   weather,
how my feet would never stink a few days in
   such socks,

how great it would be to leap from platform
   onto train,
how lullabied I would become from watching
   the terrain

rise and ebb through the window, floating up
   and down
into the air high above the rails, where storks
   would hold

sway with babies in their beaks, where clouds
   would frenzy
upward in slo-mo towers of Babel spilling out
   lost languages

that evaporated by the time they reached our
   ears, where
geese would barely flap their wings in their
   V-configurations,

where I could see below the patchwork of
   farmlands
punctuated by houses and fences, where
   roads and highways

underlined the borders once ink on an atlas,
   where
skyscrapers of glass hand-mirroring the skies
   around them

rose in a mirage that never blinked, where I
   would
discover that I didn't need a passport after all.

Raymond Luczak is the author and editor of many books, including *Chlorophyll: Poems* (forthcoming from Modern History Press), *once upon a twin: poems* (Gallaudet University Press), and *Compassion, Michigan: The Iron-wood Stories* (Modern History Press). His work has appeared in *POETRY, Prairie Schooner*, and elsewhere. An inaugural Zoeglossia Fellow and a Yooper native at heart, he lives in Minneapolis, Minnesota.

Sorrow's Lament (A Found Poem)

by Ellen Lord
—after Kwame Dawes, from: NEBRASKA

When my father died suddenly,
I sought out the villains quickly,
they kept me company for years.
the sense of doom was a comfort.
I *grew* bloated with decency;
every silence a wounding,
every poem a deep sin,
and every metaphor fell apart;
the dialect of sorrow,
the unending despair of sorrow.

Is memory merely the revenant
of flesh? Do the dead hum their decay
in the air? *Can we abandon*
the myth of home, the fear of nostalgia,
its haunting hold? Must something die
for something else to live?
Is there a lie in all sincere acts?

It was like that.
Wincing into the open sky.

Now, in the late morning light of October
everything is muted, a heavy greyness;
a gangly harbinger of shadows,
a shifting oppression of sky.
On a day as gray as this, the ending
of things seems imminent.
The wind becomes a steady moaning
and all my mind dwells on
are the deprivations; heavy weighted
with my sins, and betrayals.

Look at my eyes. Pay attention.
The sky has started to darken, to thicken.

My haunting is the failure of language.
And love does not teach us
the language we need. *But* each day,
enacting the things I have lost,
becomes another kind of holiness.
Suffering makes us pray.

I walk, ambling, ambling. The road
is empty. The heavy swoop of night
is coming. In the simplicity of it all,
and the grand silence…
I mark this day as the beginning
of my leaving.

Now I go deep into the forest
where the silence is absolute.
I have taken to talking to trees,
the light succussing, the deep hues
and filigree of wispy clouds.
The scent of rain.

Under the deluge, *I pray*
in sobbing thanksgiving, a flagellating
brusque wind that I welcome on my skin.
  Departing leaves
turn nonchalantly in the wind.
I forget to feel afraid.

Interlude

by Ellen Lord

We awaken
to the November moon, still high
over long-shadowed forest—
a primal silence.
Stormed in the night,
traces of snow remain.

I am restless
after waves of watery dreams,
searching for you again...
an old desperation.
You always say...
I'm right here. I am right here.

We walk.

Aspens stand naked, unencumbered.
I find two feathers, a stone;
you look for deer sign.

A loon sings, haunting—
from the far side of the lake
her eerie song, a comfort.

I cherish the interlude between storms.
It's easier to breathe. Breathe.

You take my hand.

The sky says another squall is pending
but right now, there is just enough breeze
to feel thoroughly kissed by nature.

I love us most when we walk—
a resilient camaraderie, a belonging.
May we go on like this forever, grateful
—up this long, rising road.

Ellen Lord is a Michigan native. Her poems have found a home in: *Dunes Review, Walloon Review, RKVRY Quarterly Journal, Peninsula Poets*/PSM, TDAL/PNO, Open Palm Print Chapbooks, and the Landmark Books Haiku contest. She is a member of UPPAA, Michigan Writers, and the Poets Society of Michigan. She wishes to thank members of the Freshwater Poets and Charlevoices for their camaraderie and support. She may be reached at ellenlordcs@gmail.com

Historical Munising - horse drawn logging

Saying Goodbye
by Tamara Lauder

It's hard to say goodbye when
  they're still with you.
The sense of loss can only be described to
  or understood by
someone else who is alone
  when someone is still with them.

The loneliness
  defies age, reason, or cause
the grief   cuts deep
the loss of what was
no longer is   or no longer can be.

Goodbye   isn't defined by leaving
Sometimes
  it requires staying right where you are
and letting go of what was
embracing what is   in a new way
so your heart and mind can rest
your soul can find peace.

It's hard to say goodbye
when someone is still with you
but sometimes
  saying goodbye is all you can do.

Novel
by Tamara Lauder

It began   novel
like any other   a <u>new</u> year.
News from afar   developing
  yet not defined,
viral   but not social

media
global   not local
urgent, emergent,
March forward. No!
Step back
lock up, cover up, wash up.

Novel   not the kind you read,
  but a virus that you breathe
corona , without the lime
    invisible, divisible, unjust for all.

The spike: protein attacks
          in cases rise
          in tension ignites
      dissention, defiance, compliance.

COVID-19, SARS-CoV-2, PPE, FDA, EUA,
  mRNA, DNA
      acronyms fly   questions arise
      confusion is high
what are they?   who are they?
what's in them?   who's got them?

2020   a misnomer for clear vision
started   a year like every other   yet
morphed   into one like no other.
Pandemic defined
novel continues.

Tamara Lauder is a professional artist in the Northwoods of Wisconsin. She combines her passion for writing with her artwork and is the author and illustrator of an inspirational pictorial book. Much of her inspiration comes from nearly forty years of visiting family and nature in the Keweenaw Peninsula, where her short story was selected for the *Houghton Selected Shorts Story Contest* performed at the Rozsa Center at Michigan Tech University. She enjoys writing, and is published in, a variety of genres.

Coffee in the Morning
by Kathleen Carlton Johnson

Mornings are difficult.
 I reenter the arena
the day gets named and events
surface, clear as marks on calendars.
Whole pathways emerge,
but not before coffee.

In other times Popes and Kings alike
Practiced some hot beverage.
Served, I am sure in bed,
steering them towards accomplishment.

Coffee, complements the cracks of light,
dispersing indigo night.
I greet my cup
with sacramental bliss.
A warm brown pool of awake
day depends on liquid taste
serene, allowing a warm glow to enter.
Another day, counted, measured
arriving in an azure cup.

Coffee.

Kathleen Carlton Johnson's work has appeared in *Aji, Diner and Phoebe, Michigan's Third Wednesday*, and *MacGuffin*. The *Origami Poems Project* has also published her. In addition, her poetry collection *Rain of Stars* will be published in May 2022 by Traprock Press.

Hunting Season
by Kathleen Carlton Johnson

He will appear, after work
going straight to the closet,
pull out a satchel and stuff it,
underwear, socks, pants and shirt.
In a plastic bag, toothbrush, paste and
    comb.
So focused he cannot speak.

I look as he enters the hall,
the light is dim, but it does not hide,
that distance growing between us.

The walls look geometric
cold in the shadows, his gear waits,
he rummages for his gun downstairs.

What is this that draws him into a wooded
    place,
To hunt and sleep amongst other males?
The primitive becomes evident.

Our homely exchanges rotate
around groceries, socks, and misplaced
    hats.
There is only one direction
and that is urgent.
the mandatory kiss
and he never looks back.

I have lost the person I know, to a wolf's
    heart,
but say nothing, as expected of the wife.
For two weeks our lives stop,
sadness and sinking rotate in awkward
    waves.

When he returns, smelling of woodstove,
Bacon, grease, and sweat.
When he has showered and melted back
into the family, he will be happy,
greeting me as his wife,
and we will continue.

Christmas Eve at the Dead Wolf Bar

by Chris Kent

The lighted wreath on the door of the Dead Wolf Bar blinked as snow fell, blanketing the parking lot. Wind gusts swirled, piling snow around the two cars outside the pub. The cement block building painted pewter gray sat just a mile from the blacktop ribbon of highway that crossed the Upper Peninsula of Michigan. Inside, tinsel icicles dangled from strings stretched in a grid across the ceiling. Faux boughs framed the mirror behind the bar. Wooden stools lined an L-shaped counter. A pool table, worn felt, in the middle of the room. A dusty artificial Christmas tree in the corner; yellow, red, green, and blue lights twinkling. Silenced on the TV, Green Bay Packers lined up against the Detroit Lions on snow covered Lambeau Field. The jukebox played "I'll Be Home for Christmas".

Vera, the bartender, leaned over, elbows resting on the bar, talking with her lone patron. Her t-shirt, stretched over her ample bosom, "I Can Get You on The Naughty List" adorning the front. The shirt separated from her snug, faded jeans exposing an intricate tramp stamp. A tall girl, well proportioned, blond hair streaked with holiday green, a broad, toothy smile, and an infectious laugh. Did well with tips when the bar was busy. Ten years ago, a college student with a career dream, met 'the love of her life'. He promised to bring her to "God's Country" north of the bridge, to a house and marriage. Live happily ever after. She came. He left. Vera and a baby girl stayed.

Only customer, Chow, somewhere north sixty, his name, like so many in the UP, a nickname. People often didn't know a man's real name, just a moniker he earned on his passage through life. Chow's Carhart pants, held up with wide red suspenders, over a faded camo shirt. His gray hair partially hidden by a wool plaid Stormy Kromer. His hands scarred and calloused. His milky blue eyes half covered by drooping lids. Several days of whisker stubble peppered his chin. "Where's the boss? Why you workin' tonight?"

"She's got a boyfriend, up in Marquette. Figured I might as well work, my kid is with her old man's mother in Florida. He don't pay attention to her, but the Grandmother does. I can use the money but it don't look like I'll get rich tonight. What you doin' here? You got kids don'tcha?" Out of habit, Vera wiped the empty bar.

"Daughter's out in California workin' at a fish cannery. Cleanin' fish all day. I barely get through a mess of bluegills. The boy's in the Army, Germany now. Nobody but me since Alice is gone. Even my ol' dog Blackie died. The best damn bird dog. I don't even have a Christmas tree, no use with just me around." His eyes filled; a tear rolled down his leathered face. He wiped it with his sleeve. Chow worked in the woods, had so many broken bones over the years he couldn't remember them all. His wife Alice died two years ago. Now he lived alone, down the road, in the house he and Alice had raised their family.

"Hey, let me buy you a beer," Vera twisted the cap off a Bud Light.

As Chow took a gulp from the longneck the door of Dead Wolf burst open, snow blew in across the floor. Vera and Chow looked toward the door as a woman in a down coat, reaching her knees, a Santa hat and flashing lights twinkling around her neck, stepped in the door. "Merry Christmas," she shouted.

Following her, a short fellow, wearing a sweater with a snowman standing on its head, the orange carrot nose dangling suggestively between his legs. "Oh, it's gettin' nasty. Thought we'd take a break. Get fueled up. How 'bout a couple whiskeys. Oughta' warm us up, don't you think? How you folks doin'?" He looked at Vera and Chow as he climbed onto a bar stool next to his wife. Taking her coat off, she exposed another Christmas sweater with more flashing lights.

Vera leaned over the bar, "I'll get those for youse but I need another look at that sweater. I think it's a winner, doncha' think, Chow? If we were havin' a contest, you'd be gettin' the prize, Buddy."

Chow looked up, "Where the hell you people goin'? Better yet, where'd you come from? Weather ain't for shit and you two do look foolish."

"Well sir, I think I'll take that as a compliment. We're headed to the Sagola Sportsman's Club for a Christmas Party. An ugly sweater contest that we are gonna' win. We live north of Bruce Crossing, well we still have a place down in Indiana, but we haven't been there for six months, having too much fun up here in the UP. Driving wasn't bad 'til we got a few miles up the road. Then it turned to crap, eh Marge? Think we better call the party, tell 'em we might be late. My name's Jerry and this here is my wife of thirty years, Marge."

Jerry had owned a Chrysler dealership in Indiana, sold it a year ago. Marge retired from being a third-grade teacher. Both had been single until their thirties when they met at a Christmas party at the dealership. That year Marge bought a new Chrysler LaBaron convertible, raspberry red, so she got an invitation to Jerry's annual party. Six months later they were married. No kids, just the two of them. Saved their money to buy a retirement place up north.

Chow took a swig from the Bud, wiped his mouth on his sleeve and replied, "Well, glad to meet you, Jerry and wife of thirty years. Welcome to the Dead Wolf."

Marge giggled. Chow cringed. Vera slid two glasses of Jack Daniel's over the bar.

"You folks gonna want anything to eat?" Vera inquired as a roar from outside turned their heads. "Sounds like a sled."

The sound died away, door opened and again the frigid wind blew snow over the plank floor. A man entered pulling his helmet off, blinking his eyes. Vera called from behind the bar, "What the hell you doin' out tonight, Pink?"

"The trail's a bitch, I'll tell ya. Well, it ain't the trail so much as you can't see a foot in front of the sled. Snowing so damn hard. I was headin' up to camp, get a fire started, everybody's supposed to come up for Christmas tomorrow." Snowmobile Trail 16 passed through the woods just south of the Dead Wolf. "I ain't tryin' it now, maybe the groomer'll get through later. I'll go then. How 'bout a Bud and a burger, Vera. Surprised to see you tonight. Thought you'd be home playin' Santa for the kid." Pink sat on a stool at the bar.

Jerry turned and called from the corner of the bar, "Did you say your name was Pink?"

"Pinky actually, I was number ten kid, might have been more in the family but the old man ran outta fingers." He wiggled his pinky finger, "So that's who I am. Who are you?"

"Jerry and this here is Marge, my wife of thirty years."

"Well Jerry that's quite a record. I don't think I know many folks that made it thirty years. She still goes places with you wearin' that sweater, eh?" Pink leaned over assessing the sweater. "Say, Jerry, did you hear about the guy that walked in here last week?"

"Pink, shut up, you moron. Nobody wants to listen to your jokes. We've heard them all a thousand times. Now, what do you want on your burger."

"Vera honey, Jerry here will think you don't love me. That the reason I'm here isn't to pick you up to go to camp with me. Ain't that right, Vera honey, you're goin' to camp with me."

"Now don't you wish, Pink. I'm not goin' any place with you. What do you want on that burger?" A swoosh as blue flames flashed under the grill behind the bar. The acrid smell of hot grease filled the air.

Pinky was single, been married a couple times but didn't work out. He ordered the priorities in life—hunting, fishing, snowmobiling, drinking and then wife. After number two kicked him out, he decided he was meant to be a single man. No more serious relationships.

"Say, Vera is it OK if I use your phone? I don't have a cell signal. Think I better call the party folks and let'um know we're gonna' to be late? While you're cookin', how about a burger, do you want one Marge?" She nodded affirmative. "Mak'em both medium, will ya?"

"Phone's on the wall by the cash register." Vera pulled three burgers out of the cooler, put them on the grill, the red meat sizzled and hissed.

The bar was quiet as Jerry punched numbers into the phone.

"No shit, looks like we won't see you tonight. Anybody hurt?" Jerry listened, then replied. "Well Merry Christmas. See you next year, I guess." The call ended. "Jez, a log truck lost it on the corner in Sagola, rolled over, logs knocked over one of the pumps at the gas station. Big fire. Roads are closed."

"Did they say who was drivin'? What color was the truck? I know most of those boys." Chow looked at Jerry, fingers wrapped around his chin, lines extending from corners of his eyes deepened.

"No, no more information. Didn't know if anyone was hurt, just said it was a mess and road's shut down. Nothin' else, sorry."

"Musta been headin' to the Quinnesec mill to dump off a load 'fore Christmas. Hurrin' to get home. Christ, I wonder who it was. Gonna fuck up somebody's Christmas, that's for sure."

Everyone in the bar turned as the door opened again. Snow was heavy behind the figure that entered. "Holy shit, it's Nanook of the North," Chow uttered as he took a swig of beer.

The man wore a fur trimmed parka, a hood that obscured most of his face. His boots laced to his knees with more fur trim around the tops. His beaver mittens reached his el-

bows. He stomped his feet, pushed the hood back exposing a tanned face, sharp, chiseled features with dark-blue eyes that sparkled. He smiled, nodded as he delivered a "Happy Holidays, folks."

"Your sled dogs outside, Nanook? Where the hell'd you come from?"

"Chow, let the poor guy get his coat off and sit down before you give him the third degree. Sorry Mister; Chow here don't get much chance to meet new folks." Vera watched as he hung his parka on a hook by Marge's puffy coat. He wore a green Nordic ski sweater and tailored jeans. He tucked the mittens in the sleeve of his parka and sat on a stool next to Marge.

"Name's Erol McPherson." He looked at the bar patrons. "And I was sure glad to see the open sign flashing. I just got back from Afghanistan a month ago. Drivin' in that God forsaken place was nothing like this."

"So, you in the army?"

"No, I'm a photographer; I work for the New York Times."

"Oh, sure buddy, and I'm special forces." Pinky sneered.

"Shut up Pinky, you don't have to be rude to everybody. Can I get you somethin' to drink Erol?" Vera leaned across the bar smiling. "What are you doin' here? From the New York Times."

"Taking photos of vacation homes off the grid. Times is doing a feature on people who have remote cabins. They're calling it 'Living Where the Neighbors Bite.' Met some interesting people."

"That could be most any place around here." Pink interrupted.

Before Erol could finish, lights from the parking lot lit up the window. A car engine died. All the bar patrons turned, expecting the door to open. Nothing.

"Probably bangin' in the backseat, quicky before they come in for a beer," Pinky editorialized.

A moment later the door opened, a couple walked in, the woman holding a black puppy. The dog nestled in her coat with only dark eyes and an ebony nose peeking out, tiny ice crystals coated the puppy's whiskers. "Does this puppy belong to any of you? Poor thing was in the snow by the side of the road. We almost ran over her. She's nearly frozen." The woman's lips tight, jaw tense, her nostrils flared. "I said, does she belong to any of you?" She was tall, a knit stocking cap tight to her head, long dark hair, streaked with gray hung straight from under the hat. She wore a red ski jacket.

Together, everyone at the bar responded, "Not mine!"

The puppy wasn't more than eight weeks old. It looked up, licking the woman's chin, then snuggled back inside her coat.

The man with her was slender, wearing a flannel shirt and ski vest. "Jackie, it's not their fault, the puppy is safe now. Good evening, folks." He took off his gloves, loosened his vest and stomped snow from his boots.

"Still snowin'?" Vera inquired.

"Oh yeah, visibility is zero and there's more than a foot of snow on the road. If your light hadn't been flashin', we never would've seen the place. And finding that puppy in the snow was some kind of Christmas miracle."

"Well come on in, join the fun. I think we're all going to get to know each other. Plows won't be out till morning. Can I get youse somethin' to drink? Where were you folks heading?"

"I'm Matt and this is my fiancé, Jackie. We're looking for property, planning to retire here. Build a place on the water. Supposed to be catching a flight back to D.C. but got a text, flight cancelled."

Erol spoke up, "I'm supposed to be flying back to New York, but I'd say we're all gonna enjoy Christmas Eve here at Dead Wolf with Vera. Right, Vera?" He touched the back of her hand, nodding his head, eyebrows raised.

"You betcha' Erol," she smiled and batted her lashes. "We might as well have some fun, enjoy ourselves. I'll fry up some poppers. Youse guys go out back in the shed, there's some chairs. Can't sit on bar stools all night. There's a sheet of plywood, put it on the pool table. Maybe we'll play some cards later. Anybody needs stuff outta their car, youse better get it."

Folding chairs set up and plywood on the pool table, Erol and Matt ventured to their cars.

Erol returned with his camera equipment, a sleeping bag, and a small suitcase. Matt had an arm full of sweatshirts and a briefcase. Vera covered the plywood with a red and green plastic Christmas tablecloth and piled cheese curds, crispy raviolis, fried zucchini, and jalapeno poppers in the center of the table.

"Vera, do you think there's a box somewhere I can put the puppy in, maybe an old towel or somethin' to wrap her up?" Jackie inquired as she stroked the still shivering puppy.

"Look in the backroom, there're some boxes and a stack of old clean up towels. Who needs somethin' to drink?" Vera called from behind the bar.

Erol stepped behind the bar, "Let me give you a hand." He stood next to Vera, shoulders touching. "I can open a bottle," smiling, he winked.

Drinks around, appetizers on the table and a deck of cards—the group gathered around for Pinky's instructions on Screw Your Neighbor. "Don't feel much like Screw Your Neighbor tonight, I'll just watch. I'm pretty comfortable right here. Know how to play cribbage?" Chow asked as Jackie put the box with the puppy on the floor next to him.

"I bet I can learn, how about you give me a lesson," Jackie pulled a chair up next to Chow.

"Fore you sit down, in my coat pocket over there on the hooks is my cribbage board. Vera, got another deck of cards? Jackie and I are goin' to play some cribbage. We can keep track of the puppy; be sure she stays warm."

"Chow, I never knew you to be such an old softie," as she tossed him a deck of cards.

A game of Screw Your Neighbor went on for hours. Between jokes and stories, they got to know each other. Pinky told some old favorites. "I was sittin' right there," he pointed to a barstool, "when this guy walked in wearin' nothin' but his work boots. I mean nothin', not a stitch of clothes and had his wallet super glued to his ass. I'm not kiddin', that happened right here, right at Dead Wolf. Funniest damn thing I ever saw."

"Well, I sure can't top that one, even the crazy things that happened in Afghanistan. Never saw anything like that."

Pinky loved the spotlight. He wasn't ready to give it up. "One day I was drivin' back from camp. A little hung over after a night drinkin', I catch a glimpse of somethin' out the corner of my eye. What the hell, I'm thinkin'. Put that old truck in reverse and backed up for another look. Sure as hell, there's a guy on the side of the road, sittin' on a truck seat, you know the bench seat outta a truck. Here's the best part. He's wearin' pajama pants, socks and flip-flops with a winter jacket pinned together with a big ol' safety pin. And oh, ya, it's 10 degrees. He tells me he was plowin' his road with his 1938 Osh Kosh road grader and it broke down. No phone signal, course. He took the seat out, dragged it two miles down the road, put it on the roadside and sat down. He was mad, a couple trucks went by and didn't stop. I said listen buddy, that's no surprise they musta' thought you were crazy." Pinky looked around the table enjoying the reaction. "So, I drove the old boy to town."

Vera stood up from the table, "Deal me out this hand and I'll get another round of drinks."

"Let me help," Erol volunteered.

Vera and Erol mixed drinks and sat at the bar watching the card game. Erol had his arm across the back of her stool, his thumb gently caressed the back of her arm. Vera spoke softly, "Bet you'd rather be in New York, not here with a bunch of crazy Yoopers."

Erol pulled her toward him, buried his face in her hair and whispered, "No place I'd rather be, Vera, than the Dead Wolf Bar."

"Hey Pinky, how come they call this place the Dead Wolf Bar," Jerry inquired. Certain Pinky would have a story.

"Here's what my ol' man said was the truth. A guy named Emil Wolf was building the place, goin' to live in it. Got the roof on and the poor bastard dropped dead right there on the floor." He pointed just inside the door. "Musta' laid there a couple days before somebody missed him. The place stood empty till a guy from up by Kenton finished it up and opened the bar."

"Good story, Pink, but this here's the truth, told to me by my Granddad," Chow spoke up from the corner of the room. "See that picture over there on the wall, the guy with the dead wolf. Well, that was the last wolf shot in the UP before they brought'm back a few years ago. It was right here, outside the bar. The guy in the picture was a friend of my Granddad's. He dropped that wolf with one shot. The hide useta' be hangin' next to the picture," he gestured toward the photo, "but somebody stole it. So that's why it's called the Dead Wolf Bar. Honest truth."

"Well, I think you're wrong but I ain't about to argue with an old man like you, Chow, you might get pissed and shoot me. Then there'd be a picture of you with me hanging in a tree on the wall. Ain't that right?" But clearly Pink hated giving up the spotlight.

"I like both those stories; guess we won't be able to prove either one of them tonight." Jerry smiled.

In the early morning hours, the stories stalled, the card players faded. Jackie covered Chow with a blanket, the puppy curled up in his arms. She and Matt settled into two chairs with shirts rolled up for pillows. Marge and Jerry the same. Pinky tried to keep the evening going but finally gave up and stretched out on his snowmobile suit on the floor. And somehow, Vera ended up spooning in the sleeping bag with Erol. Lights still twinkled on the tree in the corner.

Hours later, rays of morning sun slipped through the window bathing the room in faint light. Jackie felt along the wall beside the kitchen doorway searching for a light switch and a coffee pot. A few minutes later Vera was at the grill warming slices of ham. Jackie poured coffee. Matt mixed a pitcher of mimosas with a bottle of champagne and orange juice he found in the bar frig. Chow carried the puppy outside for a walk. Jerry and Marge set the table. "Where's Pinky?" Jerry asked.

Just then Chow came back in the door with the puppy. "He's outside shoveling off cars. The plow just made a first pass on the road. A couple more trips and it might be passable."

"Tell Pinky to get in here, breakfast is almost on the table, Vera called from behind the grill, sweat beading on her brow.

Matt and Jackie poured drinks, Vera put platters of ham, eggs, potatoes, and toast on the table. Erol set up his camera. "I want a photo of everyone; this has to be one of the best Christmas Eve's I've ever spent. Hey Chow, what's the puppy's name?"

"Eve," Chow smiled.

Breakfast dragged on, another cup of coffee, another mimosa, another serving of eggs. Finally, Erol got everyone posed for the picture. Chow in the middle with Eve on his lap. Tall in the back, short in front, making sure Jerry's sweater was visible. Then the usual, 'Cheese' everyone."

"Before we say goodbye," Jerry spoke up, "I've got a gift for Pinky, best storyteller I ever met." He took off his sweater, "I want you to wear this to camp with the family today, should make for a good story."

Vera stepped out of the kitchen wearing a different shirt, "And I want Matt to take my t-shirt with the promise he'll wear it to work in Washington, D.C."

"You folks are all being funny, this is serious. Jackie gave me Eve, my best Christmas in a lotta' years. Jackie, I want you to have my cribbage board, you were my best student ever. You remember old Chow when you get home."

Vera gave Marge, Jerry, and Erol all Dead Wolf t-shirts, making them promise to come back.

The group started drifting apart, toward original destinations, hugging and shaking hands, promising to get together sometime in the summer of 2020, wishing a Happy New Year as they went out the door until only Chow, Eve, Erol and Vera remained. "Come with me, Vera, come with me to New York. Your daughter is gone for the week. Celebrate the New Year in New York."

"Oh, I couldn't do that. I did that once; it didn't turn out so well. I just couldn't. But stay in touch. Come back."

"Are you sure?" Erol, his arm around Vera, his other hand on the door.

Chow cleared his throat, "Vera, you only go this way once. It's no dress rehearsal. Don't miss out. Look at me, an old man alone. Erol's a good fella; he knows if he don't take

good care of you, I'll come lookin' for him. Now, Vera, go."

She looked at Erol, smiled that big toothy smile, hugged Chow. "Happy New Year to you and Eve. I'll see you in a week."

Seven days later, New Year's Day of 2020, Vera stood with Erol at LaGuardia Airport. For her, a magical week: Times Square, theater, dinners, walks down Fifth Avenue as snowflakes drifted to the sparkling asphalt. Now it was time to go home. Erol held Vera, his face buried in her hair, taking in the lavender smell of her shampoo. To him she was the most authentic woman he had ever met, adventurous, sincere, and caring. And now he was saying good-bye, with a promise, we'll be together soon. She turned, blew a kiss as she moved through the security line, then she was gone. Erol sighed, adjusted his backpack, and walked toward the door.

Weeks later a virus changed everything, COVID-19 raged. Masks, social distancing, the new rules. Happy times at Dead Wolf Bar seemed so long ago. The "OPEN" light was dark.

In early June, Jerry died of COVID. Marge went back to Indiana. Pinky never had the opportunity to tell Jerry the story of wearing the sweater to camp on Christmas Day. How everyone that came in the door had to give the carrot a tug.

Matt and Jackie broke ground on the retirement home. Busy as they were, Jackie always made time to play a game of cribbage when they were in town. Eve never left Chow's side except when Jackie arrived. Then she would bound across the room, tail wagging.

New York Times employees were working from home. Erol returned to Michigan. Vera became a home-schooling Mom, living on unemployment.

The promise of gathering in the summer of 2020 was not kept; however, on Christmas Eve, two years from the night they all met, roads were clear, air was cold, and snow was deep. The lighted wreath on the door of the Dead Wolf flickered. Vera was behind the bar, Erol and Chow sat with a longneck in front of them. Eve was curled up at Chow's feet. Vera pushed the condiment trays, wiping the bar. "Youse guys want anything to eat?"

"Not yet, let's see if anybody else makes it."

"I emailed everyone. Matt, Jackie, and Pinky said they'd be here. Never heard from Marge. Probably too hard for her, drivin', bein' alone and all. Feel so bad about Jerry. What a nice guy. Poor Marge, got that retirement place up by Bruce Crossing, now she's alone. I think she's back in Indiana. Damn but we had fun that night, all of us stuck here together. Jerry with that sweater. Oh my god! What a hoot."

A new Christmas tree twinkled in the corner. The walls had a fresh coat of paint. A muted flat screen TV played the Green Bay Packers. On the wall next to the photo of the man with a dead wolf was a framed story from the New York Times. The headline *Christmas Eve at the Dead Wolf* with Erol's photo of the group snowed in at the bar two years ago. The article tells the story of the friendships established that snowy night and of the new owner of the Dead Wolf, Erol McPherson.

"Sure is good to see some fans at the game. I hope I never see another God damn cut-out sittin' in the stands." Chow bent forward scratching Eve's ears, then leaned back taking a swig from his beer.

The door opened, Jackie and Matt called, "Merry Christmas." Jackie knelt to greet Eve who bounded across the floor, then she wrapped her arms around Chow before she turned to hug Vera and Erol. Matt shook hands then hung his coat on the wall hook. "Weather sure is nicer than it was two years ago."

Jackie interrupted, "But we wouldn't have met everyone had it not been for that snowstorm. Great to see all of you. Where's Pinky? Is Marge coming? So sad about Jerry."

"Well Pinky promised he'd be here, and I didn't hear from Marge."

"You know, I've thought so many times over the last two years, sometimes it's the smallest decisions we make that change our lives forever. If I hadn't seen the flashing open sign on Christmas Eve two years ago, where would I be?" Erol mused. "And none of us would have ever met."

Just then they heard a sled in the parking lot.

"Bet that's Pink." Vera turned toward the door.

Pinky walked in with his arm around Marge, "Look who I found wandering around the parking lot. Said she was looking for a party. Told her I knew where to find one."

Vera came around the bar to give Marge a hug. "What you got under your arm girl?"

Marge held up a cut out of Jerry. "You think I'd let him miss the party?" She climbed on a bar stool next to Erol and propped the cut out on the stool next to her.

Chow sighed, "Christ, Marge, I just said I hoped I'd never see another damn cut out, but I'm glad to see Jerry."

Conversation during a game of Screw Your Neighbor turned to the past two years. "You know," Pinky said, "I felt like I was lost in the woods and didn't have my compass."

Chow sighed, "For me the days were forever. Any little noise Eve would bark, she just wanted somebody to stop by."

"Trying to be a teacher for my daughter was exhausting; I didn't know what I was doing half the time. Thank God he was around." Vera squeezed Erol's hand.

"I just feel like it didn't need to happen." Tears spilled down Marge's cheeks. Pinky put his arm around her shoulder, pulling her toward him.

"We shouldn't be bitchin'; what we all lost is nothin' to what Marge lost. I think it's time for a toast, here's to our friend Jerry, his wife of thirty years and friendships."

Chris Kent lives on the Brule River, near Iron River. She retired to the UP from a career in marketing and public relations in Lower Michigan. Chris is active in her community feeling a deep responsibility to "give back". Inspiration to write came from a local writing group and from the place she lives; a home where woods, water and sky come together to provide opportunity and motivation to create.

Lemon Cookies

by Sharon Kennedy

The air in my yellow kitchen is stifling. Even the English ivy framing the windows above the sink is drooping as if to say *spray me or put me out of my misery*. I wipe my brow with the hem of my apron. "Life's a bunghole," I say to Dodger as I dislodge the last little bit of lemon cookie dough from my Kitchen-Aid mixer.

"What's that you say?" Dodger asks. He lifts his head from yesterday's newspaper. I stare into his hazel eyes.

"Did I stutter? Did I mumble? What part of 'bunghole' do you not understand?" My tone is mocking but not unpleasant. I scrape the sides of the stainless-steel mixing bowl, carry it to the table, and roll the lemon-flavored dough into identical little balls.

"Tear off two pieces of that parchment paper, will you, and fix it so it fits on the cookie sheets. Use the scissors if you have to even it out." Dodger shoots me a look of amazement as if I had asked him to fly to the moon. He's a bachelor and although he knows his way around an outdoor barbeque, he's never baked a cookie in his life. Like me, he couldn't find anyone willing to take him on permanently. Unlike me, he has no children whereas I have a lovely teenage daughter.

Dodger and I don't see each other very often, but he loves my darling Ann. He's more affectionate toward her than her biological father who lives in California and works for a major pharmaceutical company. Dodger's in my hot kitchen on this beautiful July day instead of at Alcott Beach in Brimley swimming in Lake Superior's icy water and drink-ing wine with his buddies. He came over to play Monopoly with Ann, but she's not home. She's at the beach where anyone with an ounce of sense would be on a day as lovely as this one.

Dodger obediently picks up the parchment paper. "There's no sharp edge," he whines. "How am I supposed to tear it straight without a sharp edge?"

"That's a problem in your hands. The future of America does not depend upon parchment paper cut to perfection. Do the best you can." Dodger and I have been friends for years, but sometimes I feel like his mother. Maybe that's the way it is with all bachelors. They're basically helpless. Be that as it may, we're probably more comfortable with each other than most married people. We're non-judgmental, keep a safe emotional distance, never make demands, and our friendship will most likely follow us to the grave.

"Okay, okay, you don't have to bite off my head," he says. "Now, what do you mean about life being a—what'd you call it—a 'bunghole'? What kind of observation is that from an educated woman?" He rips off three times as much parchment as necessary.

"Hey, go easy on that stuff. It costs a fortune," I chastise him. "To answer your question, I was merely commenting on how I feel this afternoon. Give me a couple of hours, maybe even minutes depending upon how these cookies turn out, and I might feel differently. But for this moment, which is certainly not suspended in any kind of time warp, my opinion stands. Life is a bunghole.

I dare you to deny it." I continue to roll the dough into balls, place them on the sheets, and press them down with the bottom of a small glass dipped in yellow sugar.

"I like my life," Dodger replies. "If you're not happy, that's your fault, but to make a sweeping statement without any thought as to how it sounds to others, well, that's not right. What would Ann say if she were here? You've got to set an example. What's this stuff?" He finishes his mini lecture by asking about the lemon zest in the bottom of a ramekin.

"Does it look like the zest of a lemon or a dead chicken? Does it look long and stringy and yellow or does it look like a nut that fell from a tree? I forgot to put it in the dough, and it's too late now. I'll freeze it for next time." Dodger hands me the ramekin. "I like you," he says. "But I think you're crazy."

"Well, I like you, too, old buddy, and I *know* you're crazy. You'd have to be, hanging around this hot kitchen when you should be at the beach. Ann is with her friends, and I have no idea when she'll be home. Probably not before ten tonight." I flatten the last cookie and slip the sheets into the oven. The heat hits my face like a blast from a furnace. "Lordy, I'll be glad when this hot spell's over."

"Why'd you pick the hottest day of the year to bake?" Dodger asks. I take the chair opposite him. He looks the same as he did when we met thirteen years ago except now his hair is totally gray but still as thick as a lion's mane. He wears the same dark rimmed glasses, the same plaid shirts, smokes the same brown cigarettes, and still smells slightly of mothballs even in summer. Dodger never changes which is another of his endearing qualities. He loves his wine, his long-dead and never-known Civil War generals, his flower and vegetable gardens, his many friends, but most of all, he loves my daughter the way I wish her father loved her. Dodger is Ann's pseudo-dad and I thank God for him. I take a sip of the cold lemonade in front of me.

"I wanted to bake cookies and I didn't even think about the heat this morning because it wasn't hot at 6:30 when I got up. I just thought about how good a lem-on cookie would taste dunked in a cup of hot coffee. Once I decided to bake, I didn't care about the heat, just the cookies." I stir more sugar into the lemonade. "And then I didn't put the zest in the dough and the zest has all the flavor. How dumb is that?"

"Well, I guess it's not as dumb as drinking hot coffee on a hot day or calling life a bunghole," Dodger says. He sticks his nose back in the paper. "Say, did you see here it says someone got killed on Six Mile Road near Brimley. Says his Tracker tipped over and crushed him. Now that's a bunghole." Dodger shoves the paper in my face.

"I read that article yesterday and conveyed my condolences to the fellow's widow. She told me to save my sympathy for somebody else because she was in the process of divorcing him and didn't give two cents about his death—that it actually worked in her favor because now all his property and chattel belonged to her. She said he cheated on her with any female who would have him. Such is the way of life and the inhabitants who people the earth."

"Well, I'll be," he says. "You never know about people, do you?"

"Of course not. As I said, life's a bunghole." The buzzer sounds so I get up, open the oven door, and take out the cookies.

"Will you stop saying that," Dodger pleads. He lifts his head from the paper, so I give him my full attention.

"Bunghole is not a bad word. It's an essential part of a barrel. How would wine tasters know when that liquid you enjoy is ready for bottling without the bunghole? How would Jack Daniels know when his whiskey is ready? I know what you're thinking. You're thinking I'm cursing life, but I'm not." I put my elbows on the table and stare into Dodger's kind eyes. He stares back.

"It's like this," I continue. "Yesterday I took my seven-year-old nephew and his friend to town for an outing. As the air conditioning in my Blazer is on the fritz, the windows were down. Every time I stopped at a light, the boys had a blast yelling at the car next to us, 'Life's a bunghole.' I asked them to stop, but they paid no attention. By the time we reached Taco Bell, I, too, was yelling their chant out my window to the delight of the boys and the horror of strangers. So, you see, my friend of many moons, I will not stop saying what you want me to stop saying because it reminds me of the utter rejection of civility by two little intoxicatingly happy boys."

"You might be on to something," he says. "I haven't yelled out a car window since I could afford air conditioning. Next time you take those boys for a ride, let me know. Now, bag up some cookies, and I'll head home. Be sure to tell Ann I stopped by, and she owes me a small Monopoly fortune."

"You got it," I say. "See you later." After Dodger leaves, I put my lemonade and a few cookies on a tray and go to the back porch. Even without zest, the cookies are tasty. Life really is a bunghole, but as long as you know it, and don't expect much from it, you'll make out just fine. I watch the dust from the gravel road settle as Dodger drives away. Through his open window I hear him shout, "Life's a bunghole." Although he can't see me, I raise my glass in salute to the best pal a gal could have.

Historical - Ironwood bad boys

A Day at Marlene's Beauty Parlor

by Sharon Kennedy

Betty, the tall, pencil thin hairdresser who works for Marlene makes her announcement so anyone within hearing distance can hear it even if they aren't listening. "I'll wear these red heels until the day I die," she says as she perms Miss Abbot's hair. "Yessirree. I'll die with these babies on, and you can take that to the bank." Everyone laughs, including me. I can't stand Betty. She's too skinny, too pretty, and too outspoken, but you have to admire any woman who spends eight hours a day with a pair of scissors in her hands and a pair of four-inch stilettos on her feet. I can only imagine what her feet look like after the daily beating they take. My feet are my best feature—long and thin and narrow—just the way I used to look until I hit fifty-six and started aging as fast as a ball rolling downhill.

"That stuff's getting in my eyes," Miss Abbot squeals. "And it's burning my head. Get it off before all my hair falls out."

Betty assures her everything is fine. "There's nothing in your eyes," she says calmly. "It's just the ammonia making them sting, and your hair's not going to fall out. I've done this a thousand times."

"Baloney," Miss Abbot snaps. "If you don't rinse my head right now, I'm soaking it in the toilet." She jumps from her chair and heads for the bathroom. Betty grabs her arm and leads her to the sink. The smell of ammonia fills the salon. I close my eyes and relax in the chair as Marlene takes the scissors to my gray hair. I want her to surprise me with a new style, something that will give me the

appearance of youth and beauty. Quiet fills the room. At least I thought it was quiet until I stopped listening to the bustle around me. It always amazes me how much we hear when we don't listen.

Miss Abbot is breathing heavily, like we do when we're scared or cried too hard for too long. I know all about crying and a smidgen about being scared. It's like this—either you get life or life gets you. Either way you stumble along doing the right thing to all the wrong people or you let life bump you whichever way it wants. Mind you, I'm not complaining about my life and the years I've been here, but I'm at a crossroads. It's not just the gray hair that's getting me down. It's landing on the wrong side of fifty-five that irritates me.

"Miss Abbot, I've rinsed your hair and all danger of losing it went down the drain with the ammonia. Please sit still while I set it. Just a few minutes under the dryer and a quick comb-out and I'll be done. Please stop bouncing around like a headless chicken." Betty's losing patience, anyone can hear that, and the syrup has left her voice.

"Oh, go to hell," Miss Abbot says. "I'm going home." With that, she pulls the curlers from her hair, flings them on the floor, grabs her coat and cane, throws some bills on the counter, and exits the salon.

"That old bitch," Betty addresses the room. "The next time she comes in, someone else can take her. I'm done." She sweeps her station and sits in her chair and begins to cry. "I hate her," she says. "Why do we prostitute ourselves for a measly two-dollar tip? Every week I set Miss Abbot's hair and smile and pretend to be interested in what her cats did or didn't do, and every week I get the same tip she's been giving me for the past ten years. Twice a year I give her a perm. Today's the final straw. I hate that old woman, and I'll never touch her head again."

Betty dries her eyes and readies herself for her next appointment, my friend Pegs. Along with everyone else, I pretend not to have heard Betty's outburst. I glance at myself in the mirror and see the same old haircut I've been wearing for the past thirty years, a classic pageboy. So much for my surprise. I feel cheated but pay the $35.00 and a $5.00 tip. Marlene didn't earn any more than that because I look and feel the same way as I did when I came in—defeated.

I take a comfortable chair and wait for Pegs. I watch as Betty uses a small brush to paint the dye on her hair. Pegs is one of the lucky girls. She has hair as thick as a horse's mane. I don't think I've ever seen such thick hair on anyone except her four sisters. Their hairlines start just above their eyebrows. When we get together for coffee every Friday morning at Applebee's in the Soo, I tend to stare at those hairlines and wonder what genetic fluke made hair grow so thick and low on their foreheads. One day their mother joined us, and my question was answered. What I wouldn't give for just a pinch of that marvelous gene.

Eventually Betty finishes Pegs' hair. It looks nice because it's natural curly and the color suits her—sort of a reddish brown. The short cut goes good with Pegs' round face. Betty looks pleased with her efforts. Her scissors snip this way and that, and a few wayward curls land on the floor. Pegs would be very pretty if she lost seventy-five pounds.

"Well, what do you think?" Betty twirls her around in the chair so she can check the back of her hair. "Great," Pegs says. "You sure know your business." Betty smiles and clicks the heels of her red stilettos much as a drill sergeant might. She's practically beaming. She removes Pegs' cape and walks her to the till. "That'll be $75."

"Worth every penny," Pegs says and gets out her checkbook. From the look on Betty's face, I assume she got a hefty tip. "Ready to go?" Pegs asks. I tell her I've been ready for the last half-hour. We head for the door.

A blast of hot July air slaps us as we cross Ashmun Street. "Let's get lunch," I suggest, and Pegs agrees. We walk one short block to Country Kitchen. I know the head waitress. She always adds more walnuts and dried cranberries to the salad I order. She's a good old gal as my fellow would say. Of course, he says that about every waitress so it's not much of a compliment. When we enter the restaurant, Pegs takes one side of the booth, and I take the other. I like to sit with my back to the entrance. She likes to see who's coming and going because she knows half the people in Sault Ste. Marie and loves to get noticed just like my Harold does.

"Well," Pegs says after we place our orders. "What'd you think of Betty? She sure lost her cool with Miss Abbot. I bet it's those ridiculous high heels that rattle her." Pegs adds three sugar packets to her coffee. I take mine black.

"You could be right," I say. "Every time I get my hair cut, she's wearing a new pair of stilettos. Says she orders them from an outfit called Cutesy Girl on the web and gets them for a good price. I tell her she's crazy working in four-inch heels. She's ruining her back as well as her feet, but I might as well talk to the wind." I sip my coffee. If there's one drink I truly enjoy, it's a cup of hot, strong coffee and a piece of cherry pie with a scoop of vanilla ice cream. Harold would have a fit if he knew I ordered dessert whenever I lunch with Pegs. He'd ask why I complain about my weight if I'm going to eat pie and ice cream.

"Did you know her husband left her last week?" Pegs asks. She loves gossip even more than she loves food and that's saying something. She bites into her bacon cheeseburger.

"I had no idea. What happened?"

Pegs puts her elbows on the table and leans forward. "Apparently she's been having an affair with one of her customers, the one who calls her 'Cherry.' You know him. The oldest bachelor in the Soo—Ace Mince.

He's sixty if he's a day. Betty's at least twenty years his junior, but Ace is rich. Of course, the affair didn't last. As soon as Ace found out Betty was on her own, he dumped her. Everyone knows he only has affairs with married women because they're safe unless they leave their husbands, or their husbands dump them." Pegs burps. Just as she's about to tell more juicy gossip, Betty walks in and spies us. She heads for our table.

"Hey, you guys," she says. "Mind if I join you?"

"Not at all," Pegs says. She motions to the waitress. "Bring me a hot fudge sundae, will you, and top off my coffee with a swirl of whipped cream. While you're at it, bring Betty whatever she wants. Put it on my bill." She settles back in the booth, all ears to hear what Betty has to say.

"I'll just have coffee," she tells the waitress. Then she turns to us. "I quit. I told Marlene she could shove her job. I've had my fill of dealing with old bats who complain I pull their hair or cut it too short or color it too dark. I've had enough of lousy tips and jealous coworkers. I've had enough of everything."

"You can't quit," Pegs says. "Who will do my hair?" She picks the cherry off her sundae, licks the whipped cream from it, and pops it in her mouth.

"Oh, do it yourself," Betty says distractedly. She sips her drink.

"Say," Pegs whispers. "Isn't that Ace Mince sitting with Miss Abbot over there by the window? They look pretty cozy." Betty and I turn in the direction of the window and sure enough, Ace and Miss Abbot are deep in conversation.

"Well, what do you know," Betty says. "I wonder if she's his mother."

"Could be," Pegs says. "She's old enough."

Miss Abbot spies us and yells, "Hey, ladies, come here and meet my boyfriend." She can't be serious.

"Pleased to make your acquaintance, girls," Ace says. He acts like he's never seen Betty, let alone been her lover for two years. We sit in silent amazement until Pegs' enormous burp jolts us.

"Are you kidding," Betty yells. "Are you honestly kidding me?" She leaves our booth, walks to Ace, and slaps his cheek. "You devil. You dirty devil. You bastard." She turns to Miss Abbot. "If this loser is your boyfriend, you're welcome to him, but don't expect a wedding ring." She slaps Ace again. Pegs and I watch as his cheek turns bright pink. Miss Abbot reaches for her cane and whacks Betty's stilettos, breaking off the heels. Betty falls to the floor. Pegs jumps to the rescue.

"I'll sue you, you old hag," Betty yells at Miss Abbot. "I'll take every dollar you have. You ruined my new shoes and nearly broke my back." Pegs helps Betty to our booth. "I'll get that old bitch if it's the last thing I do," Betty promises.

"Calm down, Betty," Ace says. He slides next to her and slips money into her hand. "This should pay for the shoes. If there's anything left, treat yourself to something nice. Mother often confuses me with my father. Sorry to hear about your divorce, but these things happen. Good luck, Kiddo." He kisses her cheek and leaves our booth.

Betty counts the money—three hundred dollars. Her anger flees as fast as it came. "Those were cheap shoes anyway," she says as she rubs Ace's kiss from her cheek. "And I never really liked them. Guess I'll head back to the salon. You gals have a good day." She grabs her purse and goes out the door. We watch as she limps away.

"If that don't beat all, I don't know what does," Pegs says. She motions to the waitress. "Bring me a little more hot fudge," she says then turns to me. "Say, how about we head to the Goodwill when we finish here. Let's see what's on sale."

"Okay," I say. I'm in no hurry to get home. Harold's bound to be mad about something. I drink the last of my coffee and watch Pegs as she tips her glass and scoops out the remaining bit of melted ice cream and fudge sauce. As we drive to the Goodwill, I thank my lucky stars I don't have Betty's stiletto and divorce problems or Pegs' insatiable appetite. The depression I started the day with is slowly lifting. I don't have much to complain about, at least not until I get home and face Harold. Maybe I'll buy him another jacket to hang next to the twenty-five he already has in his closet. Clothes always make him happy.

I honk the horn as we drive by Marlene's. She's standing at the window with her arm around Betty. Marlene treats her hairdressers like family. By tomorrow Betty will have forgotten all about today's commotion. Maybe I'll send Harold her way. He needs a good haircut, and I need a new fellow. Things always seem to work out if you don't cash in your chips at the sight of your first gray hair. One look at the smile on Miss Abbot's old, wrinkled face is proof positive we create our own reality. It seems to be a whole lot more fun than living in the real world. Maybe I'll give it a try.

Sharon Kennedy lives in Michigan's Upper Peninsula. She's a columnist for Gannett Media newspapers. Her books are: *Life in a Tin Can: A Collection of Random Observations* and *The Side Road Kids: Tales from Chippewa County*. She's currently writing a sequel to her stories about kids growing up in rural America in the 1950s.

Historical stereoview · camping out near Lake Superior

Extinct

by Douglas Hoover

Have you ever been afraid of something your whole life? Afraid of something that has terrified you even though it never really made any sense? Some people are afraid of spiders, even the smallest of them. Some are afraid of snakes, even if they aren't poisonous, and a lot of us never got past being afraid of the dark. That's why, as adults, we keep the bedside lamp within arm length. Oh, we say it's for reading, but if we were totally honest with ourselves, it's so we can have a quick light to ward off the boggies that go bump in the night.

As for me? Ever since I can remember I have been afraid of dying alone. For some reason I've always felt that if you die alone you have to spend the rest of eternity that way. I know that all religions tell us differently, but the idea has been stuck in my head ever since I was a kid and it still haunts me. Kind of the same way some adults will make sure that their feet don't hang off the side of the bed so whatever might be hiding under there won't be able to reach on up and grab an ankle.

And now in the last few hours of my life, I am forced to face one of my worst fears, and die alone.

It's inevitable, I know. Fate has decided it and I can't change it. When it comes right down to it, I have worked hard to ensure that is exactly what happens. So if you're alive enough to read this now, please remember me, Mike Fallis, the unknown paleontologist who may have saved the world, and died alone all because of his clumsiness.

Yet, perhaps by writing this I have found a way to cheat a little. By having you in my thoughts I won't be completely alone when death finds me. I know I will die soon. I can feel my life slipping away. It will be a release. I can feel them inside of me. Alive. Growing. Eating.

There is another sore, this one on the back of my left shoulder and like the others, it burns. I know what this means. Another hatching. More have matured, and they are gnawing their way out.

As much as this hurts, I need to ignore it, (if I can). I need to fight through the pain so I can write this down, so you'll understand what has happened. How nature tricked us. My last act of defiance toward these damn things will be to sit here and type as long as I can, and die at this keyboard.

But first, let me explain while I can.

All of us were so excited when we came up here on this dig. I mean, what more could twelve dinosaur seekers ask for? An almost perfectly preserved mammoth, frozen beneath the surface, and hiding away on this Russian island. All the questions we were going to answer, we were going to learn so much. And we did accomplish that I suppose. The elusive question of how they died off, I think, has finally been answered. Most of us subscribed to the asteroid theory, but the truth turned out to be so much smaller. These damned winged demons.

We were in awe when we discovered them. So amazed that something so fragile could survive being frozen for so long. It was a scientific find that would be talked about for decades to come, and we found it! We worked so hard to save them. The care we gave them. The attention. The love. We managed to revive almost three dozen of them.

Renee was the one that was most intrigued. She was the one who actually saw them first, and devoted all of her time to them. Renee's biggest professional goal was to get her name into the history books, and she was sure that finding these things would do just that.

She was right of course. Her name will go into the books, but she'll never know it. She was the first of us to die.

It's my fault that she's dead. It's my fault that we're all dead. It was my clumsiness that stranded us here. Shortly after we got here we started moving things around to better suit our needs, and I accidentally knocked our only radio to the floor and it broke. Too cold to go anywhere without transportation, and no way to call for help, I cut us off from the outside world. Isn't it ironic that I had to watch the others die? Poetic punishment for my clumsiness!

At the time none of us really considered the loss of the radio a major problem. We had all the supplies we needed for our month stay.

Franklin Weeks, the guy who graciously funded this expedition, had supplied us with everything we needed, and the lab was totally set up by the time we got here. Weeks is a very strange guy. I think that he is rich beyond most imaginations. How else could he pull this off? He got the information about the mammoth before anyone else. He was able to get into northern Russia, and build this underground lab without interference from the Russian government and I'm not sure how. A find this big demands a certain amount of prestige, and nobody would just willingly give it up without compensation or acknowledgment. Besides, if the Russian government knew about the dig we would be above ground, not beneath it. Only loads of money has the power to do that. I can only imagine that everyone who knows about the dig received enough money to keep quiet about it.

I don't know if that makes much sense to you, or if you understand what I'm trying to tell you. It's getting hard for me to focus. I can feel the toxin slowing my mind, but my memory seems fine so far. So far.

The money I received for coming up here was enough to buy my silence. It was also enough to buy a nice house for Lynn and me.

Lynn, I feel sorry for her most of all. Our wedding is only six weeks away, all set up and ready to go. She thought out every detail, and we could hardly wait. Starting a family was an important dream that we both shared. Lynn's mother's health is not the greatest, and it's important to Lynn to give her mom the opportunity to see her grandchild in the time she has left. In my family, I am the only male born to this generation. It's up to me to pass on the proud name of Fallis. Something my dad would not let me forget. Me having a son was important to the whole family. Lynn has already stopped taking the pill, and we were going to try for a baby right out of the gate.

It is not going to be easy for her to understand why this happened, and yet, I think somehow she knew this was coming. A sixth sense perhaps, or some kind of premonition. Whatever you call it, she knew. She tried to tell me this was coming, but I wouldn't listen. We had a fight three days before I left to come up here. She was so insistent that I not go. "I just have this funny feeling that something bad is going to happen to you." She told me. I told her that it was just nervousness about being separated; we haven't spent a lot of time apart since we met. I remember she told me, "It took me a long time to find you, and I wasted a lot of time in the search so I'm making up for it now."

Man, I miss her. Whoever said that it is better to have loved and lost then never to have loved at all, never went through anything like this. Lynn is a fine woman. Smart, caring and thoughtful. She gives of herself and asks for little in return. I wonder if she will be the same wonderful, person when she learns that fate has used the man she loves to spawn demons.

What I wouldn't do for a radio now. The things I would give to trade some of my clumsiness for some of the grace of these damn bugs.

The bugs were, and I suppose still are, beautiful to look at. As if they are made of black velvet. So soft. When the light shines straight down on them, you can see the royal blue trim that high lights their delicate wings. Ancestor to the butterfly I imagine. And there's something else. The way they move their wings when they're not flying. There's a strange rhythm to the idle movement. It starts at the tip of the wing, and then rolls inward to the center of the body, crosses with the slightest movement, and then picks up in the other wing, moving from the center out. Like a ripple moving across a still pond. When the wave reaches the tip of the opposite wing, it simply changes direction and goes back the other way. There's a mesmerizing, almost hypnotic quality to it and if you look at it long enough you drift off into a peaceful, happy place. Then they kill you.

Renee was so excited when the first one started hovering around her. She held out her arm and followed its movements, almost begging it to land on her. She was so proud when it finally chose her to perch on. "It tickles." were the only words she got out before it attached. The six legs beneath its belly penetrated her skin.

It stings, you know, when they first attach. Your first reaction is to swat it and brush it off. That's what Renee did. She killed it, and died six hour later.

Wow! I just got a strange rush through my body, and it made me shake all over. That's not going to help. It's already getting hard to write, and this is taking longer than I thought. I'm a good typist but Im losing coordination in my fingers. I expected all of this, but didn't think it would happen this fast.. It's all part of the process that I've seen several times now.

When Renee got sick the rest of us started to study the bugs with new respect. Sounds noble doesn't it? Study. New respect. Self-defense is what it was. We were trying to save our own asses. But for the sake of pride I'll call it study. And studying them quickly became a morbid exchange, because what we learned, we learned from the dead. Both theirs, and ours.

Trying to catch one of the bugs is hard because they are fast and never hold a steady flight. It's like trying to catch a butterfly between your fingers, but these bugs are amazingly fast, and their endurance is incredible. They're like moths on steroids. They never land unless they want to, and usually it's on you, and that's the last thing you want to happen. We tried different tricks, bright colors, and fruit, but their not attracted to such things. They're not really attracted to light either. They have stung as many of us in the dark as they have in the light.

We wore thick clothes, and kept as much of our skin covered as possible. We set up watches and slept with the lights on. Each taking turn shouting the alarm if a bug happened to get into the room. Then we ran. I've seen them flatten out and shimmy under the door, and come through the ventilation vents. I know it sounds strange, but these bugs seem smart.

What we believe—keep in mind that we're not chemists—is that small sacks in the center on the legs manufacture poison. When the legs penetrate the skin, a small amount of this toxin is injected to help the process take place. Kind of like a lubricant. Same characteristics as a mosquito. The initial sting isn't fatal. Maybe it's their way of letting you know that they're there. The legs are barbed, and once they've penetrated the skin, the legs are folded inward like a fishing hook, so once you're on, you're on. If you brush or pull the bug off, the legs tear off above the sacks, leaving the lower part of the leg intact, muscles and all. The same way a venom sack of a honeybee will stay with the stinger. The leg muscles contract and keep pushing the venom from all six legs, and a lethal dose is administered. Brad was the second to die, his reaction being the same as Renee's, and we did not yet understand what was happening.

After you see it once or twice you start to recognize the symptoms and the effects of the toxin on the mind and body. Physically the poison works by deteriorating body functions. The victim starts to feel distant from the body. Not too long afterwards the motor control abilities are attacked. The hands start to shake, and the legs start to lose coordination. Falling down is common. Then the victim starts to sweat regardless of the room temperature. In the later stage bladder control is lost and soon after, bowel control. Near the end the eyes shut down one at a time, but the sense of smell and hearing are increased. Eventually there is a series of flash backs of ones life that are very vocal, and soon after, death.

The effects on the mind are harder to describe. It seems as if the rational is reduced slowly, but the imagination is somehow heightened. It appears that when you start to loose your sense of reality, hallucinations come in greater detail. The mind runs off without the owner and makes the victim see the illogical as logical. We termed it *Brain Flux*, because the victim fluctuates between sanity and insanity. They start to imagine certain unrealistic ends to the problems they face, and to them the solution is so simple, and they believe it so fully, that they will do some incredible things for what they believe will save them, regardless of how absurd it really is. Once the victim gets an idea stuck in what's left of their mind, they can't seem to shake it or be talked out of it.

By the time Tom got stung we had learned enough to be afraid to swat it or kill it, so he decided to let it go about its business. What choice did he have? What we didn't understand at the time is that the under belly of these things has a small slit in the skin. This slit is a cavity that houses a proboscis that looks like the tubed nose of a mosquito. It penetrates the skin, and feeds in the same manner. It sucks your blood. It seemed to us that was all it wanted. It stayed locked on Tom's arm for only a minute, then detached and flew off leaving nothing more than six small holes, and a small bump from the bite in the center.

Tom seemed to be fine, but thirty-two hours later a sore spot started to form not far from the bite. It grew red, and expanded to the size of a shot glass . Tom kept telling us how much it burned. Six hours after he showed it to us, small holes in the center of the sore started to bleed, and then opened up to let the off spring out. Larva stage of course. Looked like maggots. We humans, it seems, are the right temperature to hatch eggs.

The bugs lay their eggs through the same tube that it feeds from. Our own body temperature incubates the eggs, and the larvas are subsequently hatched into a perfect environment. Warm, protected, and with an unlimited food supply. They grow until they mature and strong enough to gnaw their way to the surface.

If you kill them as they come out, they secrete the same toxin as the adults, and the open wound is a window to the blood stream. If you allow them to crawl onto the out side of your skin, they leap off and release an odor that you can smell if you put your nose close enough to the wound. To me it smells like rotting meat. At leased I think it does. Nothing much has been done with the mammoth since we found the bugs, and it is rotting quickly. The whole place smells like dead meat. Draw a quick breath through your mouth and you can taste it.

The odor released by the young home how signals the near by adults that a suitable incubator has been found, and that the young need a lift. The adults come at you from all directions. Some flutter in a pick up as many young as they can carry. The young hold on to the small barbs of the legs, and off they go. Other adults land and attach to start the process over again. Where the adults take the young I dont know, but I can only imagine that they prepare them for the chrysalis or cocoon stage.

Tom freaked right out when the other adult bugs rushed him. He started swatting and pulling as soon as he felt a sting. Five in all. With that much toxin in his blood, he died within the hour. Moving from one deadly effect to the next so fast that we could barely tell what stage he was in.

After we learned what would happen if we got bit, we each made our own decision about what we would do if that time came. Lastthing we wanted to do was to allow more to hatch, but there is only one way to stop them from maturing once they are in your body. You're not much of an incubator when you're dead.

Bill got bit, and hung himself. "Captain of his own ship" was the way he explained it. Derek ran out into the snowy wasteland, and we never saw him again. I can only assume that he froze to death and died like a big Dereksicle. Maybe some day a group of scientist will dig up, and study Derek. Tammy tried to fight them medieval style. She slit her wrist, and tried to 'bleed out' the eggs. Just so you know it does'nt work any better today then it did then. She died all the same, just a lot bloodier.

Molly, Cliff, and Rodney simply pulled the bugs off and let the toxin take them. Each suffering the effects of the poison on the mind, all with completely different ideas on how to save their own lives. Molly's brain flux caused her to become obsessed with body heat, and was convinced that by doing things to lower the body temperature, she could keep the bugs from hatching. She said that most body heat escapes through the head, and saw her hair as a problem, so she shaved her self bald. By the time she did this there was a loss in motor control, and she cut herself several times, but she managed to cut it all off, and was bald when she died. She was also completely naked, thinking that clothes, any clothes would aid the bugs inside her. For the last three hour of her life she was exposed to the world, and packing herself in ice. Becky tried to cover her up once, but she got bit on the thumb for her effort. Not just a nibble, I'm talking about a teeth to bone kind of a bite. I'm sure if Molly had the strength left in her jaws she would have bitten Becky's thumb clean off.

Cliffs's brain flux had him setting up rows of books like dominos. He would line them up, knock them over, and then poke a small hole in his finger. He would then care fully put one drop of blood onto a slide, and look at it under the microscope. He would then release a string of curses, convinced the bugs were still alive. He would then run back to the books and start the process all over again. He was convinced that doing these actions would kill the larva inside of him. What he couldn't remember is that he pulled

the adult off as soon as it attached, and the bug never had time to lay any eggs. But he kept doing the book and blood thing over, and over.

Rodney was convinced that if he were to look more like the bugs then they would leave him alone. 'They would never kill their own kind' he said. He made antennas for his head out of some plastic zip ties, and fuzz from his socks. He tied them on his head, then tried to tape them, and then finally resorted to using the staple gun. If stapling things to your own head sounds bizarre, it's mild compared to the his next idea. He said that if he were to change hisbody to resemble the bugs he could fool them. He was convinced that if he lost his ability to walk, his body would grow wings so he could fly. That has to be the stupidest idea ever conceived, but apparently it made perfect sense to Rodney. I leaned how seriously he believed this when he tried to hack off his own feet with the edge of a screwdriver.

It's cold in here, and I'm sweating. I'm beginning to think those damn bugs inside me have found their way to my inner ear. I can hear them whispering. You know it kind of sounds crazy, but I just realized that no one has ever tried talking to these things. I wonder if they speak English. Hold on, and Ill see what I can do.

Great news! If I yell really loud with may head in a bucket, they can hear me. They do speak English and I am happy to report that I have opened a channel of communications with the bugs, and we are now in negotiations. Theses sessions are closed to the public, and Im not allowed to talk about this with anyone. So if the bugs ask, you didn't hear a thing from me. Ill try to talk them into allowing me to give you reports every now and then, but I'm sure that theyll want something in return. In the mean time, I have asked them what it would take to keep them from killing me. They said that they would have a meeting, and get back to me. They told me to just go on typing and they would let me know.

Brave Josh decided to take the fight to the enemy. He was our warrior, and survivalist. He had an emergency kit that was chocked full of stuff, and he was prepared for just about anything. He was like the ultimate boy scout. Heavy into fitness, he was in great physical shape, and he was sure that he could either catch, or kill one of the bugs without getting stung. He locked him self in a room with one, and the fight was set. Josh vs. the bug, a fight to the death. A promoter would have loved it.

Josh did his best and almost had it cornered three times, but it fluttered away and the fight went on. Five hours after it started Josh was spent, and the damn bug never landed once. Josh stopped to catch his breath and take a break. When he tried to leave he turned his back and the bug floated in and landed on the back of his neck, and attached. Josh was not amused. He tore it off, and stomped on it twelve times. Once for each of us I suppose. He used a snakebite kit in his emergency pack, and cut open the skin around the sting, and tried sucking out the poisoned blood with this plastic suction ball, fill it up, and then let it spit back out all over his shoes. I bet he spilled a half a pint, and left bloody footprints allover. Do you think anyone will complain about that? I don't know if that helped or if it was because he was in such good physical shape, but Josh lasted over twelve hours after the bite. By then he had his fingernails and toenails pulled off, jerked out most of his teeth, and discussed the problem with several dead relatives.

Hold on ! I can hear the bugs calling me from the inside. I have to answer them, and I need my bucket. I Think that its important for me to remember that I am negotiating not only for myself, but for the whole human race as well. That is an honor that you have given me, and I do not take lightly.

The bugs have just given me something to work with, and I have accepted out of love for you. They have suggested that if I were to give them something better to eat,(it seems we are not very tasty) that they would consider letting me live. I rationalize that if they were to get something that they were more accustom to that would satisfy them and suggested the mammoth. They tell me that if I eat some, they will consider letting me live.

I think that is a small price to pay to insure that the talks continue.

It was the worst thing that I have ever putin my mouth, but at least I didn't have to chew much, it was already mostly rotted and falling apart. I ate until I was full, and am hopeful to hear from the bugs again soon. I fell on the way back and hit my head. I hope when they find me they won't think I did that on purpose. I In the mean time I will continue to bring you up to speed.

If I haven't told you already, I was the last one bitten. When I was trying to comfort Becky through the last half hour of her life, one landed on my shoe, crawled up tye inside of my paint leg and bit me on the calf. I knew that there were still things that I needed to do, so I let the damn things lay its eggs. I knew that being last one alive I had things I needed to do. I think that I have done all that I can to keep people out, and protect you. If these things ever got released into the world I doubt that we could stop them. Humans would end up going the way of the dinosaur. Were not due to be picked up for four day's and I'm hoping that it will be another day before anyone can get in. I hope the bugs will freeze by then. See, I turned the heat off so it will getcold in here, but I'll probably be dead before the cold becomes a problem. (if talks go well I can always turn the heat back on. my little safety net if the bugs try to double cross me. I pulled one of the bugs off for hours ago, and now I wait for this nightmare to end. The batch of larva that will soon be crawling out of the holes they are making will be the forth hatching Ive allowed to live so I could try and save your life. The thought of those maggots eating me from the insideout makes me throw up, so I try not to think about it. Especially now that negotiation are going well. I might lose a major token of trust.

I'm so embarrassed to tellyou that I have just peed my self. please don't tell my ma. Shell beat me .

I stacked the others in one room, so they would be all together. Like soldiers killed in battle, and buried in a mass grave. That was somthing we all decided to do after tom died. Actually I only had to stack the last few. I had help for the first brunch. I put a big note on the outside of the door, telling everbody to saty out, and let these things go back to hell where they cane from. I locked and bolt the door, and then blocked it with as much stiff as I could find. It will take a bull dozer to get that door open. I broke some of the lab stuff when I did it I hope i dont have to pay for it. They might not like me bustin up his stuff.

I have to try and get a hold of the bugs and see if the mamoth was okay. If it was I'l ask then to fix the radio.

I jried for half hour and lost my voice form screaming. They wont answer.Maybe their still eating. my right eye is not working very well, and I cant feel my face, but i think Im spitting down the front of my shirt. Hope my mom do'nt see me she will no i was doing something bad.

I dont, want to die, not here , not by my-selve1 There is a tear in my left eye, but nothing is working in my right. I kant even see out it now. Ill call forthe bugs agan.

no andswer. mabye their train broke down. or their fone wont work   Bugs bugs can you read. talk to me/   I didnet mean to broke the radio mom itt just felll. pease domt tel dad

I wasnet runnning i wsajusttttttttfcxz

The Document

by Douglas Hoover

Hey Marion,
I tried to call you this morning but got no answer. You were probably already gone with the kids, so I thought I'd sit down and e-mail you, just in case.

I wanted to tell you about the dream I had last night. It scared me enough that for a short time I thought I was having a heart attack. I didn't sleep much after having it, and maybe it was for the best. As I tossed and turned, I thought about it a lot, and in the end, I cursed myself for my own imagination and finally fell asleep with a smile. And when I woke this morning, I could laugh about it.

I got to sleep okay last night, which is a rarity; you know I don't sleep well when I travel, but I fell asleep early last night. I was exhausted and I felt a little strange. That's probably what inspired the dream.

I dreamt that I woke to find a group of people in my room, businessmen and woman. A smart looking bunch, dressed in black and gray business attire, and very well kept. Needless to say, this scared the tar out of me. Imagine waking up in a strange hotel room and finding a crowd of strangers at the foot of your bed. I awoke to one of them talking.

"Mr. Kentrell? Mr. Kentrell, we need you to wake up briefly."

I opened my eyes, or thought I did, and there they were.

"Mr. Kentrell?" He said softly again bringing me awake.

I sat up, "Who are you people and how did you get in here?"

I reached over and flipped the switch to the bedside light. It came on, but the room was already lit, and the lamp didn't make it brighter.

"Please relax, Mr. Kentrell. I realize this is unusual, but I can assure you there is no reason for alarm."

"Who are you and why are you here!" I asked as I retrieved my glasses from the nightstand.

"My name is Blake, Samuel Blake."

"What do you want?" I asked, reaching for the phone.

"What we want—what we would like, is your co-operation." He said and pointed at my phone; it wasn't working by the time I got it to my ear. "What we need is your signature."

"On what?" I asked still holding the phone to my ear.

"A simple document."

A younger man moved to the dresser, set down a briefcase and opened it. A woman, in her early forties I guessed by the lines in her face, removed a piece of paper and handed it to Blake, who looked it over.

"Yes, yes, very nice." Blake told her. The document was given to another man who retrieved a silver pen from the inside breast pocket of his suit and presented them to me. Their movements were well rehearsed. I have put together some good business teams in my time, but none compared to the efficiency they exhibited, and I found myself wishing they were on my team, or I was on theirs.

"What is it?"

"I'm sure if you read it, you'll understand it completely." Blake said.

"I don't want to read it! You explain it to me." I said putting my phone in my lap.

"Very well," Blake continued. "It's a statement acknowledging the fact that you have spent your time allowance and it is your consent to proceed with the ending of your time expenditures."

"My time expenditures?"

He nodded. "Yes."

"What do you mean?"

"You've exhausted your time budget for this realm, Mr. Kentrell, it is time to end your time consumption."

"Time budget, and time consumption for this realm? Are we talking about my death?"

"Yes, Mr. Kentrell, we are."

"And just so I understand, you want me to sign this so you may proceed with killing me?"

Blake's faced soured. "Of course not, Mr. Kentrell, we are not in the business of killing people. Our responsibility is to keep the time budget balanced."

"And my allotted time allowance has reached its end, is that it?"

"That is correct."

"And if I sign this, my life will end?"

"That is also correct."

"Well forget it. I'm not signing anything that will bring about my own death."

Blake sighed. "Mr. Kentrell, I consider you to be a reasonable man, and you must understand that some things in life are unavoidable. Of these things, death is at the top of the list."

"I understand, but I'm not going to give consent to my death. On the contrary, I intend to fight it tooth and nail."

"Why, Mr. Kentrell? It is a fact that most people fear death, but I can assure you that it is quite natural. The biggest complaint we receive is in conjunction with the cold. There is a coldness that comes with death that is, unfortunately, unavoidable. With that exception most people find the experience, well, interesting and, if you are properly in line with your faith, quite enjoyable."

"That's nice to know, but I'm not doing anything to help promote my own death, so you can just take your document and go." I said flipping the back of my hand at him.

The young man holding the document didn't move.

"This is most disappointing, Mr. Kentrell," Blake said crossing his legs and sitting back in his chair. "You don't understand what this does to the greater budget. We as a species have a limited amount of time. Each one of us is given a time budget at birth and when that budget is exhausted it is time to stop spending. If you refuse to cooperate, we will have to balance the budget by taking time from someone else."

"That's fine, Mr. Blake, take time from someone else. I'm not signing that thing."

Blake held up the palm of his hand in the universal 'wait' gesture. "Before you stand firm on that decision, Mr. Kentrell, allow me to tell you the story of a Mr. James Turner. He held to the same thinking you do now. He refused to sign and was probably the most stubborn person we have ever encountered.

"He said he owed it to his twin sons not to go anywhere until he finished what he set out to do. Mr. Turner was an attorney, and both his sons were in law school. It was his ambition to open a law practice with them. That was all part of his plan from the time they were born. We visited him in the same fashion we are visiting you. He dismissed us and awoke in the morning with the familiar thought most do; we were nothing more than a bad spot of potato consumed with that night's dinner. He dressed and went to work noticing nothing unusual."

"That's fine, I'll have the same," I said.

"You need to let me finish, Mr. Kentrell," he continued and folded his hands gracefully around his knee. "Mr. Turner noticing nothing unusual, until he ordered lunch. He often ordered lunch into his office from his favorite little deli down the street. He not only liked the egg salad, he enjoyed the company of the young delivery woman whom he lusted over. He could see her crossing the road on her bicycle enroute to his office, and this would entice his…appetites. On the day after our visit, he decided to order from the deli as a way to remind himself that he had made the right choice, and there were things that he still wanted to do. However, he never got his lunch that day. The woman didn't make it to his office. He spied her from his window as she neared the street. He saw the truck coming, she did not. He watched her die in the street."

"Wait, let me guess, you're going to tell me you caused that right?"

"Not caused it, Mr. Kentrell, we don't deal with the actual removal of life; we did, however, approve the move."

"Gee, that's mighty nice of you, do you also kill puppies?"

He grinned but ignored the challenge. "We needed to balance the budget, Mr. Kentrell; Mr. Turner was spending time that was not his to spend so we were forced to take it from the woman."

"I understand; you were just moving numbers from one column to the next?"

"If it's easier for you to accept, yes. However, what Mr. Turner didn't understand, and what you must comprehend, is that this was only a temporary solution, and his continued spending would need a more permanent solution. He had already changed the future, and affected the lives of thousands, and the longer he stayed in, the worse things were going to get."

"Worse for whom?"

"Worse for the whole world, Mr. Kentrell. Turner didn't respond reasonably and sign the document when we asked, therefore, we were forced to balance the budget by allowing the woman to die early. Because of that, she was unable to do the things she needed to do, and unable to finish her tasks here. That made things much more difficult for a different committee."

"And did this woman sign the document?"

"She did. We are not allowed to proceed with the project without the proper documentation in place. Of course, there was the early exit addendum, but like most people she considered us a strange dream or hallucination and she signed in a state of disbelief."

"Oh, I get that. But are you telling me that if I don't sign, I'll have to watch others die in my place?"

"That's correct, Mr. Kentrell. And, unfortunately, some will say that watching a loved one die is harder than dying itself."

"I'd have to agree with you there, Mr. Blake."

"Most people do. However, Mr. Turner did not. We visited him the next night, and tried to persuade him to sign, and again he refused. He told me he could live with the death, said he intended to spend another fifty years or more here. He was a very determined man and deduced that by not signing, he could live forever."

"So, you took time away from someone who had more to spend?"

Blake shrugged. "It is the only way to balance things out."

"So, you killed someone else."

"Not killed, simply approved a removal."

"Nice play on words, does that make things easier for you?"

"Perhaps it does, but what choice did he leave us?"

"Don't you need their signature in order to terminate their time? I'm sure not all people agree to sign."

"Correct. Some do not. But there is a small reserve we can use if we are forced to. The problem is: time that is forcefully taken is only worth half time spent. Forty years of promise is worth only twenty years lived."

"A bird in the hand is worth two in the bush kind of a thing?"

Blake smiled. "Exactly, where do you think the concept originated?

"Why don't you just forcefully take the people you visit?"

"Oh, you miss understand, Mr. Kentrell; we don't forcefully take people, other people do. Murders, wars, and the like. This unlawful taking is the origin of our reserve. Besides, the people we visit have already spent their time. If we are forced to approach someone early, it is because someone is spending stolen time. If we take them at that time, we gain nothing back, and the budget would never balance. If everyone signed when they're asked, there would be no premature deaths. The reason children die is because an older person refused to accept their own fate and pushed the burden of death back to the next generation."

"Just like the national debt."

Blake smiled. "That's a humorous and clever comparison, Mr. Kentrell; may I use it some time?"

"By all means, Mr. Blake." Blake was a likable guy. His charisma was like an emotional magnet, and I couldn't help but to like him, regardless of what he was selling. He was good at what he did, but then I suppose he would have to be.

"So, who did you... approve to be removed, a delivery girl, or the paperboy perhaps?"

"One of his descendants, it seemed only reasonable that if he intended to live forever, it would be his family's responsibility to pay for it."

"You took who? His sons?"

"Not took, Mr. Kentrell."

"Sorry, whom did you approve for removal?"

"His first-born son. Ironic that this thought come up now, but this man was born a few minutes before his brother and was selected to be removed because of it. See how important a few minutes can be?"

Blake shook his head. "His first son had to be taken the next day for two reasons, first it gave us more time to convince Mr. Turner to sign, and second, it balanced the budget in case Mr. Turner refused to sign. Which, of course he did. We visited him every few years, and he rebuked us each time. When the time stolen from his son was nearly spent, and Mr. Turner was still not willing to surrender to the inevitable, we were forced into another agreement."

"The second son?"

"Seems logical, does it not? But we conceived one of our better ideas. Since Mr. Turner was acting on stolen time, we devised a clause in his contract that could be used by him, if he changed his mind. Anytime he called for us we would use thirty seconds of reserve time for each person near him. We agreed to stop time for those around him if he decided to sign. He exercised that clause on the fifteenth birthday of his grandson. We had already approved the removal of this young man, and when he started to choke on a piece of his birthday cake, Mr. Turner called for us. He realized what was happening, and finally surrendered to fate and signed."

"Did you release the grandson?"

"Of course, we did, it was not his time to go. Mr. Turner had finally given his consent and accepted his mortality."

"I'm guessing that Mr. Turner died later that night."

"Actually no. We have no idea when death comes to the people we visit. That, I suppose, is a blessing, but it happened fast for Mr. Turner, almost immediately. Rarely are we there when it happens, but it was so quick. You could see it in his face, the pain, the sorrow, the loss, and the cold. He clutched his chest and fell to the floor. If it's any comfort, I think he was at peace with it. He understood that he saved his grandson's life and died with a slight smile. I believe it was authentic. He had made the right decision."

"Like you gave him a choice."

"He had his choice, Mr. Kentrell, the same as you have yours."

"So, you're telling me that if I don't sign, you'll approve the removal of one of my children."

Blake made a gesture of futility. "Our hands are tied. The budget must stay balanced."

"How do you live with yourself, or the rules you make?"

"I do neither, Mr. Kentrell. I do not make the rules, nor live with them. We simply balance a budget the best we can. It's people like you who make, and change the rules."

I have to tell you, Marion, it was the weirdest dream I ever had. What choice did I have? In the end I signed the document. I know what it feels like to have a business competitor on the ropes, and it always made me smirk. I expected the same thing from Blake.

"I'll bet you just love this," I said as I signed.

"We gain no pleasure from our duties, Mr. Kentrell," Blake said.

The document bearing my signature was placed back into the briefcase. Blake stood up and moved to the edge of my bed.

"Mr. Kentrell, you have done the reasonable thing, and I commend you on your wise decision." He held out his hand for me to shake. I refused it.

"So now what?" I asked.

"Our business is done," Blake said. "I suggest that you go back to sleep, but the choice is yours, Mr. Kentrell. Good day."

That was it; they were gone. I woke up and felt a pain in my chest. It was dark; the light I thought I turned on in my dream worked fine when I flipped the switch and the phone, my phone, was back on the nightstand. It worked when I used it to call for a few aspirin and antacid to be brought up. I should have known better than to have Mexican for dinner.

It was a terrible night, but I got up this morning and everything seems the same as yesterday. Weird huh?

Anyway, I'll be home soon. The deal I've been working on here has been agreed upon, and all that remains is the signing of the paperwork. Maybe that's what triggered the dream. Once the paperwork is done, I'll catch the red eye home and see you in the morning. I'll call you later to let you know how it went. The meeting's at 1:00; until then, I'm going to try to relax, and take a hot bath. I suddenly feel chilled to the bone.

I love you!

Jerry

Douglas Hoover grew up in a suburb of Detroit before moving to Northern Michigan. He and his wife Cheryl now live in Charlevoix, Michigan. He has authored several short stories and has moved to writing novels. After a battle with cancer, Cheryl asked him to take his writing hobby to a full-time career. Titles to look for in the future include: *Atlantis, The Stones, Nighttime Visitors*, and *Ye Gods*.

historical Powers - man and woman in carriage circa 1909

Iroquois Island

by Richard Hill

David had a bone to pick with his wife of twenty-five years, but he was hesitant to come right out and ask her. For years, he'd suspected something wasn't completely honest between them; yet he couldn't clearly say what it was. Abby had seemed distant and distracted for a long time, as if her thoughts were on something else or, perhaps, someone more appealing.

In early October, as the maples and birches were bursting with color along Lake Superior, David and Abby launched their canoe a few miles west of Brimley. They paddled in the chilly waters toward Iroquois Island, about a half-mile out from shore. It was one of the last pleasant weekends in the U.P. before the predictably inclement fall weather moved in.

David needed to get something off his chest and didn't want any interruptions from cell phones or visitors. Abby didn't like confrontation, but the island seemed the perfect private spot to iron out some issues. She wouldn't be able to run out of the room, as so often happened, if she became anxious or frustrated. To sell her on the idea, David presented it as a great fall getaway, their last chance to canoe before the long winter weather took over.

When they arrived at Iroquois Island, they gathered driftwood and made a fire on the beach. Far out in the St. Mary's River channel, they could see a downbound ore freighter working its way towards the Soo Locks. Storm clouds gathered in the late-afternoon sky, but the steel-colored waters remained calm.

David reached in his knapsack and pulled out a couple glasses and a pint of Jack Daniels. As he poured the drinks, he wondered how the two of them had lost so much interest in each other. Was she growing complacent with him? She rarely laughed at his jokes anymore and seldom complimented him on anything. Maybe, he thought, we've been too nitpicky over too many little things. It all bothered him a great deal, and he wanted to clear the air.

Sipping her bourbon and poking the crackling fire with a stick, Abby asked, "Why did you want to come all the way out here to the island? A storm could come up and we'd be stranded."

David tossed another piece of driftwood in the fire. "When I was in Boy Scouts as a kid, our troop used to come camping out here in the summer. We swam and explored the island for days. Did you know last time I was here the skeleton of a wrecked schooner had washed up on shore? It was the coolest thing. You could see the dried-out ribs and the bleached, broken framework of the old ship from so long ago. Must've been a hell of a November storm that broke it apart." David was stalling for time. He paced back and forth near the burning embers, unsure of how to begin.

"I was reading some magazine article recently," he started, "about a survey on how many women were unfaithful to their husbands. So, I just started wondering... Have you ever... cheated on me since we've been married?"

The abrupt question caught Abby off guard. Her first instinct was to completely deny it, but then she decided to play coy, perhaps to gain a little more attention from her husband. "How can you ask me such a thing? Are you serious?"

"Well, it bothers me once in a while," he answered. "I've been wanting to ask you for a long time." As David hesitated, he collected some nearby driftwood and tossed it on the blaze. He thought of a few of his close friends and some of the overly friendly hugs and kisses his wife had freely given them. Usually after a few drinks. Was he half-blind, he wondered? Was something else going on and he was the last to know? "Tell me, what kind of feelings do you have for Tom or Charlie? What kind of feelings do you have for me?"

Abby looked up at him. "Don't be so jealous, David. Those are your good friends. Trust me, there's nothing serious going on. Relax."

Since their two boys had grown up and headed off to college, their nest had been bare. Just the two of them, day in, day out. Abby thought back to earlier years when they were dating, and everything was so fresh and exciting. The sex was always great back then — on quiet beaches, on the football field at night, in the back seat of the car. They had always tried to look their best for each other. After marriage, there were job responsibilities, kids to raise, a mortgage to pay off. Their sex life had diminished. During holidays and birthdays, there were in-laws' wishes to consider, and their schedules had become a management frenzy. Before they knew it, more quarrels ensued, more disagreements over petty matters followed. They showed less consideration to each other, and predictably, more hard feelings erupted. What had started out with such promise and joy had somehow withered and unraveled.

Abby stood up and skipped a stone across the flat surface of the lake. "How about you, David? Have you always been loyal to me these past twenty-five years? I've seen your wandering eyes on the pretty girls at parties sometimes, but I never said anything. And you've come home late often enough after a few drinks with your crew. You made me wonder about things."

For many years, David had worked as an independent carpenter, joining a larger crew occasionally to finish a bigger project. He'd met Abby when she was waitressing at the "Antler's Restaurant" in the Soo. He liked her beautiful smile and her easy laugh. Her strawberry blond hair brought out her deep brown eyes and dimples. Her full lips reminded him of Cindy Crawford. He soon asked her out, and within months they were inseparable.

"Well?" Abby asked.

Standing on the beach with his back to her, David finally spoke up. "Okay, I admit... I had a meaningless affair with someone. But it didn't last more than two months. Some little blond I'd met after work at the casino who invited me out for a drink."

"Do I know her?"

"No. You've never met her, I'm sure. I was feeling bored, kind of down, and she made me feel special. Don't worry; we didn't go to bed, if that's what you're wondering. I just lost interest in her — too high maintenance for me."

Abby's tears glistened in the firelight as she wiped her eyes. "I had no idea you were seeing someone. I'd always trusted you." She was quiet for a while. David was at a loss for words.

"She was nothing to me," David said. "I made a big mistake."

"Listen," she said, "I made a mistake too, a couple years back. At dinner one night with some friends, out in the bar parking lot, I shared a moonlight dance with a fellow. The radio in his pickup was playing that Neil Young song, 'Harvest Moon,' and I just got swept away romantically for a moment. I think the wine had gotten to me. Anyway, he tried to kiss me... and I let him. I know I shouldn't have, but it was all so spontaneous... We never pursued any sort of relationship together — he was married too. But, I'll admit, I've fantasized about the possibilities. I can't help it; I'm not perfect. It's just that... you don't seem to love me as much or pay attention to me like you did before."

David stared blankly into the fire in silence and poured himself another bourbon. Feeling slightly ashamed and restless, Abby walked into the nearby woods to relieve herself. She was gone for an unusually long time, and David began to worry. He called for her, but no answer. As he traced her steps, calling her name, David started to panic. Was she reconsidering what she'd just told him? Was she angry with him? He ran to the far shore on the north side of the small island, but there was no sign of her. If an animal had attacked her, he would have heard something. He looked out at the water in the late fall afternoon. No, she wouldn't do that; she was not a good swimmer. He raced through the trees and brush, down some well-worn paths into the deeper woods, calling for her, shouting her name. As he came over a higher ridge in the woods, David caught sight of Abby slumped down against a large birch, weeping to herself.

"Why didn't you answer me?" he said frantically.

"I don't know," she said. "I'm so mixed up right now. What has happened to us? We used to be so close."

David sat down next to her and put his arm around her shoulder. "I don't really know either," he said. "It just seems... like time and carelessness have worn us down... kind of like that old schooner over there. You know, the fire between us hasn't gone out just yet... but it might be smoldering."

Abby stopped weeping and smiled. "Yeah, who knows? There could still be a few live sparks under those ashes if we poked around a little. Anything's possible."

David kissed her on the forehead and hugged her closer. They walked back to the campfire and toasted with bourbon to a new beginning. Abby said she wanted to travel more — to places like New York or San Francisco, maybe take an Amtrak trip to Vegas for a few days. David agreed, if they could tent-camp and trout-fish together more often. He lived for the outdoors. She hated mosquitoes; he hated crowds. She hated the hard, cold ground of tent-camping; he hated flying in airplanes. She blew through money; he was much too thrifty for his own good.

They agreed to try harder, to be more patient.

With the sun perched low on the horizon, a slight wind gust parted a cluster of maple leaves, and they fluttered to the lake surface.

"If we don't start paddling back soon," said David, "we'll be finding our way in the dark."

They gathered their things, doused the fire, and climbed into the canoe. As they stroked their way silently towards the mainland, a half-moon rose between the shifting clouds. In the approaching darkness, a flock of Canada geese, squawking loudly, flew high overhead in a final V-formation before settling down for the night.

Steering from the stern with a J-stroke, David tried to quietly collect his thoughts. Had their confession of past lovers been an unwise move? Would it rattle their marriage or bring them closer? Only time could tell. He felt better about himself having voiced his suspicions. But a sense of violated trust, for him, had taken a mysterious new turn.

Abby, kneeling in the bow, paddled straight ahead, staring at the darkening shoreline. She, for her part, never dreamed that her husband would be interested in another woman. How naïve I've been, she thought. Why didn't I see the signs? We have been so inconsiderate of each other.

Abby stopped paddling for a moment and turned around to face David. "Do you still love me?" she asked.

A few feet from the canoe, a loon suddenly broke the surface, called into the night, dove, and disappeared. David, distracted for a moment, turned back to Abby. "Of course, I do," he said. "Very much."

•••

Over the years, gale force winds and winter blizzards have buffeted the rocky shores of Iroquois Island out in the bay. It not only survives the four seasons on Lake Superior — it flourishes. The rugged little island stands its ground, molded by trying conditions and the winds off the big lake. Yet, the dance goes on — without absolute certainty, without guarantees of any kind, thanks to the tempering value of nature and time.

Maxwell

by Richard Hill

A Lucky Match

The first thing you notice are the eyes. Big, brown, inquisitive eyes that seem to look right through you. This golden, fluffy cocker spaniel, part of a ten-week-old litter, stares back at us, patiently wagging his stubby tail, hoping we'll pick him. Of course, we do. How could we not?

A thirty-minute car ride later, he is back at the house with us, chasing a tennis ball across the living room and returning it on the first attempt. He seems to have a natural retrieving instinct. After sifting through dozens of names, we finally christen him Maxwell, after the little dog that pulled the Grinch's sled.

Max made his entrance into Michigan's cold, snowy Upper Peninsula on New Year's Eve just before the clock struck midnight. He was born in Brimley, just west of the Soo, along with several rambunctious brothers and sisters. House training Max took about a month, but we noted that when we scooted him outside to do his business in late spring, he always searched the yard for a small patch of snow to set up on. What would he do, we wondered, when winter was completely over?

Along with my wife and two sons, we adjusted our routines as necessary to accommodate our new addition to the household. Max required constant vigilance to prevent him from chewing any electrical cords, coffee table legs, or TV remotes. To distract him, we bought him some rawhide bones and a few tug-of-war toys, but for some reason he seemed to prefer the table legs.

We tried teaching Max to bark when he needed to go outside, but that was a waste of time, it seemed. However, if we were all sitting around in the evening watching a TV show, and one of the show characters happened to say something in a high-pitched voice like, "Who is it?" Max would launch off the pad and race to the front door to greet the unexpected stranger, barking all the while like the town crier. He seemed disappointed when no one was there but nevertheless stood his guard in case the intruder returned.

Cocker spaniels seem to love going for walks, and Max was no different. When we walked toward our neighborhood cul-de-sac, I would let him off the leash so he could sprint down the street after careless crows or leap back and forth over the roadside ditches. His favorite sport was chasing chipmunks and squirrels. The way they twitched their tails and chattered so teasingly drove him to distraction, and he wasn't about to let them get away with it. Max learned to freeze in midstride like a jungle cat stalking its prey. He'd creep closer and closer, step by step, then suddenly pounce. But the chipmunks and squirrels were always a split second ahead of him and scurried up a pine tree, scolding Max vindictively from an upper branch.

We had a very tall poplar tree in our backyard that we should have removed when we built the house. When the fall winds blew in off Lake Superior, we thought it might someday snap and crush part of the house. We had chainsawed nearly every nearby tree in the backyard except this particular poplar. The only reason we hesitated to remove it was because of its slight lean toward the house; if we accidently dropped it on the house, our insurance man would likely give us just a blank stare for being such imbeciles.

One summer day, Max sat with me on the back porch enjoying the leisurely afternoon when a red squirrel scampered across the yard. Max instantly scrambled down the stairs and gave chase. The squirrel scampered up the side of our poplar tree and calmly surveyed the situation from above. Max retreated to the porch but kept his eye on the wily critter. After about five minutes, the brave little squirrel quietly climbed down the back side of the tree, but Max heard him and raced off the porch to force the issue. The squirrel retreated again to a much higher branch, but there was no other nearby tree that he could leap to for escape. For what it was worth, Max had him cornered and seemed to relish this game of stalking and intrigue. For the next hour, the critter attempted twice more to outmaneuver Max, but he always caught wind of it and drove the poor creature back. It gave Max a blistering lecture from high in the tree, chattering nonstop with frustration, as if he may have had more important places to go and things to do. Finally, Max had enough of the game and pawed me for a bone and a fresh drink of water. He'd save the chase for another day.

There were a lot more dogs in our neighborhood after Max arrived on the scene. Three black labs, two Weimaraners, a Jack Russell terrier, one Chihuahua, and a few others of unknown origin. Most dogs love to chase anything that moves suspiciously—birds, rabbits, snakes, even an occasional mouse. One evening, up in my son Coleman's bedroom, Max spotted a mouse running behind the TV stand. He sprinted after him, chased the frightened critter around the room, and finally pounced on him with his big front paw, pinning him to the ground. Unsure of what to do with the helpless victim, Max gave the mouse a count of three and released him, figuring he had made his point. The mouse scampered into the closet and disappeared. Then Max looked over at Coleman as if to say, "What? I caught the little pest. Was I supposed to rehabilitate him, too?"

As a younger dog, Maxwell was a speedster. Coleman would often race him down the street on his bicycle but could not outsprint him. For a cocker spaniel, Max had blistering speed. One time, as I was walking him down the cul-de-sac, Max must have caught the alluring scent of pheromones in the air. Our neighbor's pit-bull Fifi was in heat and Max was only too willing to oblige. He broke into a dead run and would not stop or slow down as I called after him. I raced four blocks trying to keep up with him until he disappeared into the woods. He was on a mission and wasn't about to let his master interfere. When I finally tracked him down, Max was so relaxed he may as well have been smoking a cigarette and sipping a cocktail. The call of love had been answered.

On some occasions, Maxwell was unpredictable and hard to read. Working out in the yard one day when he was a younger pup, I lost sight of him and called his name. He didn't come to me, and he didn't bark. I combed both ends of our street, shouting and whistling into the woods and every yard. I asked all the neighborhood kids if they'd seen him but had no luck. Finally, after over an hour of searching, I walked into the garage to put away the rakes, and there was Max, wagging his tail and happy as ever that we could play this exciting game of hide-and-seek. Though I'd called his name repeatedly, I hadn't been able to get even a simple bark out of him for the past hour. He must have quietly followed me into the garage when I wasn't paying attention.

When it came to loud noises, Max was never shy of a roaring lawn mower, a whining chainsaw, or any other power tools. He would lounge comfortably in the grass as I cut up firewood or ran the leaf blower across the yard. But come near him with a vacuum cleaner inside the house and Max would retreat to a far corner of the room. Same with 4th of July fireworks. We took him with us once to see the annual festivities in Grand Marais, and when the colorful, booming spectacle overhead started, Max thought the world was coming to an end; he shook uncontrollably and couldn't wait to go home. We never exposed him to the shock of fireworks again.

Over the years, Max and I spent many hours together in one corner of the house that I use for reading and writing. If he noticed me writing a story in a notebook, he would know not to bother me but instead would chew on an old bone or take a quiet snooze. Afterward, I would reward him with a long walk in the woods or a car ride to the grocery store. He preferred standing on my lap, sticking his head out the window to catch a cool breeze.

Learning the Ropes

How do you describe a thirty-pound golden cocker spaniel that has held your heart and soul for more than sixteen years? In that period of time, he had become a close member of our family, whose needs and well-being were always considered whenever we made plans. Walks, camp-outs, trips out of town or to the beach—he became a part of everything. Picnics at the Iroquois lighthouse or Brimley State Park—Max was always included.

What is it about the relationship between a person and a dog that makes that bond so special, so meaningful? As time goes on, we fall under some kind of canine spell and become hopelessly attached. Unlike people, a dog doesn't ask much from us and simply accepts us as we are—no comments, no complaints. Whether you leave the house for five minutes or five hours, your dog will be there to greet you when you return, wagging his tail and licking your hand. Without any advance notice, a dog will drop whatever he's doing and gladly join you for a brisk walk or a trip to town in the truck. Total spontaneity—a trait one seldom finds in most people. Whatever it is, your dog is always up for the game and asks so little in return: he loves being petted, having his neck scratched, and being told that he's "a good boy." An occasional milk-bone doesn't hurt matters either.

Max had always been very patient, waiting vigilantly in the car for me, windows partially rolled down, while I ran my errands around town. To reward him, I sometimes stopped by the Dairy Queen on a hot day and bought him a small vanilla ice-cream cone, which he devoured in a matter of seconds. He started out with a few slow, polite licks, then shifted into high gear, gulping the entire cone in one cold, creamy rush.

In October some years, as the leaves were peaking, we would walk into town on a Sunday morning to my brother's place to watch the Lions football game. It was a ten-mile hike through the woods, down the dormant snowmobile trail, and Max would join us. He'd race twenty yards ahead, dart into the woods for a pee or to check out some new scents and then catch up with us. After three hours of hiking, we covered the ten-mile distance, but Max must have clocked twice as much mileage in all his excitement. After a light lunch of chicken and biscuits, he would sleep through the entire football game at my brother's. As often as the Lions lost, I wish I had done the same.

Living on the upper St. Mary's River, Max had plenty of opportunities to swim in the bay. Many warm summer evenings, Judy and I would be relaxing with a drink down by the deck on the water. Max would zero in on a flock of geese drifting closer and closer to our bank. Suddenly, Max decided it was time to show them who's boss. He'd scramble down the bank, plunge into the water, and begin dogpaddling swiftly after the geese. They nonchalantly turned their backs and began their ho-hum retreat, hardly ruffling a feather. Meanwhile, Max pursued them with a vengeance until we called him back from the deeper water. With an air of confidence, he swam back to shore and shook himself dry, proud that he had shown those nosey intruders he wasn't about to be pushed around.

My son Travis sometimes took Max for a kayak ride in the bay. He would sit alertly in the cockpit, front paws on the forward deck, watching the ducks and seagulls landing near him in the tall reeds, no doubt tempting him to abandon all sanity and leap into the water in hot pursuit. Travis had to warn him: "Good boy. Don't you even think about it." You could tell by his rapt attention to the ducks that he was considering his options.

Once when Judy and I took both kayaks out for a cruise around the bay, Max was first mate on her vessel. I was paddling about

twenty yards ahead and heard her say, "Do you want to go see Daddy?" Before she could blink, Max dove out of the cockpit into the bay and began a mad dash towards me. As he neared my kayak, I tried to pull him in without flipping over. It wasn't easy, and just to show his appreciation, Max stood up and shook every last drop all over me, as if to say, "I'll bet you weren't expecting that."

For a cocker spaniel, Max was usually very even-tempered. If he ever sensed any danger, he would respond quickly. One Sunday afternoon, when I was out in the garage finishing up a woodworking project, Max lay in the doorway soaking up the sunshine. He suddenly scrambled to his feet, barked excitedly, and tore through the trees after something black, about the size of our neighbor's Labrador. The black shadow galloped through the woods, with Max close behind, then suddenly scurried up a tree. When I realized the animal was a black bear cub, I looked around for the protective mama bear, knowing Max would be in big trouble if he persisted. But Max was apparently near-sighted and totally oblivious to the bear cub's mad dash up the tree. He bounced through the woods in a bewildered manner, like Pepe-Le-Pew, trying to pick up the lost scent. Fortunately, there was no mama bear in sight. The frightened cub climbed down from the tree and bolted across the road when Max wasn't looking. It could have been ugly, but Max didn't seem worried; he had stood his ground and defended his turf.

Even more dangerous was an incident down by the lower hillside deck one morning when we were enjoying a leisurely brunch. Judy and I were sipping coffee on a crisp October morning, watching the lake freighters out in the bay, and Travis was coaxing Max to sit up for a piece of his peanut butter toast. Suddenly, Travis' jaw dropped open as he gazed at something behind me moving through the brush. I quickly turned to see a large timber wolf with steely blue eyes less than twenty feet from me. He froze and stared at us for a second, realized we were no threat, then loped briskly through the hillside brush and disappeared. Meanwhile, Max, with his back to the wolf, had not seen a thing; he was more focused on the buttery toast. If he had noticed the wolf, we felt sure he would have challenged him and lost that battle. Thank goodness for the hypnotic power of peanut butter toast.

Food in general was one of Maxwell's great obsessions. I think he dreamed about it many nights. The vet said we could feed him chicken, rice, and green beans; they were all very nutritious for him. Max liked the first two but turned his nose up on the last. Sometimes, to entertain himself, he would chew a hearty hambone for two hours straight or until his jaw muscles tired out. Most of the time, I was well-armed with emergency dog snacks; Max knew I usually carried a handful of his favorite treats, some five-calorie milk-bones, in my jacket pocket and frequently pestered me for a couple handouts. When my pocket was empty, I'd wave my hands in a crisscross manner and say, "No more." He knew there was no point in persisting, so he drifted off to some other canine pursuit.

Living with us for so many years, Maxwell adjusted to our daily schedule. He got tired when we got tired, came up to bed with us, and slept on a nearby blanket; he held his bladder for the night and woke up in the morning when we woke up. Only in his later years did he wake us at 2 a.m. or 4 a.m. for a potty trip outside. Whenever I heard his telltale whimper, I would jump out of bed, pull on my jeans and sweatshirt, scoop him up and hurry down the stairs and out the back door. Like many of us as we grow older, Max could hold his bladder for only so long.

The more familiar Max became with our household routine, the more closely he kept tabs on us. He had a need to know where we were in the house at all times. If one of us stood up in the living room and wandered into the bathroom, he would soon nose the door open and stare at you with those inquisitive brown eyes while you sat on the pot, as if to say, "What are you doing sitting in here? I've been searching the entire house for you. How about a little heads-up next time?"

When it was time to stretch our legs and go for a walk, Max was always more than agreeable. But one time, after I hooked his leash to him and coaxed him down the driveway, he seemed lethargic and tired. He lay in the grass and wouldn't move. After carrying him inside, I flipped him over on his back and closely examined his belly and under his legs. Sure enough, a large tick had firmly at-tached himself. So, I lit a match, blew it out, and touched the hot ember to the tick. As I pinched him carefully with the tweezers, he released his grip on his host. Within ten minutes, Max was back on his feet, bounding energetically out the door for a walk.

Most dogs seem to follow the same protocol on a walk. They race around sniffing various scents from other animals until they find one that appeals to them. Instead of emptying their bladders in great relief, they release just a fraction of their burden and try to spread their calling card throughout the entire neighborhood. This sort of canine conduct is probably saying something like, "Yes, I'm interested," or, "This is my turf. Watch your step." And Max was no different when it came time to rolling in another dog's mess, a behavior I will never understand. He knew it meant an immediate bath in the tub, but that threat did not deter him. After all, a dog's got to do what a dog's got to do.

At Christmas and birthdays, wrapped gifts held a very special enticement for Max. He insisted on helping everyone rip the bows and paper off the presents to see what was inside. If you set the gift on the floor, he would pounce on it, grip it with his front paws, tug at the ribbons with his jaws, and claw at the paper until it was sufficiently opened. We didn't teach him this behavior; it was pure instinct. Max didn't seem to mind that there wasn't a bone or treat inside the package. This frantic ritual was a reward in itself.

Winning the Super Bowl

We each took turns walking Max nearly every day, usually a mile or two. After ten years' activity, we calculated that this energetic little spaniel had hiked more than 4500 miles, or the equivalent of walking from New York City to San Francisco and back. No wonder he stayed in such good shape. His daily outings, in turn, kept all of us quite healthy and fit.

As mentioned earlier, we included Max in most family activities, including the Super Bowl pool. The board had one hundred spots open at $2/square and paid off at the end of each quarter. Max was allowed to take the very last spot open. After the New England Patriots trounced the Kansas City Chiefs, Max seemed to be the happiest one in the room. He had just won $115, enough to buy all the chicken and bones he wanted. With great humility, Max didn't gloat but seemed to take it all in stride, knowing his friends would be envious.

As Max grew older, we left him at home less often. When he was close to ten years old, we brought him to our retail gift-gallery downtown every morning so he could have company. He eventually decided that his role at the store was to greet customers as they entered. When the front door chimed, signaling a new patron, Max would charge out of the back room with a hearty bark to see who was coming in. When he was satisfied that the customer was harmless, he would turn and wander back to the office, seemingly disappointed, as if to say, "Oh, it's just you. I was hoping for the mailman."

One winter, when Max was ten, he lost his left front leg in a quirky sort of accident. Jumping down from the back seat of my wife's car, he hit a slick patch of ice that caused an unrepairable spiral facture. After a valiant attempt to mend his broken bones, our veterinarian removed the leg and helped guide us through Max's recovery. With only three legs remaining Max was forced to adapt to a new life, eventually learning how to hop when he walked. His spirits remained as buoyant as ever, especially with all the love and support he received from us and many of our neighbors. This brought about several changes in the house. Max acquired several new sleeping and feeding stations throughout to make life a little easier for him. He soon had water bowls in the kitchen, living room, office, and upstairs bedroom. Max discovered that by moaning repeatedly, one of us would magically fetch his water bowl and bring it to him. He didn't have to lift a paw and milked it for all it was worth.

On occasion, he developed a severe case of diarrhea and required a visit to the vet. After Max had downed a week's worth of prescription pills, cleverly disguised in liverwurst, his bowel habits finally improved. Despite a carefully monitored diet, within months he would again surprise us with another bout of diarrhea. It soon occurred to us that he might be picking up some kind of bacteria from his water bowls. Upon closer examination, we detected a somewhat slimy deposit in the bowls if we didn't scour them regularly with hot, soapy water. As simple as that, after making the necessary adjustment, the problem soon disappeared for good.

For over sixteen years, Max was a loving companion to all of us. He got along well with Hazel, Moose, Delilah, and all the other dogs in the neighborhood. My brother said that Max was not "street smart" and would never make it if he lived in the city. He was much too friendly and trusting, a consequence of growing up in the U.P.

A dog's life is so short in comparison to a human's. In many ways dogs remind us of our own brief trajectory, our own mortality. They experience so many of the same elements that we do, albeit in their own ways: learning, growth, discoveries, excitement, making friends, new environments—then the inevitable slowing down, special needs, and the necessary pampering and care in old age.

Maxwell stayed with us until the first week of spring; we had endured another long U.P. winter together. He will be cremated and buried in the corner of our backyard, overlooking the St. Mary's River. We will plant a pine seedling over his plot in memory, a symbol of his love for the outdoors. As it grows over time, it will remind us of the many wonderful years we spent with him. On his final day, during the somber drive home from the vet's office, I spotted my first spring robin in the neighborhood—perhaps a hopeful sign from Max that, eventually, our broken hearts will begin to heal.

Richard Hill has lived in his native Michigan's Upper Peninsula for more than fifty years. His books include *Lake Effect, Hitchhiking After Dark, Lost in the Woods,* and most recently, *West of the River, North of the Bridge.* Richard attended the University of Michigan, Northern Michigan University, and the Great Lakes Maritime Academy, and currently lives with his wife near Sault Ste. Marie. For more information, see RichardHillBooks.com.

Three Poems Linking Emerson, Besonen, and Custer

by Mack Hassler

Classic Dualism: Family and Predation

"You know, Pap [his father B.L. Emerson], I often
used to wonder why you and all the other vets of
the last war, never talked too much of your
experience over here; now I... realize just why."
PFC R.L Emerson, 6/28/44

The epigraph above engraved
From the father of my wife's best
Friend and carefully saved
In letter boxes from the Nazi war
Features love balancing this bellicose nest.

In my overly ambitious poem,
That surname, though hardly sure of any
 line
With its descent as metaphor alone,
Represents a philosophic dualism
That communicates well as telltale sign

Of meaning. The great Emerson's father
William was a preacher who exhorted
Sons of liberty in that first civil war
Against our British brothers. His son
 fought
With equal eloquence to see slavery
 aborted.

Recently we undertook to raise twin dogs,
Males of the same litter. We watch them
 pounce
On mice and even squirrels as horrid
 predators.
But family love is manifestly evident as
 well
When they tussle into bed each night and
 bounce.

Just so our friends who somehow carry
Tracks of that Emerson line plan to hunt
Our forty acres in the North, always wary
Of what they stalk, of death in the woods
That images Empires of power only love
 can blunt.

Joanne Besonen in Her Weeds

Even with my weak vision in the rain,
The image of his widow burns my brain
With transcendent pathos. Standing apart
In strangely white pants, nearly immaculate
At the far end of the cemetery, she
Watched her husband, who was finally free
At last, buried as a hero proclaimed
As only she could know when she had named
The essence of their lives in all the years
Alone and absent children, still with fears
And stillborn hopes at all the wondrous stuff
Traveling decades with grace and joy enough.

Custer

We drove through Deadwood and down
The Custer battlefield with our dogs
To visit our son who signs his name as mine.

In a better world, the lion may lie down with the lamb.
For now, "Solaris" is the project, a polar orbit
Of our star. Our son's final signature.

Such generation is, also, the Empire
Of our dogs. Life's vitality competes and some die
To traverse more *lebensraum.*

Lem's old novel lent the one word of its title
To our trip, and our fierce puppies play
Generation games in the morning.

Young Custer from Monroe had secured
His wife, who lived another half century,
At Fort Lincoln before the final fight.

Mack Hassler has spent most of each summer with his family on Vermilac Lake in Baraga County since 1989. He worked in the English Department at Kent State in Ohio from 1965 to 2014. He publishes literary criticism under his "fuller name," Donald M. Hassler, mostly dealing with 18th century literature and modern science fiction. His poems have appeared in *Analog* and *Academic Questions*. For his 80th birthday, his two sons edited a collection of his poetry on family and the UP titled *High Latitudes*.

The Most Remarkable Thing
Starring Norwegious Ida G

by J. L. Hagen

Ida G opens the passenger door of the palm and sand green 1957 VW Microbus and hops down onto the blacktop. Her fluffy, salt-and-pepper curls are a consequence of yesterday's weekly trip to the beauty parlor. She turns, presses her glasses up from her button nose, and peeks in at my five cousins and me, crammed into the back rows like starlings on a stretch of telephone wires.

"I'll just be a minute," Ida says. She glances up at my uncle Jim in the driver's seat, then hurries toward the entrance of Wally's Superette in Great Falls, Montana.

Near the door, three young men gawk at her. Dressed in blue jeans, engineer boots, and black leather jackets, they serve as a gauntlet, blocking the path in. Their hair, laced with Brylcream, is slicked back from long sideburns, and piled high and wavy; Brando wannabes—as in *The Wild One*—evidenced by a row of Harleys parked a couple of spaces down. She peers up at the largest of the threesome, who throws a shadow over her five-foot frame. They converse a moment, then she flashes him a sweet, maternal smile. He immediately steps aside to let her enter. His two sidekicks fall back behind him, all loose-jointed and bent over, snickering. One slaps him on the back and sights down a finger in a "gotcha" moment. He twists around to see who's watching, face as red as an apple.

A few minutes later, she strides back through the entry. The outlaws are long gone.

Sliding onto the front seat, she sets a grocery sack on the floor.

Jim nudges up the bill on his ever-present green army hat, the one that reminds everybody of Fidel Castro. "What was that about?"

She blinks her round, lake-blue eyes. "Well, the young man said, 'Hello, Grandma!' So, I replied, 'I'll be your grandma—if you would like me to.'"

Uncle Jim, who is six feet tall, goes about 225, and sports dark hair and a dog face like Robert Mitchum, roars with a belly laugh. My cousins and I all fall in line and chuckle. This is classic Ida G, a tiny, fearless grandma dynamo with sufficient energy to power the entire Rocky Mountain states.

It's sweltering outside, close to a hundred degrees. But it's a dry heat, which means your ice cream melts and evaporates at equal rates. I'm not used to it, being from Upper Michigan where, if the temperature heads above seventy-five degrees, people talk seriously about emigration to Canada—even Alaska.

My parents have evidently decided I need to become more self-reliant and so have loaded me on a Greyhound bus at the eastern terminus of US-2 West on the first warm day in June 1960 for a 1,500-mile trek from St. Ignace, Michigan, to Great Falls. There are no freeways, only two-lanes, and it takes a meandering three days through every village, cow town, and hamlet to get there. My last birthday was barely three months ago. I am ten years old.

Now, I am staying at Grandma and Grandpa's for the summer. Lawrence, on the glide path to retirement for a few years, has finally landed. Ida has elected to raise two daughters, keep house, and entertain their friends. She can never retire, especially now that he is home all day.

They reside at 2908 Central, the same place where my mom grew up, a middle-class neighborhood of white, one-story bungalows. I have my own bedroom, in fact, my own apartment in the basement, when Grandpa isn't sharing it at his large wood executive desk.

On the wall are family photos, the largest of which is an eight by twelve-inch portrait in a Rococo gold frame of three-year-old Ida. Swathed in a dark dress with a ruffled white collar, she peers toward heaven, hands steepled in prayer, a perfect little golden angel.

Born in 1894, Ida Gurina Sundahl is the youngest of six children, fifteen years younger than her oldest brother, Halvor; six years younger than her youngest brother, Charlie; clearly, the baby and darling of the household.

•••

Grandma brews coffee in a percolator every morning in the kitchen, takes it with half-and-half, which she also pours on a tiny dish of cereal. She nibbles a cookie afterwards, homemade; often a "thumbprint" with a dollop in the center of gooseberry or huckleberry jam.

Grandpa takes a shot of Listerine, straight out of the bottle, and gargles in the bathroom, then spits it in the sink before he sits down to breakfast. He carries over a china soup bowl, the kind with a flat rim, heaps it with a mountain of Wheaties, then pours half-and-half over it until it nearly overflows. If I squint, it resembles one of the Rocky Mountains I have seen in picture books at home. The cream looks like melting snow on the peaks and valleys. He slides it my direction, then sits across the painted yellow kitchen table, leaning on his folded arms to watch me eat. Every bite. On more than one morning, he fills the bowl up

to five times. I don't know if he is concerned my mother has been starving me back in Michigan or if he is attempting to pump the value of his General Mills stock (the largest holding in his retirement portfolio and his former employer).

They are both Midwesterners, originally from Litchfield, Minnesota, bedrock Republicans steeled on self-reliance. He's a graduate of the University of Minnesota and a Cornell man until called by the Great War. She is an alumna of the Mankato Normal School who, before she marries Grandpa, teaches school in Owatonna, then back in Litchfield.

She has survived a bout with breast cancer. She bears a permanent red rash that spiderwebs from the base of her neck until it disappears into the collar and placket of her blouse. She never talks about it, at least around me, and I never dare to inquire.

One afternoon, I am watching a Roy Rogers movie on television. We don't have a set at our home in Michigan. My brothers, sister, and I dash across the street to our neighbors on most afternoons to view cartoons broadcast on Channel 2 from a station in Sault Ste. Marie, Ontario, the only one accessible, assuming you have a fifty-foot tower with an aerial behind your house. Television is a luxury, especially, if the picture isn't snowy like at home. Grandma switches off the set and shoos me from the couch to go outside and play.

"Grandma, I'm tired," I say.

"You can sleep when you're dead," she replies. She doesn't laugh. She knows how to take little boys in hand—and big boys, too.

•••

My Montana summer is transformative. My grandparents take my cousins and me to Glacier National Park. I see mountains for the first time and walk on a glacier. We stay on the shore of Lake McDonald in a log cabin with a stone fireplace.

Grandpa teaches me to play golf. One weekend, he takes my cousin Eric and me fly-fishing on Belt Creek, and we camp out overnight. Later in the summer, Grandpa takes me to the Montana State Fair, and we wear matching white straw Stetson hats to the rodeo.

I am learning what it means to be a Westerner, not a Midwesterner, but a Montanan—a cowboy. Grandpa sports a pencil-thin mustache that makes him look like John Steinbeck; he wears a braided, black leather bolo tie with a polished silver dollar set in its clasp.

He tells stories, the kind you hear around a campfire, like the time he encountered a drunk weaving out-of-control on the highway. Grandpa trips his high-beams twice and motions him over to the roadside, pretending to be the Sheriff. Since he drives a green and white DeSoto, this is plausible.

As he pulls up behind the vehicle, he slips the silver dollar down toward the ends of the bolo strings and wedges them into his left chest pocket. "The fellow was so inebriated," he declares, "he mistook it for my badge."

The drunk rolls down the window and commences talking fast. "Sorry, Sheriff, so sorry, I just live up the road a bit. On my way home. I'll never do it again."

"The man looked so pitiful," Grandpa says. "I gave him a stern lecture, made him pledge to go sober, and dispatched him with a warning. He thanked me." He looks alternately at me and Cousin Eric. His eyes twinkle.

He tells us other whoppers as well, like how you need to carry a pail in Minnesota in the wintertime, where it's so cold that when someone speaks, you have to catch the frozen words and bring them inside to thaw to hear what they're saying. I suppose he learned how to recount similar tales while helping around his father's saloon. He tells me once about carrying buckets of beer down to the blacksmith for the workers on their lunch break.

Toward the end of Ida's life, my sister Maren asks her what Grandpa was like when she first met him.

"He was a bit of a show-off," she says. "I liked his brother better."

•••

When Maren tells me this story, I flash on a conversation with my cousin Julie.

"When they were first married in 1920," she says. "Grandpa was kind of a 'sportsman.' He liked to hang around with his pals and play tennis and golf. Meanwhile, Grandma was stuck taking care of their babies and keeping up the house. One Saturday afternoon when he arrived home with his golf clubs, she sat him down for a little chat about being a father. That pretty much ended his days as a 'free spirit.'"

•••

Not that Lawrence, one hundred percent Swedish, can't also deliver a pointed lecture, like the morning we broke camp on our fly-fishing trip. As we pack up our gear, he says to me and Cousin Eric, "Okay, stand on either side and stretch your arms out until we're fingertip to fingertip." Then we march in line to "police" the campsite, removing debris. When I walk by a gum wrapper on the ground, he says, "Hey, pick up that tin foil."

I protest. "I didn't put it there."

"Doesn't matter," he says. "We leave the site better than we found it."

I remove it from the dirt, embarrassed but miffed that I have to clean up someone else's trash.

Unbeknownst to me, if not to him, he has handed me a splendid gift, the value of taking responsibility. Years later, I think, *maybe that's what he learned from Grandma.*

•••

I also learn that before Ida and Lawrence were married, his brother may not have been the sole rival for Ida's attention. After my mother's death a few years ago, Maren gives me some mementos relating to her and our grandparents. Included is a black leather photo album that belonged to Ida. In the album are numerous small black-and-white pictures of her and her friends taken in their teens and early twenties: several young women out for the afternoon, dressed in beautiful, flowing dresses and long hair coiled high on their heads, sometimes accompanied by young men in thick, tweed suits topped off with woolen caps or, in rare cases, fedora hats. I am reminded of illustrations from a nineteenth-century Sears and Roebucks catalog.

In every photo, she is the smallest and by far the most beautiful, always with a knowing, camera-conscious smile, as if to say, "Look at us, aren't we acting silly?" The boys have tanned faces from working in the fields. There are group photos of them sitting in buggies, swimming in a lake, and standing in front of a farmhouse porch. In one picture, Ida speaks to her students in a classroom. There are also portraits of young Indians, with long braided hair, dressed in native dress, possibly participants in a parade or traveling show. Other couples stand with their backs to the camera, an umbrella shielding their upper bodies, lending a risqué air to the captured instant.

Page after page, I flip through the book. I use a magnifying glass to examine tiny details. There are plenty of young men, but it's not clear which are brothers, which are friends, which are beaus of the other girls, and which are of special interest to Ida.

Where is Grandpa?

Finally, halfway through, I spot him. He looks so young and appears in profile, dressed in a suit in the afternoon in the yard, hands in pockets, glancing sideways toward the camera. His face is tanned, nose straight—almost Teutonic; hair terminating in a widow's peak. He is smaller than young men in other photos. But he projects the same handsome air of confidence exhibited in an early portrait I had seen in my grandparents' basement in 1960.

Then, I find him again and again in other snapshots. He is part of her circle now. And he has won a grand prize, much more valuable than the future shiny dollar set in his bolo tie.

•••

However, Grandpa is not the only one with a fondness for silver. Grandma despises bank notes. "Flimsy paper money—there's nothing to it. Gets all wadded up in my purse." She shakes her head, blowing out disgust from puffed cheeks.

I notice when she goes to the store, she spends the paper currency, but holds back the silver. When they hand her paper dollars for change, she asks if they have coins instead.

On Saturday evenings, we sometimes go to the Meadowlark Country Club for prime rib. She and Grandpa both love their beef, and Montana is "Capital C" Cattle Country. Yet even better than a slab of Montana grass-fed, medium-rare prime rib with au jus, a large Kalispell-grown roasted potato, fresh-baked dinner rolls, real butter, and a salad bar, is bingo. Especially, Silver Dollar Bingo. Most of the time, she wins nothing, but is undeterred. She knows that one Saturday, she will be the one to cash in. This amount of Scandinavian determination is a formidable weapon. In the wrong hands, it could wreak global havoc. However, she is civility and integrity personified, so, for now, the world is safe.

•••

Grandma loves games of all kinds. Even into her nineties, after Lawrence is long deceased, she is still inviting people to her house. Over time, the games change: bridge, pinochle, canasta, hearts, rummy, even cribbage. She often gives back the money she has won so that family members and guests will stay longer and continue to compete. When she can't get a decent hand, she throws down her cards.

"Phooey!" she says. "Good grief, I haven't had a decent hand... all night!"

Still, she keeps on playing. She will never give up.

•••

Only recently do I come to understand her relationship with her brother, Charlie. On more than one occasion, she speaks of riding to school in Minnesota with Charlie driving a horse-drawn sleigh.

"The snow was over top of the fences," she recalls.

Late in her life, she owns dogs. She always names them Charlie.

One Christmas, she comes to visit us. While she is here, a kitten follows my brother home from school and sits on our doorstep. At the time, we own a dog named Missy (after a girl I met at church camp the summer before I started high school). My middle brother owns a parakeet named Nicky.

The potential reality of a dog, and a cat, and a bird—not to mention four children— all together in the same small home floods my mother's vivid imagination. The result would be a literal household tornado. As the little black-and-white kitten sits out on our front porch, meowing incessantly, my mother puts her foot down.

"We are not letting that cat in this house."

It starts to snow, big fluffy white clusters, yet over the following day, she remains adamant.

Ida stares out the window of our front door. "Oh, look, its little ears are getting frosted. And its little nose too," she says.

My mother throws her hands up. "Okay... okay, let the cat in."

Three days later, she loads up the family car and takes Ida to the airport for her flight back to Montana. Then, all my mother's worst nightmares come true. The dog chases the cat, and the cat stalks the bird, except when it periodically runs away, only to limp back, face swollen from some injury which has become infected during its all-night carousing. It lays around the house for a few days, while my mother plays feline Florence Nightingale and nurses it back from the dead. Then, the entire business starts again. Eventually, the cat develops a cauliflower ear like an old prize fighter, torn claws, a broken tail, and a jagged patch on its nose where no fur will grow.

Before Ida flies back to Montana, she has presciently named the cat. Charlie. Charlie Black.

•••

It's a mystery why she names her pets after Charlie. I happen to talk with Maren about it.

"I think I stumbled on the answer," I say. "How's that?"

"I was looking online on my genealogy program, and I noticed Charlie died on November 11, 1918, the day World War I ended. I wondered if he was killed in action on the last day of the War. Maybe that had something to do with it."

"No, that's not it," she says. "Grandma told me he was living in Minnesota then, a farm implement dealer and married with children. He came down with the Spanish Flu. He developed this horrible cough and was afraid he might pass it on to his wife and kids—and they would die. So, he went upstairs in the house and barricaded himself in the bedroom. He wouldn't come out, he wouldn't eat or drink anything, and he wouldn't let anyone in. After a few days, they found him there, dead of bronchial pneumonia."

"Whoa, you make it all the way through the Great War without dying, only to be killed by a 'bug' on the day it ends."

"Yeah, he was thirty. I don't think she ever got over it."

•••

We also know the story about her maternal grandfather, Anders Olsen Bækkedok, immigrant from Kongsberg, Norway, who came to Acton Township, Minnesota, only to be ambushed, shot, and scalped by Indians while salting cattle on his farm in 1862.

He was thirty-four years old. This happened during the Great Sioux Uprising that broke out in Acton and spread through other parts of Minnesota. We hear about his wife, born Larina Maria Syversdatter Korsbakken (under Spisholt), later forced to hide her children when she went into town or gave food to hungry renegades knocking on the back door of her farmhouse.

Julie says, "It must have been bitter fruit for her."

When I mention this to Maren, she says, "You know, in a book I just read, there is another side to that."

She tells me the Uprising started in part because the Indians were desperate and starving. After a few months when the fight ended, the U.S. government held nearly four hundred trials, some lasting as short as five minutes. They sentenced 303 Indians to death. President Lincoln reviewed every case and commuted all but thirty-nine. On the day after Christmas, they hanged thirty-eight in Mankato, the largest one-day mass execution in U.S. history.

"That kind of wrecks it for me," I say.

"Yeah," Maren replies. "I wonder how much Grandma knew about the rest of the story."

•••

Julie has interviewed her in the 1970s for a college paper about the nineteenth century, which she sends to me. It contains lots of references to Norwegian food, such as *primost* (a rich, spreadable, semi-sweet cheese), *flotegrot* (a cream pudding) and *frukt suppe* (a stew of cooked dried fruits).

Every Christmas, Ida eats *lefsa*, a Norwegian potato flatbread, which resembles a soft taco, spread with butter and sugar. She also religiously eats *gjetost*, a tawny, caramelly sweet goat's milk cheese that only a Norwegian grandmother born on a farm in nineteenth-century Minnesota could love.

When my wife and I have our children, we bundle up our youngest on his first Christmas and bring him over to meet her. He's tiny, swaddled in a blanket and crowned with a yellow, cone-shaped knit hat sporting a fluffy little ball on top that sticks straight up a foot above his forehead.

"*Tomte gubbe*," she coos, taking him from my wife. "*Tomte gubbe*."

We learn this means a little elf, and a mischievous one at that, a name whose origins predate Santa Claus and Christianity.

•••

As Ida comes to live in my former hometown in her later years, I start to wonder about all the experiences she has accumulated in her life. I ask her to write about her childhood, growing up in Minnesota before there were cars, airplanes, television, computers, and a million other things. I have already caught snatches and hints in her conversations, as have my mother, my siblings, and my cous-

ins. But I am looking for something more quintessential.

One day, after pressing her for months, I receive a letter in the mail. Attached, at last, is an essay about her mother, a reminiscence that reaches back to another generation and another country. It's titled "A Blue Trunk." Beneath the words, her hidden world emerges from the past.

A Blue Trunk

A proud possession of a dignified old lady, not really old in years but in life, and its contents were practically all she had left in life after her children were gone. It stood in the corner of her bedroom where she spent most of her time, when she wasn't using the spinning wheel or knitting long black stockings for me to wear.

This trunk had had a long journey being tossed around in a sailing boat for sixteen weeks coming from Norway to the U.S. It was sturdy and strong, just as she was then and it contained her precious things, a few clothes, a shawl, a bonnet and as I remember, a box with the most lovely, old buttons, and only occasionally I was permitted to look and touch them, and usually this was after I read a small verse from a little blue book with a picture of Jesus on it and the caption was, "Se på Jesus—*look at Jesus*," Norwegian of course.

This trunk had a special aura of dignity about it—homemade by my grandmother's brothers, strong enough to last, heavy with bands of steel holding it together—and it seemed to say to me, "Do not touch." It still does.

•••

Somehow, it had not occurred to me she may have spoken Norwegian at home as her primary language.

"Yeah, I visited her a few weeks ago," Maren says. "She's been reading the Bible in Norwegian. She has a Norwegian-English dictionary sitting out on the dining room table next to it."

My ninety-year-old grandmother is relearning the language of her childhood. A language from a different country, a different age. It leads me to a deeper question. *What is the most remarkable thing she has experienced in her long life?* I am determined to know the answer.

•••

A few months later, I make a quick weekend trip from Grand Rapids to St. Ignace to see my mother, widowed after the sudden death of my father on Christmas Day, 1981. It's now 1985, and she is living alone in the retirement house he planned and built on the shore of Lake Michigan. I am up only for the weekend to check on her.

She shows me a scrapbook she has been making that captures the chronology of her life, including her parents, husband, children, and grandchildren. It's an extraordinary two-inch thick document, with news stories, drawings, photos, programs, and awards she has collected since high school. We spend the afternoon looking at it.

On the last page of the scrapbook is an intriguing newspaper account of Ida's marriage to Lawrence on August 11, 1920, held at the home of her sister.

"The bride wore a traveling suit of dark brown broadcloth, trimmed with fur, and hat to match, and carried a corsage bouquet of pink roses and sweet peas." The article goes on to say that "Both the bride and groom are well known Litchfield young people. Miss Sundahl, who taught in the Litchfield schools a number of years, is a very accomplished young woman."

Next to it—surprising and somehow prophetic—is a brochure entitled "Your 1919 Vacation." A drawing of a cruise ship steams out of the picture frame along with a list of destinations the ship will visit. Among these is Mackinac Island, across the Straits of Mackinac from St. Ignace, where my father at the age of one will move with his family in 1923.

Inside the fold-out, four-panel brochure is a black-and-white photo of a wedding party with a pretty, young woman dressed in white, seated front and center, holding a bouquet. The caption reads "Fond Recollections from

1916" and a smaller caption elaborates that the photo is of the "Home Talent Troupe on Board in 1916." Beneath the brochure, my mother has penned "Ida—'Bride' in center picture."

Ida had been a member of an acting troupe one summer onboard a Great Lakes cruise ship.

•••

On Sunday afternoon, before I leave to return home, I drive around the point of St. Ignace to see Grandma. She lives on the other side of the Straits, in an apartment on the shore of Lake Huron, rented from Florence Sims, a woman who also attends the Methodist Church.

Ida is surprised to see me. It's a spur-of-the-moment trip, and I haven't telegraphed my visit. She invites me in, makes coffee, and offers me one of her ever-present homemade cookies. On the table is the Norwegian-English dictionary and the Bible, which she restacks neatly on the kitchen counter. After the usual pleasantries about how she is doing (good), the weather (wet), my wife Joy (working hard) and our children (Pete, talking up a storm; Andy, working on potty training), I come around to the real point of my visit.

"Grandma," I say. "I have been thinking about your life and how you grew up on a farm in the nineteenth century. You used to tell me about riding in a sleigh to school with your brother Charlie, and how the snow drifted over the fence posts. I have been trying to picture what that was like."

She nods. "It was cold. I could never get my fingers and toes warm."

"I have a question that I have wanted to ask you for months," I say. "It's really been on my mind."

"Oh—what's that?"

"Well, you grew up in the horse and buggy age. You lived through World War I, the 1918 Flu Pandemic, the invention of the automobile, the telephone, and the airplane, the Great Depression, World War II, the atom bomb, the Korean War, the Vietnam War, plus a thousand other changes. So, I have been wondering, what is the most amazing thing you witnessed over your life?"

She starts to speak, but I hold up my palms. "Before you respond, I have been thinking about this, and I'm sure I know what you're going to say."

She immediately pipes up. "Okay, what's your answer? I'll tell you if you're right."

This catches me off-guard. I am thinking she would have to ponder such a momentous question for at least a *little* while.

"Uh..., well, for someone who grew up riding in a horse-drawn sleigh to school, I can't imagine anything more amazing than watching a man on television walking on the moon."

She stares intently at me. "I have to admit, that was pretty remarkable." She points with her index finger. "...But when we got rural electricity, it was really something."

Rural electricity? I am dumbfounded. All the momentous events and changes she witnessed—wars, technology, deadly diseases, economic devastation—and the most remarkable thing she has experienced in her entire, long life is lights that turn on with a switch?

"Wow, Grandma," I confess. "I never would have guessed that in a thousand years."

•••

I relate this conversation to Maren.

"It may have had less to do with electric lights," she says. "And more about indoor plumbing. She told me how she despised using the privy, especially in the middle of the night. She would try to hold on as long as possible to avoid having to go. But finally, when she couldn't wait any longer, she would hang onto a rope strung from the back door to guide herself through the darkness to the outhouse. Imagine doing that in Minnesota in the dead of winter."

•••

Since then, I have thought about Grandma and our conversation hundreds of times. I still have trouble fathoming how that could be her answer. It causes me to ask the same question of myself. Someday, if I'm lucky enough to have grandchildren, perhaps they will think about my life and all the things I have witnessed and visit me to ask the same question.

Like my grandmother said to me, I will respond, "Well, what's your answer?"

And they will talk about beaming a woman to Mars, or cloning humans, or traveling back through time.

I will stare directly at them and say, "I have to admit, that was quite remarkable." Then, I will point with my index finger. "But when we got the Internet, it was really something."

Incredulous, they will exclaim, "The Internet? The *Internet? Everybody* has the Internet!"

Then I will smile at them, but laugh to myself, and think about my grandma, the Norwegious Ida G—and Rural Electricity.

J. L. Hagen, former nonprofit executive, is the author of *Sea Stacks*, a short story collection that references the fictional town of Loyale, Michigan. His story, "Chelesea's Rescue" in the anthology, *Again, Hazardous Imaginings*, was named one of the best science fiction stories in 2020. A graduate of the University of Michigan and the University of Chicago, he grew up in St. Ignace. His email address is: j.l.hagen@outlook.com.

Historical stereoview - Chapel Rock campout by BF Childs

Finders & Keepers

by Elizabeth Fust

It's a brick building with a clapboard sunporch on the back and technically sits downtown. It's somewhat between the library, the park, the water, and the residential areas, so it is hard to tell at a glance if it is a caretaker's shack or someone's home. It is, however, neither. It has been hard for the historical society to slap a date on the construction of the building but the earliest records of the town list it for what it still is, Keepers—and then to clarify on the glass window in gold it says 'Shoppe.' Sometime over the last hundred years, and again the exact time is disputed, a small hanging wooden board was hung over the entrance that said, "Antiques and Second-hand Goods."

Keepers is the surname of the family that has run the shoppe for forever, the current Keeper being Eulalea—or so I discovered later from the Chamber of Commerce. But those who know her call her Lea. Being around her makes one feel as if their eyes have lost focus or glasses have smudges or contacts gone dry. She's there, but just beyond clarity.

The first iteration of Keepers was a sort of pawnshop on the frontier of the wilderness north of town. At least that makes sense and is what the local history books claim, with the caveat that it might have just been that the family living there would barter for goods to get by; no one really knows. To this day, Keepers maintains an air of mystery about it. The reason being that the "how" and "why" of the place are never satisfactorily answered and that if one thinks to ask these questions, they hardly ever remember to do so.

My experience happened that one day I was taking a stroll through the park lazily seeing the town through fresh eyes. My business-lunch plans with potential investors had fallen through and rather than rush back off to work, I just strolled and appreciated the speed at which the town ran when I wasn't in a hurry. I had sat down on a bench to watch the water for a while when my glances drifted to the brick shoppe. In fact, I stared at it for quite some time before my mind caught up with my gaze. I had seen it and known it for all my life. But had never been inside. So of course, I strolled over and went in.

The house was deceptively big, and filled with so much that it felt small again. Outside was peak daylight, but the interior seemed stained with an afternoon's worth of golden sunlight that bent and curved around bookshelves and china cabinets, filling empty depression glass cups with liquid light.

A bell rang as I came in, and it echoed, mingling with my footsteps and creak of the floorboards. Little particles of dust danced in the sunbeams and led me deeper into the shoppe like faeries would a lost errant knight on some quest.

"Hello," Lea said.

I was not sure if I had turned the corner and found her there, or if she had walked up to me, for it seemed we had both just appeared together in an alcove where frames of faded paintings were stacked and hung and teetering.

I replied in kind.

"Are you looking for anything in particular today?" As she asked, her hand extended and gestured across the paths diverging through the interior of the labyrinth of goods. Some of the dust faeries from before settled in Lea's hair, which is when I noticed that, as she turned to survey her realm and as the sun and shadows bounced over her, I couldn't tell if her hair was silver with age or gold with youth and if those were wrinkles or a furrowed brow or smile on her face.

But I told her no, I was just looking.

"You never know what you may find. Please let me know if there is anything I can do."

The floorboards did not creak for her as she walked away.

I wandered. Carefully I picked up old photographs by their edges and read the barest trace of cursive names on the backs of them. With delicate hands, I opened leather volumes, and quickly and gently put them back when their spines creaked loudly. Out of curiosity, I picked up antique kitchen tools and home goods wondering what this and that ever could have been used for.

But of course, even as old as I was then, the toy section was the most fascinating. And it is a generous statement to call the alcoves and cubbies throughout the shoppe "sections" as everything was scattered about with duplicates of items appearing now and again haphazardly. But the toys, the children's books, these were all together.

For a time, I was invested in toys recalled from my own long-ago youth and toys which predated that time. I quickly read several of the short children's stories. And then I came across the trading cards.

I wondered. And I looked.

My older brother had been a great collector of sports cards, and I had collected only a few. Sports were not my forte, but secretly, I enjoyed the cards for the stories of the athletes on them. We had our initials on the cards to tell whose were whose. It was my grandfather, seeing my blossoming interest, who had given me a trading card of an underdog sports star who had gone on to play for the state with great success. This athlete's name was Knight, which thrilled me because of the comparison I drew. Like modern-day warriors, we told athletes' stories around the dinner table whereas our medieval counterparts would tell legends of knights. Grandfather could tell stories of all the players on the cards, but I liked these stories the best: the underdogs who saved the day. But the trading card had been lost. A bully had stolen my book bag one day and thrown it into the swamp off a deer path we took as a shortcut to school. I stuck to the main ways after that. The bag and its contents were never recovered.

Yet there was no trading card like that in the box I flipped through. I hadn't really expected it to be. My sports hero was a successful underdog, but he was not popular enough for his trading card to be saved by anyone and end up in a vintage collection.

When I turned, the sunlight caught on a perfect rectangular patch on the floor. I had dropped one of the trading cards and when I bent to pick it up, my breath caught and didn't release until I was standing upright again and well enough in the sunbeam to see it clearly.

I flipped the trading card over and squinted at the familiar scribble on the back. They were my initials; it was my handwriting.

"Where did you get this?" I said taking it to Lea at the counter, a bulky wood thing like at an old general store or bar, and probably with a step up behind it because Lea seemed taller than usual.

She tipped her head and her lips fell into a little curve. "I couldn't tell you all the ways things end up in this shop."

I told her the story and pointed out my initials. I laid it on the counter so she could get a better look.

"I'm so glad." She said and pushed it towards me again.

With hesitating hands, I reached for my wallet. Lea laughed. I didn't ask why she laughed but jumped a little at the unexpected noise—like wind chimes on a windless day, I thought.

"You can't pay me for what's yours." And with that graceful hand she waved me out of the store, led by a path of golden faerie dust.

When I arrived back at the office I put the trading card in my top desk drawer, then sat there and stared into the corner until an hour before closing, when I managed to cram an afternoon's worth of work into the hour. The card sat in that desk drawer for months. Every time there was a complication with running the paper, I took out the trading card, looked at it, breathed a bit deeper, and continued fighting for the life of the local journal. Straights became desperate and I needed a miracle. Miracles. Those were hard to come by. I opened the desk drawer, and there was my miracle.

I sold the trading card, and its worth was much more than I expected. Everybody does love an underdog after all, especially those childhood heroes that you can't forget even as adults. I turned around and invested the money into the little journal, which was just enough to bring it into a digital age with a small complement of staff to keep it running ad infinitum. The first story of the new edition, right below the headlines declaring the new edition, was about Keepers Shoppe and the trading card that saved the newspaper. While I had been researching and writing the cover story about Keepers, I came to find many others about town, and across the region, had similar experiences at Keepers Shoppe. Things once lost long ago, found again amidst the dust and gold light cluttering the space. Or things never lost but found in the nick of time for this or that to save the day—presents and tools and somethings borrowed and somethings blue—and trading cards. Lea never responded to my request for comment for that article.

This was all many years ago now, and I still often forget the story. But sometimes I find myself with a free lunch hour in the park and absentmindedly staring at the little brick shoppe with the clapboard sunporch on the back. And on this particular lunch hour, I decided to write the story down. Just in case the next time I forget the story I forget forever so that someone else will be able to remember. "Finders keepers" being what it may, sometimes when things are lost or missing, they are not lost and missing forever.

Elizabeth Fust graduated from NMU and refused to leave the U.P. Now she is the author of two children's books and a coloring book, gets to write about space for her day job, and has been a contributor to the *Marquette Monthly*, *Michigan History Magazine*, and several of the *UP Reader* anthologies. You can learn more about her writing on Facebook and Instagram @elizabethfustbooks

historical stereoview · Munising old town · circa 1892

The Stubborn Snowblower

by Deborah K. Frontiera

I sat on the floor all shiny and new that first fall. I wasn't the biggest or fanciest snowblower ready for sale, but neither was I the smallest. A lot of other power machines sat around, too: riding lawn mowers, green tractors with yellow trim, plows ready to attach to the front of pick-up trucks...

A snowblower attached to the front of one of those green and yellow tractors looked down at me. "Humph!" he said. "I can blow twice as much snow as you in half the time!"

I tried to keep a bit of dignity. "Yes, but you cost a whole lot more. Besides, not everybody wants something your size."

He ignored me the rest of our time in the store, and I wasn't unhappy to see him be loaded into the back of a truck. But I did try not to knock the blowers smaller than I was. A few days later, an older man came into the shop and looked at several blowers. The salesman talked with him quite a while as the man described what he thought he needed and had room to store. The salesman led him to me! They talked about my features, how far and high I could shoot snow—apparently as the banks get higher and higher over the winter, the person using me must change the angle of my chute. The man went to the counter and filled out all the papers, whipped out a plastic card and then the salesman and he loaded me into his truck.

Hills and trees went by, still displaying their gold, red and yellow leaves, so I guessed it would be a while before I would be put to use. He unloaded me and rolled me into a shed behind his house. I could see I'd have quite a job: a path from the shed to the back door, the place alongside the house where a car was parked, and, oh, yes, a path from the street to the front steps. He also spoke of a garage with its driveway which was a fair distance from the house. I looked forward to the first snow and all the work I'd be able to accomplish.

A few weeks later, still before snow, the older man tried to show a younger man how to use me. "Hey, is this guy going to use me, not you?" I asked politely, but they didn't seem to hear me. The older one went on explaining. Irritated that they were pushing me on soft, unfrozen ground, I refused to budge!

"That's weird," the older man said. "It rolled just fine on the showroom floor."

The younger man gave me a try. I sunk lower, made myself as heavy as possible. "Probably because the ground is soft here. Probably be fine when the ground is covered with snow."

"Yeah, probably."

The two shoved me back into the shed and closed the door. Weeks passed. Either the other tools in the shed didn't like me, or they had no sense of being. It was terribly lonely. There was one window, and by and by, I could see the first snowflakes drift down. I grew more hopeful, but no one came to use me. Maybe there wasn't enough snow that time to bother with me, but I was still hurt.

Days passed, more and more snow, but still no one came and opened the shed door. Not even the younger man! "What's going on?" I yelled. But no one answered. The wind howled many nights and constant snow blew by the window. I could hear the people next door plowing out their driveway and heaping up snow between my shed and their garage. But no one came for me. Months went by. My hurt and loneliness turned into anger.

"Just you wait. See what I don't do when you DO show up," I shouted at the silent walls. Discouraged, I began sleeping on and off, only waking when I heard the neighbor piling the snow higher. I began to notice that the light coming in the window lasted a bit longer each day. Two or three times, for a few days, snow melted and formed icicles along the roof edge. Once, even those melted. Would I EVER be used?

But more snow came, then a thaw, then snow again...

I could hear the very first returning spring birds singing when the shed door finally opened. There stood the older man, and behind him a HUGE snow drift between my shed and the back porch of the house. The man must have had a doozy of a time getting through it to get to me.

At long last, I was going to be used! But as he fired up my engine, I looked in terror at that pile of snow I was expected to blow through. "Are you kidding me? That drift is twice as tall as my rotors; it's almost as tall as you are!" The man didn't seem to hear me.

I was torn between tackling the job and my continued resentment over being left alone all winter. I tried, I truly did! I got about ten feet into that huge drift, hit one of those layers of ice—bogged down my rotors like you wouldn't believe—and then my anger took over. "No! I'm not doing this!" I screamed and promptly shut myself down!

The man fussed, yelled, tried to get me started again. Prodded, pleaded, cussed, and finally gave up and went back into the house—fighting his way through the drift again.

"Yeah, I showed you!" I said as he disappeared into the back porch.

He came back out a while later and tried me again. I refused to start up!

More cuss words from the man and then he shoved me back in the shed. Because of so much snow, the shed door wouldn't quite close, so I could see out the crack of the door. Later still, he and an older lady, bundled up and with shovels and an ice ax, dug into the drift going toward the side of the neighbor's neatly plowed driveway. They chopped and shoveled, and chopped and shoveled, stopped to rest, groaned, and continued. The man would chop through the ice layers and break them into pieces small enough for the woman to shovel over the top of the drift. They managed maybe a dozen feet before they gave it up for the day. I had no sympathy for them after being alone so long.

The next day they went at it again and managed to break through to the neighbor's driveway. The day after that, the man from the shop that sold me came and loaded me into the store's truck. The shop man said, "Of course it's still under warranty, but we don't actually do the work at the store. I'll hold it there for you until you can get it to this place—they do the warranty work." He handed the older man a small card.

Off I went, back to where I'd started. But not to the sales floor—to the back room to sit in humiliation among other broken-down machines. Nobody touched me for weeks and weeks. I watched as other employees worked on lawn mowers of all kinds—the snow was nearly gone, and these machines would now be needed by their owners. Nobody even looked at me! So, humiliating.

It was midsummer before my owner finally returned, loaded me up and took me on a long drive over hills, through woods, seemed like forever, to a place where I was supposed to be fixed. I sat and sat again, waiting for some new parts. The talk around me was that some parts of me not related to grinding up that ice layer had been faulty from the start. So, it wasn't all my fault, not really.

The other machines at this place were friendlier. They laughed with me when I told them about my temper tantrum over the size of the drift.

"I've always been used and appreciated," the oldest snowblower said, "because I strived to do my best no matter how tough the job. Every year, my owner brings me in for a good going-over to be sure I'm in shape for the coming winter."

"But were you ever ignored for practically the whole winter?" I asked.

"No, but I'm owned by a young man with a family who has to get out every day to work, no matter what."

"Don't take it so hard," another blower said. "My owner is older like yours. I get used early in the winter and then he and his wife go someplace warmer for a few months. Yes, it's tough to get rid of the accumulated snow of a few months, but I understand. My conversations with the fishing boat in my garage pass the time. Did you even try talking to the other tools in the shed? Or did you wait for them to talk first?"

Well, he had me there. "No, I didn't try."

"There you are, see? Maybe if you put forth more effort, you'll find yourself used more."

I hung my chute a bit lower and remained silent.

The leaves had turned when my parts finally came in and I was fixed. I ran contentedly on the repair shop floor, starting up every time. When my owner returned a few days later and took me home, I tried harder to enjoy the view from the truck bed. This time, he unloaded me into the garage instead of the shed.

Once it was quiet, I said to a new truck parked there, "Hi, I'm Snow Blower. How are you?"

He told me about himself and the many trips from north to south and back again he'd done with his people and their cat. So, the other blower was right—they did go away for part of the winter. The first snow came in the middle of October that fall—not a huge amount, but the man came out and gave me my first workout of the season. "Just to make sure you work right," I heard him say. I hummed along and blew that few inches of snow off the driveway in no time.

I got used once more before the truck was loaded up and an old brown car moved into the garage next to me. I watched the man put some pink stuff in his gas tank and disconnect his battery. He did the same to another older truck, closed the garage door and there we all were. We had a lot of great conversations that winter, and I learned all about many trips the old truck had taken with those people before the new truck came along.

"I don't resent the new truck," the old truck said. "Quite frankly, I'm tired and enjoy the winter rest—let the new guy drive thousands of miles! The old car had even more tales to tell since he'd been around for over thirty years! He even told how he'd gone from one family member to another over those years but was hardly ever used in the winter.

It was still the "dead of winter" when the man and his wife returned; I wasn't sure why but I was happy to see them. I started right up and worked hard to blow off about three feet of snow from the driveway. Then I blew out a path from the back of the garage all the way to the shed, the back porch, and a front drive where the old car would sit. (He was pretty happy to have some winter use, too.)

The snow came down and down and down and I blew it all out almost every day! There was one day when it was so cold my electronic starter wouldn't work. But the moment my man pulled the starter cord by hand, I roared right up and went to work! I plan to outlive my warranty by many years.

Deborah K. Frontiera grew up in Michigan's Upper Peninsula. From 1985 through 2008, she taught in public schools in Houston Texas. She has published fiction, nonfiction, poetry, and children's books. Frontiera serves on the UPPAA board. She finds it fun to bring objects like Snowblower to life and has an entire book, *Superior Tapestry: Weaving the Threads of Upper Michigan History*, in which she lets artifacts, rocks, trees and rivers tell their stories. Learn more at www.authorsden.com/deborahkfrontiera

Silent Witness

by Tricia Carr

Ben smiled at Mrs. Schultz, holding her eyes with his own, the old excitement unexpectedly stirring in him. He'd noticed many small valuables as he came through the old-fashioned first-floor rooms, and the isolation of the house and this woman's great age were rapidly jelling a plan in his mind.

"Pixie and Smokey like to watch," Mrs. Schultz said, nodding at the two elderly cats coming in from the family room. "Nosy, really! Well, I'll leave you to the furnace repair then. I have some letters to finish and a friend coming at two."

Ben watched her as she opened the door to the basement and flicked on the light. Give her a few minutes, then go back up, calling out that he needed something from the truck. He opened his toolbox, hefted the wrenches, slid the flat end of one into a work glove. A little tap—not too hard, he sure didn't want to do time for murder! Besides, she was a nice old bird. Reminded him of a teacher he'd once had. He just hoped he still had the old deft touch. If he did this right, she wouldn't even remember him; they said people hit on the head forgot everything that had happened for a while. He'd seen this call listed on the whiteboard at work just when he was leaving, and since it wasn't even on his list, no one need ever know he'd been here at all. He thought back quickly. The only thing he had touched had been the doorbell out front. Ben shook his head, feeling almost devout. You take on an extra repair job during your lunch hour to show your new boss that he was right to take a chance on an ex-con, and you get handed a piece of cake like this. It was enough to make you really believe that what goes around comes around.

He heard a chair scrape briefly above him in the kitchen and then after a moment, water gushing with a hollow sound into something metal. Probably making coffee; probably for him. He slipped the wrench with its cover into his jacket pocket. Hard enough but not too hard; that was the ticket. She wasn't a bad old bird.

He opened the door to the stairway and started up.

Eighteen minutes later he was ready to leave. He'd been cool, collected, bringing small valuables quickly into the front hall, wrapping them in hand towels from the linen closet and packing them into pillowcases.

He frowned as he looked at Mrs. Schultz. He had caught her as she slumped and eased her carefully to the couch, and then brought a pillow and afghan to guard against shock. The old bird was really out, he thought worriedly. Her breathing sounded a little funny. Well, her friend who was coming at two would have to see to her.

She had said something—letters. He looked keenly around the kitchen. A bulky old-fashioned typewriter sat on the sunny desk in the corner, the little screen across the front blank. On the kitchen table lay one of those fat romance novels face down, and an address book beside it. No papers, no envelopes. Clear.

He went out into the foyer and picked up the pillowcases. Behind him in the quiet kitchen, lost in the bright sunlight, a tiny red light blinked slowly.

Chief Rumney stood watching the EMTs and then put his hand on Janet Tasson's arm. "Let's go in here." She went with him into the living room. "Did your friend say anything when you talked to her earlier?"

Janet shook her head. "Nothing. Just that she'd see me at two. And she'd never let just anybody in." Her voice quivered and her hands clenched "Sorry." She cleared her throat. "It's just—finding her like that. Makes me so damned mad."

Rumney grunted. "Me too. Always." He nodded at the empty display shelves. "Do you have any idea what's missing?"

Janet sighed. "Most of her 'pretties'. Marion's, I mean. My neighbor, Marion Stokes, owns the house. She's away for a few weeks and her sister Lena—Mrs. Schultz—is staying here to take care of the cats. So, what was stolen were Marion's collectibles. She does have quite a few rare old Hummels; but I think it was mostly eggs."

Rumney blinked. "Eggs?"

Janet nodded. "Special eggs. You know. Unusual materials. Works of art, some of them."

"Special! You mean like those Faberge eggs?"

"Well, nothing that elaborate. But she does have some really nice pieces. Jewel cases, and tiny ring cases, made in the form of an egg. Quite a few Chinese eggs. Jade, alabaster; silver ones set with amethyst or mother-of-pearl. A matching pair of lovely old carved ivory eggs. That kind of thing. It's really special. Marion doesn't indulge herself, it's always 'if it still works why change it?' But this collection was begun for her years ago by her late husband, and it's her heart. She'll hate that Lena was hurt because of it."

Rumney made notes, thinking quickly. A clean job. Someone who not only knew the value of these small items, but who knew how to sell them. A careful personality; careful for himself and also careful about Lena Schultz. That was sufficiently unusual in itself to be interesting. Kind of—old fashioned.

As the word came to him something moved in the back of his mind and he paused, but the thought remained just out of reach. He put a mental check mark next to it and looked at the shelves thoughtfully.

"Is there anything else you can think of that might help us, Ms. Tasson?"

She shook her head, starting for the hall. "Oh, they're taking Lena. I want to ride with her. I'll be at the hospital, Chief, and then back here later to take care of the cats and close up the house. If you need me-" the front door closed on her voice.

Janet returned to the house a few hours later. Lena was fairly comfortable now and drifting in and out of wakefulness. All the bright sunlight of the day was gone, thunder grumbled, and water was falling in sheets from the sky. "The windows!" Janet moaned, and hurried squelching up the path. Before she reached the door, it opened, and she blinked through the rain at Chief Rumney. He raised an eyebrow and smiled. She stood suddenly still, and her heart lifted. "You got him!"

Rumney stepped aside to let her pass and stood her dripping umbrella on a rubber mat in the foyer for her.

"Well, almost. We know who it is. There's a local man who went to prison way back who specialized in this kind of knowledge and robbery. He's out now. He's been gone so long I didn't quite recognize the look of this thing right away. We haven't picked him up yet, but we know."

"But—how?"

"Actually, she told us. Your friend. The place was so clean of evidence we were stuck at first. But then we found she had told us." Janet looked at him blankly and he laughed. "Come and see." She kicked off her wet sandy shoes and followed him.

"We were still here when the storm came up. It got real dark and I'm dogged—all the sudden that funny typewriter in the kitchen is blinking this tiny red light. Blink, blink, blink. Wasn't a typewriter at all, it was an old word processor with one of those black out features where if you don't type for a few minutes the screen goes blank."

"Screensaver," Janet said faintly.

"Right. So, we touch a key and up on that little screen comes a letter—a sort of running letter to this Mrs. Stokes, keeping her up with everything that happens each day. And because it's an ongoing sort of thing she doesn't just have the date, she has the time at the start of each new entry."

The chief touched the spacebar and the small screen filled with words.

12:45 pm: Marion, you'll be happy to know that the man has come out about the furnace! I was just sitting down to write to you when the doorbell rang and there he was. I'll get him a cup of coffee in a minute. Do you know this man is using his own lunch hour to come out here! You might want to mention that to the company bigwigs. He's new there and seems so anxious to do well. Ben something his name is. He didn't say his last name but just 'Ben' should let them know who you mean....

I'm So Sorry Margaret

by Tricia Carr

Your cheerful little hat pin with a toboggan at the end
Should never have served in such a way.

Through the breast of a stuffed bird, yes;
Or riding hills of snowy tulle
On your favorite hat.

But—slid to the base of Matthew's brain?
I'm so sorry Margaret.

Tricia Carr, a long-time Gwinn area resident, grew up reading Agatha Christie and her first loves in writing are the traditional and cozy mysteries, especially short stories. Her husband and daughters, her three cats, and her Pomeranian, Sir TripsALot, (called so because he does) cheer her on.

Troubled Waters

by Larry Buege

"We have to leave," I said. "The river's rising." Standing in two feet of water, I was explaining the obvious. The woman stared at me as if she did not hear. Judging by a few gray roots in her otherwise brown hair, I assumed she was in her late thirties or early forties. Not all her hair was gray, just enough to justify trips to the hairdresser. She did not bother to introduce herself nor did I. My name was embroidered on my fatigue jacket if she really needed to know. This was day three with little sleep, and I no longer cared whom I was rescuing. She was one more warm body, one more piece of baggage to load into my johnboat and drag back to the armory for three squares and a cot. Someday—when I look back through the warped prism of time—I may remember my actions as passionate, perhaps even heroic. Today, I only want to sleep. The sky was dull and opaque, giving no indication of time, although my watch confirmed the lateness of the day. By the time the woman joined the host of other refugees, it would be too dark for further rescue efforts. Then I could sleep.

The current was mild in the two feet of water in which I now stood, but the drag on the johnboat strained against the rope I held. The boat was painted in a confusion of greens intended to render the boat invisible, but it looked silly against the brown river water. The only identifying mark was the battalion designator painted on the bow. I pushed the boat against the front porch where the woman stood ankle-deep in water.

She had her jeans rolled up to her knees, but they were still wet. Behind her, through the open door, I could see water covering a brown thick-piled carpet. It might have been a different color on a different day, at a different time. Now it was ruined. There was no way to remove the mud and silt that would remain after the river receded, providing the house was still standing. The current had eroded much of the foundation, and the house was on the verge of collapse. I assumed it would be gone by morning.

"Ma'am, do you need help getting into the boat?" I asked.

My question was met with silence. The woman stared into the distance as if discerning some speck on the horizon, but her eyes transmitted no images to her brain. I had seen it before—during the war. Educated people called it the *thousand-yard stare*. The rest of us called it shellshock, burn out...hitting the wall. The woman's brain was in sensory overload and blocking further input. It was the equivalent of an ostrich inserting its head into the sand in hopes the world would go away. If her brain were a computer, we would say it crashed and needed rebooting. Other than her upright posture, the only evidence of life was the slow undulating motion of her hands as she washed away imaginary stains. Her fingers were chaffed from long hours of physical labor. Large veins protruded from the backs of her hands. They were covered with skin thinned with middle age. Perhaps she was older than I had originally presumed, or maybe life's misfortunes had aged her prematurely. I really didn't care. I had a job to do. I needed sleep.

"Ma'am, we need to leave. The river's washing away your house. It's no longer safe." I said it louder than need be. It was almost a yell, but it got her attention. She looked at me as if she had seen me for the first time. "Your house can't last much longer. It's washing away. We need to leave."

"I have to stay with my quilt. I can't leave my quilt. My husband gave it to me." She spoke softly, almost a whisper. Her voice was void of inflection and emotion, and she refused to look at me as if she were talking to someone else.

I looked at her hand and found a simple wedding band. I don't know why I hadn't noticed it earlier. "Where's your husband?"

"He left to find work. He's coming back. I promised to care for the quilt until he returns. He gave me the quilt."

"You won't need the quilt. I'm taking you to the armory. They'll have cots and warm blankets and hot soup. You won't need the quilt."

"I can't leave my quilt." She looked at me as if I were the one insane.

The rain had stopped, but it was only temporary. I looked up at the sky, which remained uniformly gray and shapeless. I could see no clouds, but I knew they were there, somewhere above me. That could be three hundred feet or three thousand feet. There was no sense of depth, just grayness.

If I were physically capable, I would have carried her to the boat just to get on with it, but I couldn't steady the boat and carry a struggling adult even if it was a woman. She was breaking no laws. I had no right to force her into my boat.

"Ma'am, where's your quilt? If I get your quilt, will you leave with me?"

"I can't leave my quilt. My husband gave it to me. I promised I would care for the quilt."

"What does the quilt look like?"

"It's very pretty. It's pink and soft and cuddly. My husband gave it to me."

With the water eroding the foundation, I couldn't leave her. The woman and her house would be gone by morning. Neither could I waste time. There were others in need. The johnboat had no oars or motor and was meant to be towed. That was fine when the water was low, but there were already areas waist deep in water, and the force of the current was increasing. The river wouldn't crest for another two days. I needed to leave now.

"Wait here. I'll get your quilt."

"I can't leave my quilt."

I tied the johnboat to the porch railing, hoping it would hold. The woman, oblivious to my actions, returned to her thousand-yard stare, tuning reality out of her sphere of consciousness. I headed into the house. It stunk with the odor of damp mold. The electricity had been out for two days, and the house was dark even though the sun, somewhere beyond the storm clouds, had yet to set. I turned on my flashlight and began a search for anything pink and resembling cloth. It occurred to me that its existence was in doubt. I found nothing on the ground floor, but a foot of water now covered the floor. If the woman had left the quilt on the floor, I would never find it. Leading off from what had been a living room was a staircase. The railing was still intact. Even in the dim light, I could appreciate the fine craftsmanship of the cherry woodwork. At one time—perhaps last week—this had been an attractive home. I started up the steps and found them solid although warped from the listing of the house. If I didn't find the quilt during a cursory exam of the bedrooms, I would leave—with or without the woman.

The bedrooms were capacious and decorated with a feminine touch. Pictures of landscapes hung on the walls. Lacy curtains, now soggy and smelling of mold, draped the windows. In the first room—I assumed to be the master bedroom—I found a wedding picture taken not many years ago. A woman dressed in a white wedding gown stood in front of a late model car, smiling up at her new husband. I studied the picture for a moment before convincing myself that the bride in the picture was the same woman now standing in six inches of water on the front porch. Maybe she was not as old as I had thought, or perhaps she married late in life. She looked happy, ready to take on the world—how quickly our dreams shatter.

The second room was smaller but still large by most standards. A double bed made up and prepared for company was the cynosure of the room. The bedspread was hand embroidered in reds and yellows, but that was not what drew my attention. Lying wadded up on the bed was a pink quilt. It looked soft and cuddly, as the woman had described. This, too, appeared hand embroidered—not a typical store-bought gift a husband would buy. I had assumed the quilt, if found, would be neatly folded consistent with its obsessive-compulsive owner; but then, she was a study in inconsistencies. I scooped up the quilt and prepared to leave. It was heavy—too heavy for a quilt. I peeled away the layers of quilt until I stared into the inquisitive gray-blue eyes of a young infant—the gift from her husband.

🐚 🐚 🐚

Larry Buege's short stories have received regional and national (English) awards. He has authored nine novels including the ever-popular *Chogan* Native American Series. His most recent work, *Growing Up in Sparta*, tells of fifteen-cent movies with double features and newsreels, Halloweens without fear of needles and razorblades, as well as home deliveries and doctors who make house calls. Learn more at Gastropodpublishing.com or email him LSBuege@aol.com

Historical Neebish Island fishing - circa 1913

The Pasty Smuggling Ring

by Sharon Brunner

Tension was high at the remote area of the Mystery Spot, the location of a secret government operation. Evan and Jenny worked undercover at the Mystery Spot, Mackinac Bridge, and the Truck Stop Restaurant in St. Ignace, Michigan. Their families agreed to keep their FBI employment a secret and told their friends in St. Ignace they returned to St. Ignace because they missed their family. An illegal pasty smuggling ring, under investigation by the FBI, had all law enforcement personnel in the area on alert in search of any suspicious behavior. The FBI learned that pasties were being transported from Mackinac City and were being dispersed all over Upper Peninsula and into the hands of people of all ages, including children. Part of the illegal activity included the making and selling of illegal pasties, pasties that were not made in the Upper Peninsula. The businesses were claiming the pasties were made in the U.P.

Pasties were discovered and made for miners a long time ago to serve as a meal when they were working in the U.P. mines. They were meat pies surrounded by a crust and usually included potatoes and rutabagas. The goal of the secret government mission was to preserve the integrity and authenticity of U.P. businesses selling pasties.

The Mystery Spot served as the perfect spot for the secret government building which provided the FBI with a top-secret meeting facility. The building was located behind the world renown tourist attraction known for its optical illusions. It was hidden in the woods.

A large building built of bricks to withstand the wet weather. The building did not get a lot of sun, hidden amongst a heavy growth of trees. A two-track dirt road led to the secret hideout. The road looked like any of the roads used by people who enjoyed traveling by four wheelers all over the scenic U.P. The large building had offices, meeting rooms and a place for people to sleep when they came from out-of-town, or they worked on projects in the area. Jenny and Evan stayed at the building and drove older all terrain jeeps, so they did not stand out from the rest of residents.

Evan enjoyed his part time job at the Mystery Spot. He fit into the Upper Peninsula's Yooper persona. He had long dark hair that was tied back with a ponytail, had a beard and wore flannel plaid shirts, t-shirts and blue jeans. Evan was born and raised in St. Ignace and knew a lot of the locals. He went away to college to fulfill his desire to work in law enforcement. He sought employment with the FBI after fulfilling a role as the local sheriff in another U.P. town. He had an eye for picking out suspicious characters and solved many crimes in his previous position. He built a name for himself when he worked closely with the FBI on many cases. He considered his current job, his dream job. Solving the crime of the decade and saving the Upper Peninsula (U.P.) pasty business was of the utmost importance.

Jenny had a similar background. She was also born and raised in St. Ignace. Took a similar path of going away to college and working in Marquette as a City Police Officer. She ended up working with the FBI on many occasions to solve high profile cases. Jenny also fit the U.P. persona. She was tall and lean, had freckles and brown hair. She wore her hair long and it was tied back in a ponytail. She wore t-shirts, flannel shirts and jeans. She could hunt deer with the best of the hunters in the area. She also built a name for herself, so when she applied to join the FBI, they welcomed her with open arms. Her heart went out to the U.P. businesses that tried to sell locally made pasties. "People need to be told the truth," was one of her favorite sayings. She hated lies. It was discovered that people were entering local establishments in pairs from the Lower Peninsula to sell pasties saying they were from the U.P. Their pasties were tasty, so the authenticity of the goods was not questioned.

Jenny and Evan traveled to Marquette to locate the address listed on the billing statement provided to the businesses that sold the pasties in question. The address was the location of an automobile body repair shop. The owners of the shop never heard of the pasty business. Their phones were tapped, and they were under surveillance. These efforts proved they were telling the truth. Businesses ordered additional pasties by using a webpage or leaving a message at a phone number with the 906 area code. The business owners were told to leave a business name, address, and the number of pasties they wanted to purchase. The business owners thought they were busy, that's why they had to use that method to order additional pasties. The pasty company underpriced other pasty providers.

Jenny and Evan met at Bentleys, a favored local restaurant, to discuss their plans.

"I want the fish sandwich and a pop," said Evan to the waitress.

"I will have the same," said Jenny.

"We should be having a pasty, but I have been eating so many to compare that I am getting tired of them," said Jenny.

"I never get sick of pasties. So far, they are all tasting the same to some degree. I haven't tasted one that raised my radar, yet."

"I haven't either."

"When are we holding our stakeout at the Mackinac Bridge again?" asked Jenny.

"I think we need to be at the bridge tonight. It's Thursday night. Before the weekend. We may spot some suspicious activity," replied Evan.

"I will meet you at the regular spot?" asked Jenny.

"Yes, meet me at the bridge lookout."

The townsfolk thought Jenny and Evan were dating. They went to high school together and were in the same grade. He played the role of a jock who happened to be a closet book worm and she was openly a book worm. She hated jocks when she attended high school. He did not get any of her attention. They were seen together a lot lately and everyone thought there was a romance brewing. It was a small town and the longtime residents liked watching the relationship grow. Some of them were bold enough to ask if wedding bells were in their future. They really didn't know how they felt about each other. They were too busy working lots of hours at their part time jobs and doing surveillance which kept them tied up for hours each day. Jenny and Evan discovered they had a lot in common. They both liked hunting deer, hiking in the woods, and fishing. The perfect ingredients for a successful relationship.

"I have to get to work. Working as a maintenance worker for the Mackinac Bridge Authority provides me with an opportunity to see a lot of people as they cross the bridge. I have to clean windows today outside. Perfect opportunity for me to see people crossing the bridge. Keep your ear bud in just in case I have to reach you." Evan preferred working at the Mystery Spot, but the Mackinac Bridge job afforded better opportunities to spy on people coming from the Lower Peninsula. At the Mystery Spot, he got to fool people by rolling a ball up hill with ease, having people sit on chairs or stand on walls and lean out like they were floating and how they looked taller than one another when they stood on cement platforms. A wife would appear taller than her husband. It was a fun place to work. Only one of them was able to work at this location to be close to the government building and he drew the lucky straw.

"I will keep my earbud in. My work at the Truck Stop gives me plenty of opportunity to spy on people who travel from the Lower Peninsula," said Jenny. Jenny was settling into her job at the restaurant but felt some of the truckers could be crude and offensive. She considered the source and did not try to place too much importance on their advances. Both Jenny and Evan did what a lot of St. Ignace residences did to get by, work a variety of jobs to make ends meet. No one knew what they did before they returned to St. Ignace.

They both climbed into aged jeeps and headed to their jobs. Smiling and waving at each other as they departed their parking spaces. Betsy, one of the Bentley waitresses, watched them leave. She was a long-time St. Ignace resident. She smiled and told Sally about what she saw. They had a wager going about how long it would take for them to get married. Betsy thought it would be a year and Sally thought within six months. They kept checking out Jenny's stomach to see if there was a bun in the oven. Both Sally and Betsy had to get married.

The Truck Stop was especially busy today, the weekend before the famous car show the end of June. Jenny was watching and listening as she served the customers. One of the customers got her attention. He was talking about pasties and how he was traveling to a town further north to deliver some pasties. Jenny headed to the kitchen to tell Evan through their earbuds. At the same time, Evan spotted people traveling north with lots of coolers sitting on the back seat of the car. He took out his binoculars and took down the license plate number. They looked suspiciously guilty like they were looking for the police. Things were happening fast. He called in the license plate number to the main office.

Evan's phone rang soon after he sent in the license plate number. It was George from the main office.

"Hello. What did you find out George?" asked Evan.

"The number you called in belonged to a man named Ethan Edwards who was brought in for smuggling illegal souvenirs into the U.P. last year. He had alibis for the times he was suspected of delivering the goods so they could not pin the illegal activity on him. I wouldn't put it past him concerning the illegal pasties and fudge. People had made a lot of money selling pasties and fudge in the U.P. for many years. He probably wants to make a profit, too. We put out an alert and will have him located and followed. We had a tracking unit attached to the bottom of their vehicle last year when they were under suspicion. They should be easy to locate if he has the same vehicle," said George.

"I can't believe we finally have leads. Jenny overheard a conversation at the Truck Stop."

"She plans on watching them when they leave to take down their vehicle information."

"Do you think there might be more than one person involved in this smuggling?" asked Evan.

"It wouldn't surprise me. There's money to be made in the pasty and fudge business."

George gave Evan the web information to seek the location of the possible criminal. Evan entered the information into his phone and saw the car approach a wooded area in the U.P., possibly the location of a cabin.

"I am going to pick you up and we are headed to a place where the smugglers may be," said Evan to Jenny.

"I just phoned in the license number of the man I overheard talking about delivering pasties. I got an earful about how this man was associated with a possible illegal souvenir ring. He had an alibi for the times he may have been seen in the U.P. so they could not pin it on him."

"George gave me the same information about the man I saw crossing the bridge with coolers in his back seat. I think they may be working together. I think we are finally going to break this case and be able to turn our focus on other cases in the U.P.," said Evan.

"I sure hope so. We owe it to the people who lived in the U.P. all their lives to be represented by people who only make the pasties in the U.P. You know my motto."

"I know. People must be told the truth."

Evan picked up Jenny at the Truck Stop and they headed to where the tracking device led them to near the small town of Trout Lake. They called for backup while they headed toward a dirt road in the middle of nowhere, the middle of the woods. They gave their coordinates, so they could be located.

"I see a cabin with a light on over there," Jenny said. She pointed to the far left of where they were driving.

"I see it, too," replied Evan.

They parked the jeep in a small area near the side of the road and walked towards the cabin. They pulled their guns and walked as quietly as possible.

Evan stepped on a twig, and it sounded like it echoed throughout the woods. Jenny glared at him. He looked at her with an apologetic look. She motioned for him to walk behind her on the moss-covered ground. He followed her. They approached the cabin which appeared to be quiet and looked inside one of the back windows. They saw a light on in the front room and two men were sitting on a couch staring ahead. Evan and Jenny crept to the front of the cabin to look in. Both men were watching the television and laughing at what they saw. It appeared to be a movie about the *Three Stooges*. Jenny frowned. She thought shows about ridiculous antics were below her. The two men did not look familiar to her. They were not at the Truck Stop earlier. They knocked on the front door and decided to pretend they got lost and were looking for the main road.

"Hi, my name is John, and this is Sally. We were out exploring some of the dirt roads and we can't find our way back to the main road," said Evan. Jenny tried to look forlorn and nervous.

"Come in. We are just enjoying some TV before we turn in. We are hunters who come up here to hunt and explore the back woods," said one of the men.

"Can I use your bathroom? We've been on the road for a while," asked Jenny.

"Sure. It's over there," said the other man. He pointed down a hall.

Jenny walked down the hall to the bathroom and while Evan was distracting them; she explored the back rooms and discovered coolers of pasties in one of the rooms. She motioned to Evan that she made the discovery. They planned on waiting for back up before the men were questioned.

"How long have you been coming to this cabin?" asked Evan. Jenny looked at him surprised that she didn't think of asking them the same question.

"We've been coming here for years," lied one of the men.

"What do you hunt for?" asked Jenny. She wanted to find out if they knew where they were and what people hunted for in the U.P.

"We are hunting elk?" said one of the men.

They fell for the trap. Elk are not hunted in the U.P.

"Have you had any success?" asked Evan.

"Yes, we bagged two last year," lied the man.

Just as the man got those words out, vehicles pulled up outside the cabin. The men looked at each other with surprise. FBI and the sheriff's department stormed into the cabin.

"We have a warrant to search your cabin said one of the officers."

Jenny pointed to the back room and two of the men headed in the direction she pointed. They called out that they found the pasties.

"Give us your drivers' licenses," ordered Evan. They looked confused and angry at the same time.

"I work for the FBI, and we have been on the trail of the smuggling of illegal pasties for a couple of years. We know that some of the businesses have been tricked into believing they were purchasing pasties made in the U.P. but they were actually made in the Lower Peninsula. The people in the U.P. deserve the truth and should not be swindled into thinking they are buying locally made goods," said Gary, an FBI officer.

The ID they provided had an address of Marquette, Michigan, and the names on the ID's were Ethan Edwards and Ely Goodman. Their fingerprints were taken, and it was discovered that they had different names and came from a small town near Petoskey, Michigan. They broke and confessed that they have been selling pasties pretending they were made in the U.P. for a couple of years and they told the officers that they were a part of the phony U.P. souvenir racket. They folded and sat on the couch heavily like the world was lifted off their shoulders.

"We really like the U.P. and we are sorry we tried to trick the people here. What's going to happen to us?"

"Passing off goods by false advertisement is a federal offense. You will at the very least be facing some heavy fines," responded Gary.

The night ended with hauling both men off to spend time in the St. Ignace jail pending their day in court. The pasties were confiscated as evidence. They also found some of the illegal souvenirs in same room where the pasties were stored.

"I think things ended just the way they needed to end. We saved the reputation of the people of the U.P. and captured the culprits who were passing off goods that were not made in the U.P. Their business with the phony Marquette address has been closed down for good. We do good work, my friend," said Evan as he tapped Jenny's hand. They were sitting at their favorite restaurant eating an authentically made pastie.

"This was a case against the trolls who live below the bridge and the Yoopers in the U.P.

and we won," exclaimed Jenny. Evan smiled back at her.

"Why don't you try ketchup on your pastie next time?" asked Evan.

"No, thanks. I like salt and pepper."

Disclaimer: Actual names of places and towns have been used. The characters and actions in this book are fiction. There is no secret government facility located behind the Mystery Spot in St. Ignace, Michigan. Or is there? The author worked at the Mystery Spot when she was a teenager and enjoyed the experience. She remembers saying, "You have heard of Isaac Newton's theory, what goes up must come down. Not at the Mystery Spot," as she rolled a ball what appeared to be up hill. The author was also aware of places of business that claimed they made the pasties they were selling. She felt that was false advertisement.

Sharon Brunner has self-published seven books. One is called *Lake Superior in the Moonlight* and is about Yoopers. You can learn more about her from her web page: SharonBrunner.com. which she will be updating soon regarding her books. Visit her blog at sharonbrunnerwrites.blogspot.com.

Historical Sault Ste Marie · Hotel Iroquois

Kid

by Don Bodey

Must be the smell of onions cooking that is responsible for me being in this shiny diner at two in the afternoon. The whole place smelled like sautéed onions. Three small tables under the window, and a counter eight feet long. A one-man joint on a level with the road, with red rock cliffs 100 feet behind it. He'd been laying low for four months, working as a laborer on construction sites for the last two months, mostly shagging concrete forms, hitching up payloads for cranes, digging mud out of bulldozer treads.

Hard to make a living selling cigarettes. Maybe if you were legal, or almost, like the shops he sometimes sold, after he had bought them from the shop in the first place. But he was taking the risk and that suited him, until he got this job. Kick-in-the-nuts hard work for the minimum. He didn't need the money; he needed the job. He was thinking about going back into the military, because he hadn't been able to feel comfortable since he became a civilian.

When he was working, he didn't think about it. He worked. But when the workday was over, it was a different world.

.... bedtime .... BEDTIME THE NEXT NIGHT.

I can't find the guts.

•••

I think the smell of onions got me sitting in this dinky diner in the middle of the afternoon. Right after I got fired. Walking south toward a railroad I thought about laying down on, above the smell of the street there was a layer of onions being sautéed. A six-stooled-at-the-counter joint without lights that I've been going to for twenty years. Jake the Jaw owns it, bought the little house trailer diner about a hundred years ago and paid it off selling hamburgers for forty years. He had a garden behind the hamburger joint that was four times the size of his diner, with hundreds of onions "from the old country" that he ground into his hamburger meat.

Jaw was behind the counter today. That is, every part of him except his chin and half the lower jaw that jutted from the bottom of his face like the hull of a racing boat. The counter was full except for the bent-up one on the end. Sitting in it is like riding a tired bronco, but I'm hungry.

"Two or three, kid," he says.

"Three."

The hamburgers are about the size of the end of a beer can and come in a piece of wax paper. Most times the paper was a peach color. Today it was pumpkin color and crumply. The orders on the counter in front of the stools looked like three kids' baseball mitts.

"Off early or playin' hookey?"

"Off period. I got fired."

"Good for you."

He worked the takeout crowd for a few minutes. Takeout came in grease-proof sacks that held a dozen burgers. Twenty years ago, a bag was two bucks. I used to come here midnights on my way out of town to drive a paper route spreading bundles in smaller towns, for a two-dollar bag to last me through the night. In the winter, the heater fan circulated the onion smell that started out sweet and was funky after 80 miles. A few months later I was picking up half a dozen of the bags, delivering them to the small-town night cops and making 6 bucks' profit.

Then I didn't see Jake for years. So, it surprises me that he doesn't look as old as he is. Maybe 70-75. He went back to the kitchen and his daughter took the counter over. The row of stools next to me was like a painting. Old guy next to me was picking the bottom of his nose with a yellow fingernail, nursing a cup of coffee and doing the paper's crossword with a pencil shorter than a cigarette; young guy next to him skipping school and high from huffing, his pimply face like a balloon on a stick staring at the ceiling; then a bag lady with teeth she must have gotten from a morgue.

Sly, on the stool next to take-out with his grease board on the counter in front of him. He never talked, never even made sounds in his throat. He gestured and wrote on that board and talked with his face if you were looking at him. Right now, he was either swatting insects or talking to himself.

The kitchen door and the back door are both open and I can see a slice of the onion garden. Across the alley used to be warehouses. Jake's out there in his apron walking with his hands behind his back and a cigar even longer than his chin whose smoke bursts in small puffs against the skyline of the buildings that will soon cut off the light into his onion garden.

I stick two fingers up when the girl looks down the counter. There are three burgers in the corner of the grill that she throws in the garbage, then puts a double handful of onions on the grill and trowels that heap like a mason mixing mud: halves it, quarters it, chops it, flips it, moves it across the grill.

"Let's go!" she says.

It's the time of day to get rid of these people, loafers, and they know it. Within a couple minutes the stools emptied. Sly slid out, went left; the lady with morgue teeth went to her cart alongside the front door, and turned right, and after the cook pointed her spatula at the balloon headed kid, he left. I'd guess he was thinking how far to his next huff. I was still waiting for my order, slid off the crooked stool just when the in-crowd started coming, and these were people who might know I got fired.

I have to pee. Thirty years ago, there was an empty lot next door. On Saturday mornings, after us kids had paid our paper bill, the Jaw's place was always on the way home, and we ate two onion burgers for half a buck. When us paperboys were done, two burgers were 85 cents and the clientele shifted to across-the-alley guys in sweat suits. Those days you went through the back door and "tinkled" between the diner and the onion garden. Nowadays there was a bathroom around the corner; technically it qualified for a six-stool joint, could have been close to the required square footage, but the only two dinky tables were up against the bathroom door. The door itself had a permanent sign saying the bathroom is being cleaned.

•••

Jake the Jaw:
From out here, in the garden, the encroaching buildings, the change of garden shade, the hum of the city that never ceased bouncing around the alleys sometimes makes me feel alive and sometimes I feel like these onions have already killed me. With the back door of the diner open, I'm in touch if anything blows up. I can see into the grill and through the serving window: I can watch people walk down the other side of the street. I have a knack for spotting troublemakers, which is a lot of the reason I've held onto this half acre that grows onions in the middle of downtown. Used to have a pay phone on the back outside wall, which made me a little money, but then the kids started hanging around it four at a time.

Eventually somebody ripped the whole thing off the wall. Bought another one from the phone company for about a hundred eighty bucks, and when I figured I made that back, I ripped it off the wall myself and collected insurance, sold it to some guy to make it into a lamp.

The guy who came in an hour ago is still there. I remember him. No kind of trouble-maker. Came in here with his dad when he was a kid, then didn't come in for a long time, until he started driving a truck at night, and going to college. A year or so ago he came in because his car broke down, so he was walking home. Wore a coat and tie, worked in one of these buildings. He's got a goof jaw. Not like me, maybe a step down, but when you look at him, you look at the bottom of his face because it juts into the space between us.

Eight rows of onions and this time of year it looks like a small grid of volcanic eruptions, so many healthy plants like stunted palm trees, each in its own mound. Simple plant that I cared for, and it has been good to me. Nobody else could grow these without going to a lot of trouble, so meanwhile I grow them, have harvested, sliced, chopped, diced, then sold them on a bun and a mix of burger, sold, preserved, and protected their seeds. And time after time I've told people I don't know where they came from, but if I believe my mother, I do.

I need to get out my pitching wedge.

•••

Kid:
I don't remember having to piss this bad for a long time. Being downtown and full bladder up is the worst kind of fear. *Could I leak it down a pants leg?* I keep my knees knocking under the counter. She fucks my order up somehow. Maybe burned the on-ions while she was on her neon green phone. She scrapes one pile off the grill and plops another pile on. Even the smell of burned onions can't quit me thinking of pissing my pants. Yesterday I'd walk across the street to that building's lobby rest room. Now I'm fired and I figure everybody I see between here and there will see a tag hanging off my jaw like in the cartoons.

I feel like I'm being cool, but I almost got my dick out by the time I pass the grill and get outside. Turn left and piss against the back of the building, on the small foundation, which is half big rocks and half concrete, so

there is no sound. Ten feet away is the same gate that was there when I pissed here after my morning paper route. There is a lot more noise than there used to be. Traffic and con-struction noise. *Thump-thump-thumps* and twangs of car music bounce off the build-ings. Somebody is yelling across the street to somebody who is yelling back. From my right and not too far away, there's a cough. So, I fold myself into my zipper.

"Ya get fired, ya got the right to piss on my house?"

Jake is twenty feet away in the onion patch with something in his hand. The sun has just gone behind a building behind him. His face isn't plain, but he doesn't look mad. The jaw looks at rest.

"Jake. I'm sorry. I had to go—"

"—so bad your back teeth are floating? I know all about it." He looks away a little when he's talking but when he's done talk-ing, he looks directly, exactly, into my eyes. It's a warm look, doesn't make me uncom-fortable.

"I was thinking about stuffing half of one of those napkin dispensers down my pants."

Just then his daughter shows up at the back door with a grease bag so I give her five bucks and wave off the change, about what she should expect from a guy pissing outside her kitchen door. Jake comes up and it's a golf club in his hand, probably a wedge.

"I haven't seen you for a long time. Don't remember your name."

Jack has got whiffle golf balls stuffed into the big pocket on his apron, bright colors. His hands are pretty big, and his knuckles are all gnarled-looking. His arms are long and just now they're helping his hands rum-mage through that apron pocket. He brings out half a cigarette stubbed in a bullet cas-ing.

Jake is easy to like, for some reason. He's solid built, stands up straight and still looks relaxed. That jab-jaw of his has teeth in it, and mine has a horseshoe of plastic I have to glue to my gums every morning.

"Well, Jack, now what for you? I never been fired. Never had a job to get fired from. What now?"

Jack had a clean apron hanging on the wall that he changed into while he talked. His eyes go to mine. "I'll have to find a job. And I've got some other things to take care of."

"I got a job for you, minimum wage, cash. Nothing to 'move up' to." He moves his red eyebrows into parentheses when he says 'move up.' Like Groucho Marx with an extra chin.

"When?"

"Four-thirty."

"Tomorrow?"

"Morning. Or you can start now and go find the kid who should've been here to cut onions and bring him back. Help me whelp his ass."

He probably didn't notice, but he moved towards me, so we are both under the little roof where aprons and garden tools hang. We can about have a duel of chins. His gaze is intense, but there is a sort of twinkle in his eyes, until his gaze goes to my jaw. And I look at his.

"What'd you get fired for?"

The girl came to the door and Jake seemed to signal her with his chin, then he pointed it at me. "I'm takin' over, Jack."

"OK, I'll tell you about getting fired tomorrow, 4:30. Can I still get out that gate on the other end of the garden?"

•••

When the alarm goes off, I can accept the fact it is four in the morning. Hell of a lot harder to accept the fact that I have to be at work chopping onions in half an hour. And a little bit harder than that to accept the fact I got fired. Getting rightfully fired is one thing, but ...

I've not walked these seven or eight blocks for a while because I drove to work. The sidewalk is fairly new all the way downtown. It's strange to be walking the street at this time. A little wind comes into my face, and everything is so quiet I hear my own steps. The only smell I pick up is from the city street cleaner trucks. By now they are two blocks over, but the clean smell of their passing here ten minutes ago is part of the night. Their

blinking blue lights slice the air between the buildings and their particular high-pitched motor sounds seem like they belong to a city before it wakes up.

The inside of the diner is lit up on its bottom. Running lights. There's a cop car at the next stoplight and some light from the construction site when I first start knocking on the door. Jake finally comes, looks like I woke him up, but he has an apron on.

"I said four-thirty, right?"

"Yeah."

"I meant it. You're fired for being early. Sweep up the joint. Coffee is almost ready."

He looks big in the confines of the diner. I keep expecting him to have to duck his head as he ranges from handing me a broom to the kitchen. There is a radio in the kitchen. I sweep the floor: straw rappers and chunks of grease bags, a nickel and two pennies and the top half of a syringe. While I am sweeping up the lunchroom, I notice light coming on in the buildings across the street. Janitors going from one floor to another ... I notice later that the buildings look like it never happened, like they were never groomed.

When I worked there, there was nothing hollow about the building, but from here the array of buildings looks weird-fragile, temporary, which is about how I feel. Jake was way ahead of me. When I finished sweeping, he had a mop bucket sitting on the floor at the end of the counter. Old floor, small tile that was elegant fifty years ago had now been broken over and over again but was still a good floor. Under where the counter people sit is a curve of linoleum, so all the junk is easy to get rid of.

The diner is about 50 years old. The outside kept its shape, like an old-time Airstream. Inside has been through some changes, like the bathroom that is inadequate, yet isn't serious enough to condemn the operation. On one side is a construction site fenced off and idle. The street front is the intersection of two busy streets, the lesser of the two dead ends at Jake's front window. Now, about 6:30, the streets are beginning to look like the arteries they are. There are two taxis idling where the streets meet. A city bus sits half a block away with its interior lights on. Three women are smoking cigarettes under the plastic bus stop roof. The bus driver yacks with the women a few minutes, then they all stub their smokes and get on the bus, and it rounds the corner in a wave of diesel smoke. I wonder what time the driver's watch says.

Jake has been prepping since I got here. The idling grill is half little meat patties, and half a mountain of onions divided into maybe eight parts. The aroma is sweet. The joint is clean. He says something I don't quite hear on his way to unlock the street door. I'm wringing out the mop and wonder if he even remembers I'm here. Out of a slit between the door frame and the dusty cold air return vent, he pulls out a plastic sign and shows it to me.

Help Wanted, it says. He hangs it from a big clothespin made out of plastic so that it is in the middle of the window. No help coming this morning.

"My queen-you know her? —got a case of the Breeze. So, I want you to put on an apron and work back there—he jerks his chin towards the kitchen—until noon or so when Chubs comes in. An extra couple bucks. Tomorrow we'll get it straight, eh?"

•••

Jake:
He's a shy guy, doesn't flaunt his shit. Only need to tell him something once. Nothing pussy about his hands. Too late for Queenie to show up so it's going to be the Jake and Jack shift if he lasts to noon.

"There'll be a swarm of customers in about half an hour. There's aprons next to the kitchen door. I'll give you a rundown on how to put a burger together. Thanks for scrubbing us up here."

The daughter came about noon. Way before I knew she was his daughter, she sometimes struck me as confused. She hardly ever said anything but did everything that side of the counter had to do. The first cup was a dime. Small ceramic cup on a small ceramic saucer. Next cup was two-bits, in a plastic cup without a saucer. Sometimes she gave a grease bag of leftovers to someone in the doorway to stay out of the wind until the bus came.

The next day is different. Jake's jaw tells it all when I show up. His eyes rivet mine when we talk, but he spends two hours in the shed cutting, dicing, mashing onions he gathered in a small straw basket, and the big pockets in his apron. He gets phone calls and keeps a homemade cell-phone-turned-old-fashioned receiver wedged between his shoulder and his ear. Queenie is here at 6:30.

It seems ceremonial when he sees her, kisses her cheek, then takes the help sign out of the window. She has her own pile of onions on the grill, and she mops the tiny kitchen floor with a wring-out sponge on a stick. I keep busy scraping grunge from around where the chrome stools meet the floor then leave for two hours to close my bank accounts, and do a paltry load of laundry, and when I get back, I see I wasn't missed. Jake is in the back part of the onion patch, chipping those Day-Glo whiffle balls into his onion plants, little old-lady hats that poked out of the soil a month before and were limp baskets a few days before but are now sturdy plants whose purple/green leaves vary from one row to the next because of his planting schedule.

He only chips at the big plants. I see him land two, a yellow and a pink the same plant. He gives himself a thumbs-up, and picks up a dozen balls that lie scattered like an Easter egg hunt. Behind him is the city all around. Twenty-story buildings that haven't been here half as long as he has begin to cast their shadows into the onion patch.

"Did I pay you yesterday? Didn't, did I? Here's yesterday and today. Here's tomorrow too. I'm behind out here. When you get here, take a hoe to them far rows. Take you a couple hours. Here's a key to that gate, there." He gave me a wad of bills and stood there." I guess he thought I'd count it, but it didn't matter to me.

The next night he paid me for three days in advance. I did everything he did. We dug the onions individually, and a three-incher was a nice surprise. Mostly we got 2-inchers. Brilliant white knobs like small Russian churches. Something about them felt tender. We cut, washed, sliced, chopped, and saved the juices before they went to the kitchen. The smell changed often during the process, from raw vegetable and dirt to a sweet aroma inside the kitchen and diner.

That smell is what got me in here the day I got fired, and now that I make the smell, I feel like a boss instead of a *fire-ee*. Jake trusts me. I act like he would when he has to leave. I'm never in charge of the counter when it gets busy, because I couldn't handle it, not because he doesn't trust me.

•••

So next thing I know it has been two weeks. I have put some of my things inside boxes, stacked the boxes around my apartment, figuring it will be easier to move, which I see as my next step, and working jaw to jaw with Jake. He pays every night. I never figured out how he determined the amount. Most nights it was heavy, couple nights it was light. About half my time is scrubbing the diner. The other half is in the onion patch. The skyscrapers are three blocks from the patch, which ends at an alley full of construction equipment, yet all day long there are kids on bikes in the alley, sitting, watching the equipment going to work, a block away. Usually big shovels on tracks, or medium-size bulldozers, but there are 100-foot cranes that get pieced together too. The onion patch is like a scab on the arm of renovation. Briefcase types come in and Queenie writes their information on the last page of her order book every day and gives it to Jake before she leaves in a taxi. Jake hops around in taxis too, usually the same driver. Sometimes he gets in a cab with his apron on and is back in twenty minutes.

He trusts me. Every day I see him talking to people and I think I can tell who he trusts and who he doesn't, like I can feel the movement in my jaw to echo the movement of his. When you've got your arms in dishwater, it's easy to stare. A time or two I get to stare at tits. The clientele is a total mixed bag: secretaries and thin-tie guys and janitors and cabbies and newspaper boys, two bag ladies every day.

The carry out business pays the bills. We go through a big box of the bags every day. This morning Jake followed a guy outside and when the guy threw the bag down on the other side of the street, Jake screamed at him, called him ass-wipe, then fielded the bag after it blew across the street. Then he gave the guy the finger.

He has a little shed at the end of the patch. Mostly tools, but he will sit on a stool out there and whittle onions, or talk on his phone, or tweedle his golf club. A lot of times he chips his Day-Glo whiffle balls into the onions, always the same plant. Queenie takes her smoke break out the back door where my onion operation is and we watch him together: knee-length apron, rolled up sleeves, nine Day-Glo whiffle balls on the ground in front of him.

"Crazy old bastard," she says.

Queenie is a woman who was never pretty and never sexy, but part of every crowd she was ever in. Curly red hair and a face from a gravestone, she was here every day, ran her shift, passed messages to Jake, and seemed like a good friend of every person in the diner. The guy she meets on the corner after her shift reminds me of a porcupine or groundhog, a step above a rat. They meet cattie-cornered from the corner in front of the diner. Sometimes he leans on a miniature grocery cart until she gets there; they turn left at the first alley.

Crazy? Crazy how?

Don Bodey was a draftee mortarman in Vietnam. The idea for *F.N.G.*, his award-winning novel about the war, took root when he was washing dishes in a restaurant in Florida. Then he earned an MFA in the writing program at the University of Oregon, taught university classes and bought a bar in Chicago. Afterwards, he worked as a carpenter until his retirement. Learn more about him at www.DonBodey.com

Snow Child

by T. Marie Bertineau

◆❖◆

We had a big snowstorm the other day, one that held healing in its wake.

It all started slow. A flake here. A flake there. *This won't be bad*, my husband assured me—wishful thinking. We live in Michigan's Upper Peninsula, and a midwinter storm was forecast. One could smell it in the air, the Jack Frost breath. *This WILL be bad*, the weatherman warned, but who was he to burst my husband's bubble? A key component of any U.P. winter survival kit is optimism, and that's clearly what was at play here. You see, U.P. snowfalls are still somewhat of a novelty to us. We recently relocated and it was my husband's first winter in the area—*my* first winter here since I was a child. I had moved away with my family eons ago, and though my parents and siblings all gradually migrated back to our home state, for the most part, I stayed away. This winter wonderland, though beautiful, had always reminded me of a less happy time, *a childhood lost*—but that's another story. Now, the past behind me, aging parents and an empty nest had brought me back home. I was working to reestablish roots in this snow globe, and Mother Nature was about to shake things up.

We watched out our kitchen window as it happened, as the silvery sky appeared to collapse, the clouds weary of hoarding the moisture. Big, luscious, snowball-like clumps plummeted. They fell for hours and hours. They buried the yard, the rooftops, the drive, the patio. They buried the Christmas gar-land still draped from our picket fence and the miniature tree on the uncovered porch. They buried the frozen jack-o-lantern which sat atop compost behind the garage. They buried the tiny path which leads from the street to the front stoop—a path solely used by the FedEx man on occasion. Flakes paved the road between our house and the market, muted the whoosh of traffic, erased the sound of snow tires on concrete.

It was heaven.

When the storm was spent and the plow had passed, we dressed in coveralls and snow bibs. We pulled on insulated boots, swaddled our necks in fleece, propped chooks on our heads, and sheathed hands in mittens (gloves rarely keep hands toasty). "Well, ya ready?" my husband asked as we stood at the side door. It was as though we were about to make our first moonwalk.

For two hours we blew and scooped snow back and forth across the drive and patio. We shoveled and swept the stairs. We shook the garland and the mini tree to set it free of the weight. Panting, damp with perspiration, we cleared away all that had accumulated. All looked civilized again, all except the tiny path between the street and the front stoop. That poor path had been obliterated by the township's evil grader, an enormous mustard-hued monster with the bite of a T. Rex and the rumble of a herd of bison on the run. It was as though it had dumped a town-load of ice and snow right there in that one spot. Recovery would not be easy, but I had to start somewhere. And so I scrambled on all fours to the peak—a dogged queen of the hill—and flung what fresh snow I could from the summit. It didn't take long for me to reach the 'berg—the solid, crystallized rock of snowpack and street-scrape refreeze which made up the core of the mountain. There was no shoveling this mass. It would have to be broken apart and rolled away, like an unwitting snowman caught up in a crude relocation package.

I began chipping and chopping, hoisting, and tossing. I discovered the coal shovel was my best defense at breaking it into smaller, more manageable chunks. I was doing this on my own because my husband thinks it's a losing battle, this keeping a path clear to a door we rarely used. "There's no sense doing it," he said. "The plow's just gonna pack it all back in." This was true—we live on a corner lot and our house sits too close to the street. But I was adamant. The front door must be kept open. "Just one more time," I said. "You don't have to help." I didn't really mean that, but he took me at my word.

An hour or so passed and I grew weak. I had not toiled this hard in years—maybe since I was a kid. My hat was gone, tossed upon the cleared stoop, my jacket unzipped, my nose dripping like a Mr. Coffee. I was most definitely wearing out but would not give up. I was about to hit pay dirt. I felt it in my bones. In my joints. In the pain and fatigue of my wrists.

Then, at the edge of my blade I saw it: the first glimpse of sidewalk. Relieved, I tossed my tool and dropped to my knees, a weary woman at pause. The walls of the snowy passage towered over me, surrounded me, their height diminished me. There was a magic to the space, a near reverence. I *knew* this—I'd been here before. This familiarity tapped a tender vein. Thoughts of path clearing vanished as I caught my second wind. A new goal surfaced, an alternate mission. It commenced in a frenzy, a regression of sorts. Hidden by the snowbank, no one could see me, my crazy antics, my hyperfocus. Fueled by obsession, I scooped up armfuls of frozen debris and slung it in whatever direction was daylight. I patted and panked, clawed at white, my mittens glistening with beads of ice, my breath rapid and cloudlike, bent on creation.

At last, when only crumbs remained beneath me, I gazed in awe at my surroundings—at what had become the best damn snow fort EVER. I propped my back against an icy wall and tilted my face skyward. Light fell upon my cold, damp cheeks—cheeks of memory. A warmth spread through my tummy and chest, a glow, a wonder. I felt the blanket of youth, like I was five or six or maybe even seven. A smile spread from my soul to my lips.

Maybe childhood wasn't lost after all.

T. Marie Bertineau's work can be found in print and online, including her quarterly column, "Hankies in My Pocket: Tender Thoughts from the Keweenaw" (carrotranch.com). Her debut memoir *The Mason House* (Lanternfish Press 2020) received a 2021 Michigan Notable Book award and the 2021-2022 Stuart D. and Vernice M. Gross Award for Literature (Saginaw Valley State University). Learn more at tmariebertineau. com; Facebook @tmbertineau; or Instagram @t.mariebertineau.

Historical stereoview - Jackson Mine

Nimishoome: Chronicle of A Life Untold – Questions for Curt, the Uncle I Never Knew

by Phil Bellfy

Nimishoome, Uncle, did you know you were named after Charles Curtis the famous Kaw Indian who was a member of Congress when you were born on or near the rez in 1921, who later became VP under Hoover?

When I talk about your death, do I say
 that you died?
Or should I say that you were killed
on December 30, in 1943?

I prefer to say that you were killed
To say that you died sounds like
You simply 'passed on'
And says nothing of the means of
Your death.

Did you know that the pilot of your plane
 would
Put it down in the English Channel?
With only one engine, did you think that
 this
Your fifth mission
Would be your last?

When you flew over Germany to drop your
 bombs
On that chemical factory,
and the fighters attacked you, did they do
 much damage?
Is it true that the last fighter
To attack you
Could have brought you down, but
Instead, turned back to Germany

And let you all live?

Did you hear of this kind of 'mercy' before
In those two months you flew
Before you were killed?
I heard of that kind of story once.
The US-ian pilot saw the German fighter
Not only the plane, but the pilot, too
And would never forget the name on the
 side of the plane
Or his face
He shot a few holes in the B-17
But then flew up to the US pilot and
 waved him a goodbye
(or whatever it is in German)
After the war, the US pilot
Was it for the 50th or 60th anniversary of
 the war's end?
Sought out that German pilot, whom he
 never forgot,
And he was still alive
Too
And they met, tearfully
In France, or wherever they held those
 ceremonies.

If it is true that some German pilot in a
 sense let you all live, did you memorize
 his plane's number, did you see his face,
 did he 'wave' to you,
Sitting there in the bombardier's seat
Only hours after you dropped bombs on
 one of his cities?

And how did you feel about those bombs?

Is it true that you wrote your regrets to
    Grandma
Regretting dropping those bombs on
    places where her/your/our
Relatives may be living
Or dying?
Possibly at your hands.

Did you feel odd, as a White Earth warrior
Fighting a war against the Nazis
Who, since Karl May, who wrote all those
    "Indian" stories,
Were enamored of American Indians
Who modeled their own (imagined)
    oppression
On the oppression of Indians by the same
    US government
Who was dropping bombs on them
And, in your case, by your brown Indian
    hands?

Did you admit to your brown-ness
Your indigeneity
Your White Earth ancestry?
Or did Grandpa
Insist that you were French
(never Metis
never Anishinaabe)?

Or did they call you
Chief?
Did they ask about your brown smiling
    face?
Did they even notice?
Or did you declare it so proudly
That they could never even consider a
    taunt
Is that why they called you Lieutenant
Whenever you were not in the plane
But always Curt
When you were on that plane
With them?
Did they appreciate your practice
Of always shaking the hands of each and
    every one of them
As they deplaned?

Or at least for those four missions that
    you flew
Before December 30 of 1943?

Is it true that before each mission
That you went to the briefing room
To play cards with your friends
And did you play cards to pass the time
Or to test your luck before each mission?

On the morning of December 30, 1943,
Did you lose
And saw this as some sort of sign?

Did you pay attention
To signs, in that old Indigenous tradition?
Did you put down tobacco for Kichi-
    Manito
Every day
Or just on those days that you flew
    missions in Germany?
Or did you never?
Did you pray to god
Instead?
The Christian god
That catholic god
Of the Metis?

Or was it that Christian god of Louis Riel
The Metis leader and revolutionary
That they hung
The self-proclaimed Pope of the New
    World
Catholics?
Or were you an apostate
Calling those cat-lickers
Calling yourself a pagan?
I'm going to guess not.

While we always knew and acknowledged
our White Earth connection
Grandpa leaving there with Grandma
Pregnant
With your older brother, Neil
My father
Conceived without benefit of clergy
As they would say in those days,
Did you even know that?
So what was your
Mental/spiritual/physical
Connection to White Earth?

Would you, today
Had you lived
Would you be Anishinaabe

Or would you be
Simply
A browner shade of white?

Today, this is a big
Huge
Question.
What kind of Indian were you?
What kind of Indian would you have
    become?
Had you lived.

Would you be the Right Kind of Indian?
Would you be Indian enough?
Or would you be an apple?
Or would you simply be American?

Did you know that Grandpa left the
    reservation
With the taunts of our brothers
And sisters (?)
Who berated him for marrying up
Marrying a white woman
And an educated one at that?
Did they know that she was pregnant
Would that have been a bad thing?
Did you know many of those back at
    White Earth
Who drove Grandpa
And his pregnant wife
Off the reserve?
Did you get back there often
To visit with relatives?

Of course you were killed
But did you know that when Grandpa
Went back to White Earth
After you were killed
With his blood money
From the government
As compensation for
Your death
Our relatives were all over him
Asking for money
Money that represented your life?
Apparently Grandpa never forgave them
Was disgusted in fact
But they were poor
They were relatives
And it was the old way
They were seeking solace

From you
To share your
Good fortune (?)
With your relatives.
Did you know that
Grandpa refused
Then turned his back on our relatives
Never looking back only forward?

Did he ever talk about what had happened
About the time that Grandma got
    pregnant
And they left White Earth for Detroit?
Did he talk about being named as one of
    the
Forty-four
Or so
Bellefeuille family members
Considered to be
By some,
Illegitimate tribal members?
With my dad truly
In their eyes anyway
Illegitimate?
That he, Grandpa, his brothers and
    sisters,
Aunts, uncles, cousins
Were named as others attempted to
"purify"
the White Earth Rolls?

Did you know that the issue was a boil
Just at that time that he left for
Detroit
To have my dad be born
Away from White Earth
To save Grandma from her own shame
For having conceived a child
Out of wedlock
So that only a few would actually know
That dad was born
On time
Although the wedding was late?

Did you know that Grandma
Carried that shame to her death?
Although there was little to be ashamed of
She still was.
Did you know that she accused my
    mother of telling
Me and my siblings about

This self-claimed
Shameful act
And that she hated my mother for this
Supposed breach of trust?
Well, when I finally saw the dates, long
    after she died
I felt no shame for her at all
In fact, I was rather pleased
Pleased to know that my Grandma, your
    mother,
Was simply a human being
Who gave way to her passion
And love
For your dad, my Grandpa,
Joseph Homer, one of forty-four
    Bellefeuilles
Or was it forty-five
Out of ninety
Along with the Beaulieus
And the Fairbanks
All relatives
All 'mixed-bloods'
Subject to the
Purification of the White Earth Rolls?

Did you know about this
Purification affair,
Did you know that it failed?
Did that affect how you thought of
    yourself
Or how your friends
Thought of you?

Or did you know about
The assassination
Of chief Half-a-day
Leader of the so-called
Full-blood
Faction, years earlier?
Did you know about the
Role of the Beaulieu family, our family,
In his assassination?
Did you know about the sordid
History
Of the perfidy of many mixed-bloods
At White Earth
Over many years?
Did you know about their manipulation
Of the reserve's resource base to
Line their own pockets?

Did you know how long these problems
    stewed
Did you know how all of this affected
    Grandpa
Is this what drove him to drink?
And his sons, Grant and Neil.

Were you, too, an alcoholic,
A young Indian with a drinking problem
Or didn't it matter
Alcoholism that is
In the war
Constantly facing death?

Was your spirit there,
Where, when cousins Susie and Curt
And Curt's wife Margaret and I
Went to England
To accompany your
Uniform
And medals
To the Isle of Wight Military Museum
And stopped in Coney Weston
Rabbit West Town
And went to the pub where you
And others from Knettishall Airfield
Drank away the nights
Before your bombing raids,
Did you become an alcoholic there
Or were you one already
If at all?

Did you drink
While you were at
Bombardier training?
And just where was that
California?
Was that someplace exotic
For a young man from the rez?
Or were you simply a young man
From Detroit
Going to school out west?
Was it the only way out for you?
Did you think that you would somehow
    escape the
Poverty brown people faced?
Was being a bombardier
Glorious and much
Better than being a timber-nigger back
    home
In Minnesota?

Did you really have a thing going with
  Anita Louise
When you were at bombardier school in
  California
Did she talk about the movies she made
Did she care that you were younger than
  her
Did you care?
Did you drink with her
Dance with her
A brown man from the rez in Minnesota
Dancing drinking with the blue-eyed
  blonde star
Of Hollywood B-grade movies
Did she complain about never getting top
  billing
Even though she auditioned for the role of
Scarlet
In 'Gone With the Wind'
Did she complain that her blonde-blue-
  eyed good looks
Got in the way of her talent
In the blonde-blue-eyes of Hollywood
  directors?

How did you meet her anyway
At some USO dance?
Did they do that kind of thing where you
  were?
Did people from Hollywood go to the
  airbase slumming
Blue-eyed-blonde movie actresses
Looking for handsome young brown men
To share some time with
Before they went off to be killed in the war
The men that is, not the actresses
Knowing that they would never actually
  have to do anything
More than flirt dance drink with them
Have some fun with them
Show them a good time
Then send them off to their deaths?

Curtis Charles Bellfy

Phil Bellfy is an enrolled member of the White Earth Band of Minnesota Chippewa, and Professor Emeritus of American Indian Studies at Michigan State University. His book, *Three Fires Unity: The Anishnaabeg of the Lake Huron Borderlands*, won the University of Nebraska Press' North American Indian Prose Award in 2010. Dr. Bellfy has been involved in environmental activism at the local, state, national, and international levels for almost 50 years. He lives in rural Sault Ste. Marie.

Nimishoome means "My Uncle" in the Ojibway language.

U.P. Publishers & Authors Association Announces 3rd Annual U.P. Notable Books List

MARQUETTE, MI (January 4th, 2022)— the **Upper Peninsula Publishers & Authors Association** (UPPAA) announces the 3rd Annual U.P. Notable Books List this week. UPPAA board member **Mikel Classen** (Sault Ste. Marie) initiated the effort as a response to the lack of representation of U.P. writers in other Michigan state literary circles. Classen said, "Traditionally, recognition of Michigan books has been dominated by the university presses downstate and we would like to take this opportunity to highlight literature that focuses closer to home for us."

Evelyn Gathu, Director of the Crystal Falls District Community Library, will continue the library's alliance with UPPAA to co-sponsor the U.P. Notable Book Club (http://www.upnotable.com/bookclub/) . The club is available to any U.P. resident and features monthly Zoom meetups with national bestselling U.P. Notable authors including **Karen Dionne** (*The Wicked Sister*). Members borrow the books from their local libraries or purchase at local stores prior to discussions. Presentations include author readings, a conversation on the making of the book, and a live Q&A with the audience.

To build this third annual list, UPPAA consulted with Upper Michigan booksellers, book reviewers, writers, and publishers to winnow down the notable books to a bare ten titles. You can find reviews of many of these books on the UP Book Review. It must be emphasized that the list is unranked, each title deserves equal merit as U.P. Notable Book. These ten books have been deemed essential reading for every U.P. lover and we highly recommend you ask your local librarian or booksellers for them today!

1. *Firekeeper's Daughter* – Angeline Boulley (Henry Holt & Co., 2021)
2. *Great Lakes Monsters and Mysteries* – Brad Blair & Tim Ellis (Visionary Living, 2021)
3. *Tin Camp Road* – Ellen Airgood (Riverhead Books, 2021)
4. *The Wicked Sister* – Karen Dionne (G.P. Putnam, 2021)
5. *The Sideroad Kids: Tales from Chippewa County* – Sharon Kennedy (Modern History Press, 2021)
6. *U.P. Colony: The Story of Resource Exploitation in Upper Michigan* – Phil Belfy (Ziibi Press, 2021)
7. *Woodburnings: Highlights from the First Five Years* – Joanna Walitalo (Modern History Press, 2021)
8. *The Home Wind* by Terri Martin (Gnarly Woods Pub, 2021)
9. *Once Upon a Twin: Poems* – Raymond Luczak (Gallaudet University Press, 2021)
10. *Legend of Kitch-iti-kipii* by Carole Hare (self-published, 2021)

New Feature for 2022 – *U.P. Notable Classics*
The U.P. Notable Books Committee is proud to announce a new initiative called *U.P. Notable Classics* that highlights significant U.P. themed literature that has remained essential for at least 10 years. It is the committee's hope that these books can bring enjoyment to a new generation of readers.

- *Danny and the Boys: Being Some Legends of Hungry Hollow* – Robert Traver (a.k.a. John Voelker) (World Pub, 1951)
- *You Wouldn't Like It Here: A Guide to the Real Upper Peninsula of Michigan* – Lon Emerick (Avery, 2007)

Established in 1998 to support authors and publishers who live in or write about Michigan's Upper Peninsula, UPPAA is a Michigan nonprofit association with more than 100 members, many of whose books are featured on the organization's website at www.uppaa.org. UPPAA welcomes membership and participation from anyone with a UP connection who is interested in writing.

•••

The *U.P Book Review* project is honored to present a selection of reviews of three of this year's winners of the U.P. Notable Books List: *Firekeeper's Daughter, Tin Camp Road,* and *The Sideroad Kids*.
All books submitted to the *U.P. Book Review* are considered for nomination to the U.P. Notable Books list. You can find the latest reviews and subscribe to be notified of future reviews by visiting www.UPBookReview.com

Firekeeper's Daughter

by Angeline Boulley
Review by Tyler Tichelaar

Angeline Boulley's debut novel *Firekeeper's Daughter tells* the first-person story of Daunis Fontaine, an eighteen-year-old from Sault Sainte Marie, who is part Anishinaabe (Ojibwa) and part-Caucasian. Her mother, daughter to one of the wealthiest families in the community, got herself pregnant by Daunis' father, a Native American hockey player. Unfortunately, by the time Daunis' mother told her father she was pregnant, he had already hooked up with another woman. Consequently, Daunis has a half-brother, Levi, who is close to the same age.

Daunis grew up with her mother. Her maternal grandparents refused to list Daunis' father's name on the birth certificate. Daunis, however, has managed to remain close to her Native American relatives and their community on nearby Sugar Island, even though the tribe does not recognize her because her Native blood is not documented.

Add to this background the distribution of meth in the Sault and Daunis finds herself caught up in a situation that will test her loyalties to her community and her family. She soon learns that a new boy in town, Jamie, who is on her brother's hockey team, is not all he appears to be, and neither is his uncle Ron, who has taken over the teaching position at the high school that Daunis' Uncle David had held until his recent untimely death.

Death seems to be everywhere for Daunis. Both her father and her uncle have died, and her grandmother has just gone to a nursing home. As the novel progresses, more tragedies will mark her young life. Daunis has had a lot thrown at her for her young age, including the secret of her birth. Toward the end of the novel, she states: "The weight of my secrets is exhausting. My whole life has been filled with them. Even as a zygote, I floated in an embryonic sac of secrecy" (394).

What makes Daunis' life even more difficult is that everyone around her also appears to have secrets, beginning with Jamie, whom she begins to have romantic feelings for, only to learn he's not eighteen but twenty-two and working for the FBI, as is his uncle. They are investigating the meth dealers in the Sault who appear to be part of the Native American community. Before she knows it, Daunis finds herself caught up in the investigation, agreeing to pose as Jamie's girlfriend and to keep her eyes open for hints of who might be involved in the drug dealing.

Further description of the plot would spoil the surprises Boulley has in store for the reader. Daunis experiences one shock after another, gradually becoming wiser about the secrets in her community. But being wiser also makes her sadder, as she states: "Wisdom is not bestowed. In its raw state, it is the heartbreak of knowing things you wish you didn't" (393).

Boulley's novel has already received a lot of attention because it is going to be made into an upcoming Netflix series. The critics have also raved about it. While I enjoyed it, I personally felt in many ways it was a typical crime thriller, and at 494 pages, a bit too long. While I was interested for the first hundred pages, the pacing kind of fell off throughout the middle, but then the last hundred pages were gripping. While I feel it could have been shorter, so much was happening in the novel that I am not sure what could have been cut. Maybe I just don't enjoy reading about drugs, but admittedly, they make for a plausible plot and are unfortunately a reality especially for many young people today.

Criticisms aside, what made *Firekeeper's Daughter* stand out for me was its setting in Sault Sainte Marie, which is depicted as an interesting multicultural community across the river from Canada, and consequently, an entrance spot for crime into the United States. The depictions of the Native American community add a lot of flavor and color to the novel. At times, the use of Anishinaabemowin words felt a little overdone and I wished a glossary had been included, but most of the words and phrases could be understood from their context. Boulley certainly knows what she writes about, being herself a member of the Sault Ste. Marie Tribe of Chippewa Indians, and she captures the unique culture of the Ojibwa while realizing—and readers should also—that she cannot possibly speak for or depict

all 574 federally recognized Native American tribes.

The Author's Note in the back of the book is worth reading to understand Boulley's inspiration for writing the book, from her early fascination with Nancy Drew to her own desire, as a Native American, to read books with contemporary characters she could identify with. Perhaps most importantly, she wants to raise awareness of the rampant violence that is still part of Native American women's experiences. She states that 84 percent of Native women have experienced violence in their lifetime and 56 percent have experienced sexual violence. As a "young adult" novel, *Firekeeper's Daughter* does not shy away from violence, sex, or drugs, revealing how much they may be part of young people's lives.

I deeply respect Boulley's desire to capture a time and place in UP and Native American history that has been too long neglected. Boulley talks about how when making decisions for their tribes, Native Americans ask how those decisions will influence the next seven generations. Boulley is, undoubtedly, at the forefront of a twenty-first century golden age of Native American literature that will help to make a difference in the lives of Native Americans and all Americans for generations to come.

Historical stereoview - Mackinac Island national Park - Maniboujo Bay

Tin Camp Road

by Ellen Airgood
Review by Tyler Tichelaar

The wait is over. Fans of Ellen Airgood's *South of Superior* have waited a decade for her new novel *Tin Camp Road*. In the interim, Airgood published two young adult novels, *Prairie Evers* and its sequel *The Education of Ivy Blake*, but this is her first adult novel in a decade, and it has been well worth the wait.

Airgood, who owns a diner in Grand Marais, Michigan, might be called the UP's version of bestselling novelist Anne Tyler because she writes about real people, living real and often messy lives, in realistic places. In this case, her main character, Laurel Hill, lives in the small tourist town of Gallion on Lake Superior's shore, where she makes a living cleaning motel rooms, working for the people who now own her own family's home, and generally struggling to make a living as a single mother. Her daughter, Skye, is ten years old and a creative, intelligent spirit who is the center of Laurel's life.

Skye makes friends easily, including adults who want to help Laurel to give her a better life. However, their offers to help often place Laurel in a difficult position where she is torn between wanting what is best for her daughter and not surrendering her daughter to others' care. She feels bad that she cannot send her daughter to summer camps or buy her the things she would like to. It is all Laurel can do to keep a roof over their head, and for a time, she even finds herself homeless. Add to that Skye's dog and guinea pig to care for and Laurel has her hands full.

Several colorful and kind characters fill the pages, including an old man Laurel chops wood for to make some extra money, a divorced woman who runs a grocery store where Laurel helps out, and the people who own her family home that they have turned into a B&B and who almost seem to want to adopt Skye. And then there is Jen, Laurel's best friend since the third grade who finds herself in bad relationships with men and keeps expecting Laurel to rescue her when Laurel already has enough to deal with.

Airgood's style is one that penetrates to the hearts of her characters, showing us their strengths and weaknesses and especially the strengths they have that they do not always recognize. We feel the struggle that Laurel faces, while at the same time understanding why she chooses to stay in her hometown, even if work is often hard to come by or not well paying, even if she has a car that constantly stalls, and she has to shovel snow and live in a trailer out in the woods to get by. Laurel draws on fond memories of a perfect childhood and her grandmother to give her the strength to keep going, plus she is determined that she and Skye will stay together, no matter what anyone says.

Nor is *Tin Camp Road* a story all about sadness and difficulties. Skye and Laurel have a special relationship that is really filled with some wonderful moments of love, trust, and just having fun. While other adults don't always understand their situation, mother and daughter know they belong together and their bond of love is unbreakable.

The Upper Peninsula is depicted accurately in the novel. Airgood obviously knows and loves the area, not painting it at all as idyllic, yet reflecting its beauty, its power, its economic struggles, and the dangers that can exist from living along Lake Superior.

I kept hoping for a happy ending because I cared about the characters, but I also knew there would be no *deus ex machina* stepping in to save the day for Laurel, nothing that would be unlikely. I did not foresee how the book did end, yet Airgood planted the seed for the ending early in the novel like a good novelist should, and when the end did arrive, I couldn't help feeling it was perfect. It did not neatly wrap up the story but rather opened it up for the next adventure in the characters' lives.

Airgood sums up the novel's message a page or so from the end when she writes:

"Happiness was a net—that was it. You had to build a life that happiness would snag in. When it did, you took it up and used it. Ate it, salted it, relished it. Then you put the net down again. Nothing guaranteed you'd haul it up full every time. You wouldn't. But sometimes happiness would catch, and you'd have what you needed, at least for a while. Long enough to tide you over until the next time."

If you have not read an Airgood novel before, *Tin Camp Road* is a great one to start with. These are real characters you come to care about, and it reads so quickly that you will regret parting with them so soon. Hopefully, we won't have to wait another ten years for the next one.

Historical Sault Ste Marie - Native American Rapids Pilot

The Sideroad Kids: Tales from Chippewa County

by Sharon M. Kennedy
Review by Brad Gischia

There are many books that detail the history of the Upper Peninsula of Michigan. These are often rigorously researched and documented (some may be less so) and they represent an important aspect of the way we understand this strange little corner of the world.

The SideRoad Kids: Tales from Chippewa County is not that kind of book. It is a fictional retelling of the life of Sharon M. Kennedy, the stories of the time she spent growing up on the east end of the U.P., and the myriad characters that she grew up with.

Each chapter is a story about Yooper life, a mixture of back-country living and 1950's nostalgia that is reminiscent of Jean Shepherd's *A Christmas Story*. And Kennedy does indeed include a Christmas story in her book, one that takes the kids on a trip that is a little more like *Gift of the Magi* than they bargain for.

The kids in the book, with names like Flint, Candy, and Squeaky, could easily be any of the kids we all grew up with, familiar in their idiosyncrasies, lovable in their innocence. Most of the chapters are centered around the months of the year, the school year in particular focuses on notable dates as prescribed by the children's teacher, Valentine's Day, President's Day, and the like.

The way in which children experience the world is something we often forget as we get older. Kennedy convincingly recreates that and makes the reader remember how it was to be a kid again. Do you remember how easy it was to make friends? How quickly you forgot or overlooked differences that might be overwhelming for adults? Also, how fast you got over slights and arguments as a child?

Just like real life, it's not all wild capering and fun times. Kennedy tells stories of death, of loss and heartache, and of the dark thoughts that can pervade a child's mind, and she tells it with that same realism that reminds you about the real-life events and how kids try to deal with those stresses.

The setting, not just the Upper Peninsula but the specific towns and areas around it, lends a dash of realism to a native Yooper story that is sometimes lacking in other fiction about the area. Kennedy is writing about *her* hometown and the places *she* knew as a child. Because of that, it makes everything seem more real to the reader.

SideRoad Kids: Tales from Chippewa County is a great little slice of the Upper Peninsula. Even though it's set in the 50's I can see similarities to the people that I grew up around in the 80's, so I expect that those would be familiar to anyone from the area. This book is great for readers of all ages, a short story collection that is part non-fiction, part fiction, and all enjoyable.

U.P. Reader is Accepting Submissions for Volume 7

The *U.P. Reader* is an annual publication that represents the cross-section of writers that are the membership of the Upper Peninsula Publishers and Authors Association. This annual anthology will be used as a vehicle to showcase and promote the writers of the Upper Peninsula. Each issue is released in paperback, hardcover, eBook, and audiobook editions in early Spring following the deadline. Copies of the *U.P. Reader* will be made available to booksellers, UPPAA members, libraries, and news services. The *U.P. Reader* has received more media coverage each year since the inclusion of the Dandelion Cottage Award. We hope the *U.P. Reader* will be a great place for you to showcase original short works, too.

Submission Guidelines

- **Email submissions are no longer allowed.** Please submit your work through our submissions gateway which is www.uppaa.org/submit/ If you email your submission, you may be asked to re-send it through the gateway.

- Submissions will receive a receipt that the submission has been received. If a receipt is not received within three business days of submission either resubmit or contact editor@UPReader.org

- Must be a **current member of the UPPAA** to submit.

- Submissions **must be original** with no prior appearance in web or print. Submissions will be accepted for **up to 5,000 words**. Writers who submit work which has previously appeared in blog posts, web pages, eBooks, social media, or in print will be disqualified.

- Submissions **can be any genre**: fiction, nonfiction (memoirs, history, essays, feature articles, interviews, opinions) and poetry.

- All submissions will be **reviewed through a jury** and the submissions will be chosen through this process. Writers will be notified as to acceptance or rejection, but reasons for rejection will not be discussed.

- We prefer **Microsoft Word Document** (.DOC) files only or plain text files (.TXT). Do not submit PDF files. If you have some other type of text file, please inquire.

- **Please include a 50-75-word bio** at the end of the submission. Bios longer than 75 words will be trimmed by the editor. Any web addresses or email address in bios must be the most simplified form possible. (Do not include the http://)

- **Authors may only submit photos as part of a written submission** with the understanding that they will be converted to black-and-white. We reserve the right to limit the number of photos per story that will be used. Photos should be at least 300 DPI and no smaller than 2 inches on a sided (i.e. 600px minimum). If the Author is not the photographer, we may ask for a simple one-page "Photo Release" form to be sent in. Contact us in advance if you think you need more than 3 photos for your story. Author headshots are neither required nor used.

- **No more than 3 submissions will be accepted** from one person. If more than 3 are received, the jury may choose to disregard all of them. We are looking for quality, not quantity.

- **Poetry submissions count as one submission per poem. If a poem cycle is submitted it needs to be formatted either as one poem with multiple sections or as separate poems not numbering more than three.**

The U.P. Reader will require FIRST time rights in all formats, including but not limited to print, eBook, and audiobook for 12 months after publication. After 12 months, the author may use the work in any form they desire, including on the internet, print, and digital media. UPPAA retains the right to use it in perpetuity. For Example, we anticipate a "Best of U.P. Reader" to be issued for the 10th anniversary.

Publication Schedule for *U.P. Reader* Volume 7

- Submission deadline: Nov. 15th, 2022
- Dec 21, 2022   Jury / peer-review process begins
- Jan 15th, 2023 announcement of selected submissions
- April 1, 2023, official publication date

Young U.P. Author Section

UPPAA is extremely pleased to announce the winners of the 5th Annual Dandelion Cottage Contest that celebrates the creative writing of the U.P.'s newest generation of writers! Each winner will take home a cash prize, a commemorative medallion, and a hardcover edition of the *U.P. Reader* in which their submission appears. Additionally, the winner of the Senior Division will have their name inscribed on the traveling trophy which will reside in their school in the coming year. Starting in 2019, we inaugurated two divisions for the contest: Senior (grades 9-12) and Junior (grades 5-8).

This year's participants came from 9 different schools around the U.P. Some schools submitted up to 3 entries from their students. The judges would like to thank each and every student who submitted their work. There were so many great entries in each division that the judges had a difficult time whittling down the list to just three winners for the Senior division and one winner for the Junior division.

Junior Division Winner

- **Paige Griffin**, Grade 8 (Lake Linden-Hubbell Middle School) for "The Olive Branch". Sponsor: Jessica Klein

Senior Division Winners

- **First Place: Lauryn Ramme,** Grade 11 (Luther L. Wright High School, Ironwood) for "Birdie". Sponsor: Trisha Winn.
- **Second Place: Siena Goodney,** *Grade 9 (Marquette High School) for "Letters Under the Floorboards". Sponsor: Tony Parlato*
- **Third Place: Heidi Helppi,** Grade 11 (Negaunee High School) for "The Blood of My Love". Sponsor: Gina Sorenssen.

Participating Schools

Marquette County
- Marquette High School
- Bothwell Middle School, Marquette
- Republic-Michigamme Middle School
- Forrest View Academy
- Negaunee High School

Schoolcraft County
- Manistique Middle School

Houghton County
- Lake Linden-Hubbell Middle School

Delta County
- Escanaba High School

Gogebic County
- Ironwood

Iron River
- Michigan Great Lakes Virtual Academy

Birdie

by Lauryn Ramme

◆ ❖ ◆

ake Superior never gives up her dead. It's a saying I've heard my whole life, and one I know to be true. One only needs to take a single look at her violent, thrashing waters before they believe it themselves. She's as large as an ocean, stretching for miles and miles. Her waters are the dark blue of the depths where sunlight doesn't reach and are prone to swallowing up sailors whenever she gets restless.

This isn't to say I am afraid of the old lake. Not in the slightest. I have simply grown to respect it. Once you understand that you will never understand, it gets a little easier.

The rocks along the shore are cold under my bare feet. The water is chilled against my toes, but not frigid; not yet is it that time of year.

It takes longer than it should for me to realize that I'm not alone.

My head snaps up, and I observe the stranger who has broken my peaceful moment. The intruder waves.

"Hey there," he calls. "Got a minute?"

The boy—and he is a boy, not a man—trots over to where I am, seeming both eager and nervous at the same time. He's got floppy blond hair, eyes the color of muddy ice. He walks with a false sense of confidence, as though he's trying to seem more sure of himself than he is. I see right through it, as I do with most things.

"So, I'm—"The boy frowns. "Aren't you cold?"

I look down at the thick flannel jacket covering my white dress. "Not particularly," I say.

"I think I would be," he jokes. He's trying to make the conversation seem easy, using this tactic to move into another topic. I wonder what he wants from me.

The boy clears his throat. "Listen, have you seen a guy around here? About six-foot, hair a little darker than mine?"

There it is.

I haven't, and I tell him so. His demeanor changes immediately, a crease of worry making itself known between his eyes. He runs a hand through his sandy hair, swallowing.

"Really? You're sure?"

"I've been out here all day," I tell him. "You're the first person that's come through."

He squints. "You live out here?" I nod. It's not a lie.

There's silence for a few seconds, making it clear he's not exactly sure how to proceed. After a bit, he sighs.

"Well, alright. I hate to ask, but, if you see anybody like that, will you give me a call?" He pulls a semi-crumpled sticky note out of his pocket. "Just the number right here."

I nod again, and he pauses, waiting for a verbal confirmation that I don't give.

Finally, he turns, starting to walk away.

"Who're you looking for?" I ask when his back is turned. The boy doesn't stop. "My brother."

•••

The house is small. It's a ways off the shoreline, perched high enough that the lake can't do much but mist the windows. I hop up the stairs, the wood beneath my feet worn soft with use. There are divots where my toes have made a familiar pattern.

The record player has been turned on, Bob Dylan's soothing voice echoing throughout the walls. Honey-colored light emanates from the kitchen.

Turning, I walk carefully to my room, shivering a bit. I wasn't lying when I told the boy I wasn't particularly cold; it's simply a never-ending state.

The pale pink wallpaper is forever peeling, its small red roses curled over and hidden. I stare at them from my bed, trying to place new shapes and patterns in the shadows.

I lie there, and I don't think about the boy.

•••

It stormed last night. The wind howled and screamed, and the lake was angered, its rough waves rising higher and higher in their fury. I thought for a moment that it would be a bad one, one that ripped apart the coast and stole lives. But it stopped almost as soon as it began, as though Mother Nature instantly regretted her temper tantrum.

I don't mind a little tempest, not when they bring me great treasures. Scouring the shoreline, I search for pretty rocks and discarded objects, anything that catches my eye. A couple weeks ago, I found a shiny ring. I tried to wear it, but it wouldn't stick.

Shaking off a bit of sand, I observe my bounty. Some soft pieces of green sea glass, and a rock, colored bright pink. Probably not a rock at all, but a man-made item someone tossed away. That's okay. It is still beautiful.

I hear dull footsteps against the sand and know who it is without looking. "Hey again," the boy says.

I shove my treasures into my pocket, feeling the way leftover sand coats the inside.
"Hi."

He sits down next to me, making use of a dry spot along the shore. "See anyone today?"

I blink at him. "It's still early."

"Well, maybe you saw someone last night?" he tries. "I know there was a storm, so, someone could have got swept in, or..."

He trails off.

"I haven't seen anyone," I say truthfully. "I'm sorry."

The boy nods. I expect that to be the end of it, for him to move on and continue searching the coast. But he stays where he is.

"Shouldn't you be in school?" he asks, after a moment of silence.

I tilt my head. Sometimes, I forget that I look school-age. "Shouldn't you be?"

"I'm searching for a missing family member," he points out. "As far as I know, you don't have that same excuse."

"Homeschooled," I say. It's an explanation I've had prepared, but one I haven't had to use in a long time.

"Oh."

We watch the lake, the waves gently rolling over, a contrast to their violent night. A seagull cries out in the distance, likely hoping for a morning snack. I wonder when the boy is planning on leaving.

"Cole," he says, quietly.

I furrow my brow. "What?"

"That's my name," he mumbles. "You never asked, so I just...yeah." I rest my cheek on my knees.

"I'm Birdie," I tell him, finally.

Cole smiles. "That's a pretty name. Very classic." I suppose he would think so.

"Cole is a nice name too," I say, after a beat.

He laughs a little, his eyes crinkling at the corners. "Just nice? Not pretty?" I duck my head, so he doesn't see me smile.

•••

I hold my mug of tea, feeling the heat seep from the ceramic to my hands. I can't drink it, but I savor its fleeting warmth.

Cole stayed for a while longer. Talking to me.

He won't come back, My mind repeats. *Now that he knows his brother isn't here, he's going to stay far, far away.*

The thought comforts me through the night.

•••

Cole comes back.

Every morning, he comes to my small slice of coast and asks if I've seen his brother. I say *no,* he sits and chats, and then is on his merry way to do more searching.

I don't like it. Names are one thing. I have collected plenty of them. Taylor, Harry, Dorothea, Inez. Rebekah, James, Betty, August. Names, I have in no short supply.

Time, however, is more dangerous. Time leads to pain.

The more time I spend with Cole, the more it's going to hurt when he's gone.

"Heya, Birdie," he greets, all too chipper for a morning like this.

The sky is a pale gray, the kind that makes me doubt the sun has risen at all. The autumn chill has set in, and the lake's waters are starting to become littered with the browns and reds of dead leaves. I don't hate the fall itself, but what comes after: the months of loneliness when Lake Superior is barren but for scattered ice fishermen. I shouldn't mourn the autumn before it's passed, but I can't quite help myself.

"Hello."

Cole makes a *brrrr* noise, rubbing his hands together and blowing on them. "Cold today, huh?"

I nod. He grins. "But that doesn't stop you from coming out here, huh?" Shrugging, I say, "It's routine. And I like the fresh air."

"Can't blame you," Cole agrees. "Winter's coming fast. Pretty soon, we'll all be stuck inside."

Oh, don't I know it.

His cheeks are pink, and his nose is getting there too. His lips are chapped, and small tremors keep going through his body. I look at his thin jacket and lack of gloves.

"Why don't we go inside now?" I ask.

Mine might not beat anymore, but I am not heartless.

Relief fills his features, and he gets up without question.

I'm not embarrassed of the house, but I feel a sense of...something, leading Cole up the rickety stairs. I bite my lip at the chipped gray paint, the crack in the front window that's never been fixed.

He breathes out when we get inside. I tighten my flannel against my shoulders.

Whatever reprieve he gets from the chill isn't for me.

"Do you want tea?" I ask, already heading to the kitchen.

"Oh, no, you don't have to do all that," he protests, following me. I shake my head. "I'm making you tea."

I put the kettle on. Cole looks around. I see his eyes linger on the walls, and for a moment, I am confused; until I realize what he's noticed.

"You don't have any family pictures," he points out. I lean against the counter. "No."

Cole bites his lip. "Where are your parents?" He asks. "I've never seen anyone else here. Are they always at work?"

Closing my eyes, I say, "My parents aren't with us anymore."

"Oh, I'm—I'm so sorry," Cole breathes, looking immediately regretful. "I didn't mean to—I just— "

"It's okay," I tell him. "You were just curious."

He looks like he wants to apologize again, but the kettle whistles, silencing him.

Pouring the tea into mugs, I bring them to the table. Cole slides into a chair, the old wood creaking under his weight.

The dining table sits directly across from the front window, giving a picturesque view of the lake. Cole watches it now. He doesn't drink.

"Drew went fishing," he says, quietly. "It was a clear day. Perfect. We were nervous about him going alone, but he was so put-together, and he'd done it so many times before."

He clears his throat. "It wasn't—there was no *reason* to stop him."

He sounds anguished. I let him sit with his grief for a moment, feeling as though he needs it.

"I lost my parents out there," I say, finally. There were more. But he knows too much already. "That lake...it can turn on a dime. Even the most experienced can falter." I'm not sure why I feel the need to comfort him, but when I see the tension in his shoulders lessen, I can breathe easier. "It's not your fault, Cole." His fingers trace a pattern on the table.

"Birdie," he murmurs. "Do you think he'll come back?"

I should tell him no. I should tell him that Drew is long gone, and that he should run, get as far away from this lake as his legs will take him. He should leave, and never come back. I should do one thing right.

"Yes," I tell him. "I do."

• • •

Cole never breaks his routine. For two weeks, he continues to come to the coast. He questions me. I pretend to look for Drew. He helps me scour for treasures along the shore and brings me gifts of his own. Yesterday, he brought me a bright yellow flower he'd seen on the side of the road. I held it in my hands the whole time he was here. It died when I tried to bring it to the house, its petals wilted and gray.

We look for shapes in the clouds and in the shadows of my room. He fiddles with my record player, marveling at its condition, and tells me I should play records of artists I've never heard of. He lists off new, better sound technology that I don't understand, and wonders aloud why I still have a radio.

Without realizing it, he's become a part of my daily life.

Until the morning he doesn't show.

I sit patiently out by the rocks, my hands shoved deep into my pockets, waiting for him to appear so we can go inside. The house is always warmer when he's there.

But he never does. The sun rises higher and higher, its brightness stabbing my eyes like a dagger, and still Cole is gone.

Curling my arms around myself, I sit and think. The thoughts I've fought for weeks slowly start to creep in, like ivy on an old brick home.

Every day, I watch his spirit grow weaker. For all I've tried to deny it, I have not gotten this far without being observant. The light behind his eyes dims more every time I tell him I've seen no other person. His heart loses one more piece.

This missed morning will soon be one of many.

The lake's water nips at my feet, and I'm reminded that Cole isn't the only one who's patience is wearing thin.

She grows more restless with every passing hour, her waters hungry and agitated. Dead fish continue to wash up on her shores, and flies hover just out of her grasp. She is waiting. I have sealed my fate, and it's not one I can shed as easily as my jacket.

"Tomorrow," I tell her. I shove a lock of hair out of my face, grown tangled from the misty air. "Tomorrow."

• • •

The dull *thud thud* of his footfalls alerts me the next morning. Cole is out of breath, looking repentant.

"Hi," he gasps. "Sorry I missed you yesterday. I overslept, and I had to rush to school, and then—"

"It's okay," I cut him off, placing a saccharine smile on my face. "You have a life. I understand."

His shoulders sag with relief. "Okay, good. I'm sorry again." He flops down next to me. "Any sightings?"

I shake my head no. His jaw tightens minusculey, but he says nothing.

I lift my hand, shielding my eyes from the morning sun. Today is warm for autumn, and I've removed my flannel. Cole has arrived in only jeans and a t-shirt. I touch the water with my toes. They've remained painted all this time.

Smiling, I take a step in. Cole eyes me warily.

I raise an innocent eyebrow. "What?"

He frowns, looking at the lake. "It's Lake Superior. In October."

I shrug. "It's hot out, and I've been out here all day. I'm just cooling off."

He doesn't look satisfied with that answer, picking up a small rock and rolling it between his fingers. It's silent for a moment too long.

"Birdie," he says, finally. "What's going on?"

A chill runs through me. "What do you mean?"

He drops the pebble, running a hand through his hair. "I don't get it. You—you stay out here, every day, by yourself, I'm pretty sure. I tried to let it go, but...it's weird. It's really weird."

Cold dread tightens its hold across my chest, its slimy fingers feeling their way through my skull.

He gestures to my white dress. "I've never seen you wear anything else. Your house... it's always *freezing.* That day you made tea? You didn't drink it. I've never seen any other food in your house, either." His eyes fix on me, pleading.

The waves pulse around me. I can feel them, pulling the rocks out from under my feet. The bottom of my dress is soaked as I'm pulled farther in by the currents.

I swallow. "You didn't oversleep yesterday, did you?" Cole shakes his head. He looks down.

"I didn't want to," he says, quietly. "But...I went to the police. I *had* to." I feel like my world is tipping upside down. "What?"

He takes a shuddery breath.

"Birdie....did someone hurt you? Is that why you came out here?" This gives my brain a moment of pause. Hurt me?

"Did you have to run away to this place?" he repeats. The nerves are gone from his face, replaced with sympathy. He pities me.

"I don't know your story. I don't know if you had no choice, or, if it's rebellion, or...whatever, but you can't stay here. The house is old. It has no heat, and you've gotta be running out of food. Your clothes won't keep you warm out here." He jerks his head at the flannel I've discarded on the beach.

"I think you should come with me," Cole finishes. "You need to be somewhere safe. You need to be in *school.*"

I pause, and he must see it as worry, rather than the confusion it is, because he says earnestly, "We'll help you, don't worry. My family and I. Whatever you're running from, it won't get you."

Oh. He hasn't figured it out, then. Cole thinks I'm hiding from something. How naive he must be.

It makes it a little easier to go through with what I'm about to do, knowing that something else simply would have gotten him anyway.

I sink into the water, bowing my head like I've been caught. Cole steps in, kneeling down next to me. He pulls me into a hug. He is so warm.

"It's okay," he murmurs, the words I've told him so many times. "Everything is gonna be okay."

I lean into him, my shoulders shaking. He brushes my hair off of my face. And I grab his wrist.

Cole jerks back, momentarily stunned. "Wha—"

I whip around, grabbing him by his shoulders. The water is starting to rise around us.

"Birdie, what are you *doing?*" He is panicked, his voice rising in pitch. He struggles, no longer being gentle, trying his hardest to throw me off. Like his brother, he is a fighter.

The water goes up my nose and into my eyelids, making the world a disoriented, blurry mess. I can't hear anything but splashing, can't feel anything but the heat of Cole's skin through his t-shirt.

His nails scratch at my skin. "*Why?*"

The word is interrupted by choking as he's pushed further under, still fighting to grab me, to save himself.

The current pulls, stronger than anything man could ever make. The sign that my work is done. Cole is dragged down, down, down, to a place cold enough that dead bodies never rot. The last thing I see is his skinny hand, trying to reach me.

I stay in the lake for a long time. Now, she is calm. A bird chirps in the distance. Far off, I see a fisherman hoping to get a morning catch. He is in no danger; she has gotten what she wanted.

I pull myself out of her waters, once again sitting on the shore. I should feel satisfied, drunk off the feeling of a job well done. But I've long since grown immune to her charms, and all I feel is a tiredness, deep and in my bones.

I'm not sure how many years it's been since I made the deal. Time is hard to follow when you have no mortal markers, even short increments. My best guess is about a century.

I've always said I would do anything for the ones I love. I'm sure you would, too.

So you can't fault me for the choices I've made.

My parents fell victim to her violent temperament. They knew better, truly, they did, but they still took us out that day. Me, my sister, and my brother. We piled on the boat, watching it glide across her waters, cutting through them as if they were butter.

I don't remember the specifics of what happened. My mind has only been able to keep the memory of darkness, and cold, of trying to breathe, and feeling myself choke on water. The storm had flipped our boat, waves rising feet above us. I watched my younger sister flail, saw my brother try to pull her to safety and fall victim to the water in the process. My mother reached for my father, grabbing nothing but lake water.

I felt the current begin to drag me down.

"Not them!" I'd choked out. I wasn't sure if the words were audible over the raging wind, but I called out anyway, the cries of a desperate, dying girl. "Not them. *Please.*

Take me. But not them."

I kicked out, seeing my family disappear beneath the waves. "Please," I whimpered. "I will do *anything.*"

The darkness swallowed me. A voice, ancient and true, rang out in my mind. I could not describe that voice if I tried. It was like the crash of the waves against the earth, the sound of stones splashing across the sea. It was a voice no mortal should hear.

You would trade your soul for the lives of your family? The lake asked. I sobbed. "Yes."

Then you will do me the task of bringing me more.

I awoke on the beach, dry, and in the same clothes I had worn on the boat. I wasn't sure how long ago that was, now.

I never saw my family again.

But I knew they lived, for the lake never breaks a promise. Now, neither could I.

For years, I've fulfilled my end of the bargain. I don't know what she does with the bodies, or the souls they contain. I don't care to ask. All I'm sure of is this: *Lake Superior never gives up her dead.*

Lauryn Ramme is a junior at Luther L. Wright High School in Ironwood. After many years of reading, Lauryn decided to try her hand at writing. Her other hobbies include painting, listening to music, and hanging out with friends.

LAKE SUPERIOR COPPER MINES—HOISTING ORE TO THE HEAD HOUSE.

Lake Superior Copper Mines - Hoisting Ore to the Head House

The Letters Under the Floorboards

by Siena Goodney

◆❖◆

I n two years, I have lived in seven different houses and four different states, and those numbers are about to get bigger.

"Welcome to Charlotte, Missouri," said my mom as we drove over the city limits.

I didn't say anything. I was still upset we had to move again. I was beginning to fit in, in our last town. Then my mom's job forced us to move again, and here we are. My mom works as a traveling nurse and is constantly being relocated. I love my mom, but I really wish we could stay in one place. We pulled up to our new house. It is white with a small front porch and black shutters. It has an eerie look with the cracked paint and the vines crawling up the siding like snakes. It looked like a house from a horror movie.

I grabbed a box from the back of our car and went inside.

"This is your room; you can start unpacking but don't be up too late. You have school tomorrow," said my mom.

My room was a pale yellow with lace curtains surrounding a window. It has a small dresser, and a twin sized bed. I set down the box and started unpacking. The box was mostly filled with clothes, so I moved to the closet. The door screeched as I pulled it open, revealing a big walk-in closet. I walked in and started putting the clothes on the shelves. Beneath me I heard a floorboard squeak, curiously, I bent down to examine it. One side was slightly lifted, so I decided to try and pry it open. I was easily able to lift the floorboard. I was filled with a mix of excitement and anticipation as I looked inside the little space. There was a tarnished metal box. I carefully took it out and opened the box, eager to see what was inside. I opened the lid and found a dozen written letters. I took one out and started to read.

Monday, September 9th
Dear diary,
Yesterday I moved in. I don't like it here. The house freaks me out. Today was my first day of school. It went

ok. But I was late for the first hour. And ended up with homework in that class. I met this one girl named Emma. I had a few classes with her, and she asked if I wanted to sit by her at lunch. Well, I should probably go do my homework. I will write later.

I don't know what I was expecting, but it definitely was not that. It just seemed so normal and modern, like something someone my age would write. I decided not to worry since I do start school tomorrow and it was getting late. I stumbled downstairs and grabbed another box labeled "Leah's bedroom stuff" and brought it to my new room. I made my bed with the contents of the box and quickly fell asleep.

•••

"MOM! Do you know where my blue shirt is?" I yelled to my mom who was in the kitchen making breakfast. I woke up late this morning and now had to rush.

"I have it right here, Leah," she replied calmly as she walked out with it in her hands.

"Thank you!" I said, relieved.

"Also, here is your lunch, have a good first day," said my mom.

"Thank you."

I ran to my car, nearly slipping on the wet grass, and drove away quickly. Naturally I hit every light driving to school and ran in late to my first hour. My teacher, Mr. Higgins, had already started teaching. He gave me a look that made me shrink into myself. *Man, was I off to a great start!* Keeping my head down, I went to a seat in the back.

"Hi, I'm Emma. You must be new," whispered the brunette girl sitting next to me.

"Y-yeah, um, I'm Leah," I stuttered.

"So, what do you think of Charlotte High?" she asked.

"Umm, it's ok, I guess." I replied.

She had just opened her mouth to ask another question, when Mr. Higgins bellowed at us to stop talking.

"He seems like a great guy," I whispered sarcastically after a minute or two.

"Yeah, all the other teachers are fine, but he is a nightmare. Hey, do you want to sit with me at lunch?" she asked.

"Sure," I replied.

•••

I walked into the cafeteria and searched the room for Emma. The cafeteria was dingy with the dim lighting and plain walls. The fluorescence made it feel like a dream. Finally, I found her sitting alone at a round table. She was reading a book and had an untouched tray of food in front of her.

"Hey," I murmured.

"Oh hey," she said excitedly. "How is your first day going?"

"Pretty good," I replied.

"So, tell me about yourself."

"Well, I am an only child and I live with my mom. My dad is not really in the picture. But my mom and I are super close. She is my best friend; we do everything together. She is a travelling nurse, and we have to move a lot because of that. Which is kind of annoying."

"Where did you move?" she asked.

"Oh, um, we got a really good deal on the white house on the corner of Fair and Main Street." Emma's face went pale. "Why are you looking at me like that?" I asked skeptically.

"Because that house is haunted!" she whispered.

"Haha, very funny," I said, rolling my eyes.

"No, I am not kidding. Bad things always happen to the people who live there. There is a reason you got a good deal."

•••

I drove home unseeingly. Though my first day of school was pretty normal, except for lunch, something about it made me feel uneasy. I had this strange sense of déjà vu after my first hour. I couldn't figure out why; it frustrated me that I didn't know what it was. Just then I pulled into the driveway of my new house, though I didn't remember driving there. I grabbed my backpack and went inside. Once I got into my room, I started on my homework from Mr. Higgins class.

Finally, finished with my homework I started unpacking again. I opened my closet door and it instantly hit me why I had the feeling of déjà vu. The letters! I threw down the box and pried open the floorboard. I reread the letter I read last night.

Monday, September 9th
Dear diary,
Yesterday I moved in. I don't like it here. The house freaks me out. Today was my first day of school. It went ok. But I was late for the first hour. And ended up with homework in that class. I met this one girl named Emma. I had a few classes with her and she asked if I wanted to sit by her at lunch. Well, I should probably go do my homework. I will write later.
Everything that happened in the letter happened to me! I couldn't breathe. It couldn't be a coincidence. It was too specific. No! It has to be a coincidence. There is no reason to freak out. I decided that the only way to test it was to read another letter. If that one came true, then I could freak out. I grabbed another letter and started to read.

Monday, September 9th
Dear diary,
The new neighbors brought over chocolate chip muffins as a house-warming gift. My mom said they are super nice, they have a boy around my age and mom says we should get to know each other. Anyways, that's all for now.
This letter was written on the same day as the other one. If all this happens by tonight, then I will know it is true.

•••

"Hey, honey! How was your first day of school?"
"It was good," I replied. I didn't want to tell her about the letters just yet.

"That's good. Ooh look what the neighbors brought over while you were at school," she exclaimed. In her hands was a plate full of chocolate chip muffins. I wanted to scream, or cry, but no sound came out of my mouth.
"They have a boy around your age, you should hang out with him sometimes. If he's anything like his parents, he is probably really nice." She rambled. I sprinted for the stairs, tripping on the way up. I slammed the door and locked it hastily. I opened the closet door and grabbed the tin box. I felt anxious and sort of excited to see what the other letters said. Yes, the situation is pretty scary, but the letters can tell me my future! *Who wouldn't want to know what would happen to them throughout the day?* I could hear my mom yelling for me to open up my door, but I ignored her. I grabbed the next letter and read it.

Tuesday, September 10th
Dear diary,
I don't feel anything. I just feel numb. Maybe I am in denial. Maybe I will realize she is truly gone at the funeral next week. I just refuse to believe my mom is dead.

My blood turns to ice. Emma was right, bad things do happen to the people who live here. If the letters do tell the future, and if the date on the top of the letter is right, I have 24 hours until my mom dies.

Siena Goodney is a freshman at Marquette Senior High School. Siena loves to read all types of books and continually has more than one going at a time. She also loves school and math is her favorite subject. She has many interests, but her favorites are singing, playing soccer, and playing her guitar. She also sings at Redeemer Lutheran Church on as many weekends as she can with her busy schedule.

The Blood of My Love

by Heidi Helppi

◆❖◆

My father is dead. My mother is dying. I'm supposed to become the next queen. I've understood that's how it goes my whole life, when my parents die, I take over. But that's not supposed to happen for years. I'm supposed to get married first, have a few kids and let my parents become grandparents. But I guess the universe had other plans. Well, the people had other plans. My dad's throat was slit, my mother's wrists slashed. How she's alive is beyond me, she'd been left to drain out and die for the better half of the night. When the sun began to rise and Avenlie was waking up, the first thing they saw was the town square bathed in light gray blood.

My name is Charlotte Anderdale, and I am the crowned princess of Avenlie, a kingdom of judgmental blood.

It's been two days since the attack and my mother is officially dead. She tried to hold on, but at 3 a.m. I was called into her room. I was sobbing so hard they had to drag me there. I don't know why, but I felt that if I didn't go to say goodbye, she wouldn't die. She couldn't. She lived for 16 hours after be-ing drained of half of her blood. And now she is dead.

The older generation thought my parents were ruining tradition, letting me learn in real schools and not assigning me to marry into a neighboring kingdom. They thought we'd be punished for going against tradition and that our crops would stop growing. The younger generation thought we didn't need a monarch. They didn't want anyone to rule. I wonder which group decided to kill them, a good old sacrifice.

My mom's death comes with lots of things, not just crushing sadness and a feeling of coldness in my very soul; it also comes with a coronation. Since there is now officially no monarch, I must become the queen. *Ironic, isn't it?* Almost makes one think that's not why someone would kill my parents. Everyone in the kingdom knew my dad changed the laws of the monarch months ago to make it, so I didn't have to be married, so killing them would mean an automatic promotion for me. Whatever the reason they were killed, it's too late to change it now.

We have six days to organize everything, but I have no interest in any of it. *How could I be concerned with how I look, and who is invited, when I'm replacing my own parents?* Thus, I know this week is going to slip past like the sun on a cloudy day. That's something nice that I've noticed. Time doesn't work correctly, it more so just happens. I don't feel days passing or meals missed, they are simply gone. Like a forgotten memory, you know it happened, but there's nothing left to remember.

It's been two weeks since I last talked to you, and I've lost six pounds. The nurses are starting to worry about me and have started talking about an IV drip. This would take hours of my time, though, and since I was officially crowned last week, I don't really have any extra. That's right, I'm now queen. It was less of an event than I expected, which I was thankful for. The entire kingdom was there, of course, but there weren't any extra visitors. And it happened quite quickly. I honestly haven't quite processed it.

I walked down the grand hall in what could be a wedding dress, a long training white gown with streaks of red blood on the train, a nod to our ancestors. Avenlie is obsessed with tradition, remembering the ones that came before, always making sure we're "worthy" of their sacrifice. The dress is beautiful nonetheless, made completely of silk, but I barely looked at it. The only thing I could see was my parents' crowns, draped in the traditional black mesh, displayed on the sides of my waiting throne. I floated down the hall, caught in a ghost-like trance of reality, and accepted my role. And then it was over. The people danced and drank wine, but I sat with my parents' crowns.

•••

My parents have been dead for two months and I finally kept down a meal. Today is meant for more gown fittings. Like that's right. My parents are six feet in the ground, and I'm playing dress-up. Sitting up from my bed, I look around, my hole of depression. Maids make it hard to be a slob, but I think it's an important part of the grieving process.

I need to be able to see the chaos. See my life falling apart, so I have an incentive to save it. So, I told them to stay out of my room. Actually, I screamed at them. Blind, scorching hot rage that had been left to bubble too long. Finally, cracking open and seeping onto my poor handmaid that came to make the bed. Nevertheless, I don't think I'll be seeing them any time soon.

The floor is cold when I step down onto the hardwood. The sun is just rising, and the sky is soft. Pinks blending into baby blue on the horizon of my kingdom. *My kingdom.* It still doesn't feel real. My breakfast tray lies half-eaten on my bed, sunny side up eggs running onto cinnamon toast. I debate cleaning it up, but eventually lose the motivation and walk to the bathroom. I've been very angry lately, but my room has become my safe place. I think it has to do with the fact that I'm the only one that comes in here now. After kicking my maids off cleaning duty, I changed my lock to only let in myself. It feels nice to have something completely to myself when everything in my life is so public.

Running the hot water for a shower, I turn to the mirror. Bags under my eyes make them look bluer. My long brown hair no longer looks like silk but crumpled leaves. I'm definitely thinner. Sharper cheeks and sunken eyes. At least my skin looks good. It's a light olive and has adopted a milky glow in the last few days. My skin looks okay, but everything else is in bad shape. That's not good for our reputation. A sickly ruler means a weak government, which means takeovers would be easy. It's time to start caring again. The green tiles of my bathroom mixed with the assortment of plants and flowers I keep on the walls create a peaceful environment. I slip off my silk sleeping dress and step under the stream of steaming water. It's almost uncomfortably hot, but that's just how I like it, a subtle bite on the skin. Bubbles and the sweet smell of pea flowers fill the muggy room, and I almost feel like humming. Today feels like a good day.

Changing into my day dress is harder without maids, so I've been wearing lighter gowns. Today's dress is a soft green and ankle length. It cuts across my shoulders nicely to show off my collarbones, while also extenuating my thinning waist. It's almost shimmery, a light swish of color and shine. Slipping on a pair of flats, I open the door and head downstairs. Sir Benard—formerly known as Ben to me—head of the royal guard and my lifelong sparring partner, catches my attention as I turn to the great hall.

"Your majesty, this is Dakota. He's going to be your new personal guard." I almost rolled my eyes. *Of course, I have a new guard. At least this one is my age.* He's tall, and you can definitely see Ben has been making them hit the gym, hard. Lean, but with broad shoulders and strong arms. Actually, he's not bad looking. Slightly curly brown hair, (almost too long for regulation) and a strong jaw meeting well-defined collarbones. Flicking my gaze to his face, I see his eyes. Perfect green eyes. Mossy and inviting, with a hint of a dark ocean blue. Finding my guard good-looking is probably not the best, but if anything happened, Benard would have no trouble replacing him. He probably has ten in line behind him already.

I'm not surprised by all the added security, but it feels excessive. I know Ben feels responsible for my parents' death but keeping me locked up like a Faberge egg isn't going to bring them back. He was so close with my dad. You'd almost thought they were brothers. That caring relationship definitely lapped over to me, as Ben was always there when I needed him. I don't think a personal guard would save me if they decided to strike again. My parents had been taken in their sleep, in the middle of the night, from a part of the castle that only the royal family is supposed to be able to get into. Security and locks line the walls, but they still snuck in, drawn to the blood beating in their hearts.

Blood is very important to our culture, explaining why, when killing my parents, their executioner made sure the blood was the most memorable part. Everyone's blood is a different color, from snow-white to ashy gray, to the deadly, foreboding black. Blood color is based on morals, good and bad deeds. If one lies, your blood adds a drop of gray into the stream. Something bigger, like stealing, knocks one down a whole shade. But *black*?

Black can only come from death. A permanent mark of one's blatant disregard of human life; the greatest gift of all.

This system of shades and colors has been around for a long time, but not forever. A hundred of years ago, Avenlie was but a small town, and we were starving. The full world was starving. The nannies say we were being punished by the gods for our sins. No crops would grow, the rivers were dry. This went on for years. The young died and the old suffered through life, living off scraps and odd twigs. And then my great, great, great, great, bunch of greats, grandmother had a baby. And she fell in love. He was her light in the dark and a blanket in a cold room. She hated seeing him suffer like she was, hated seeing his tears and hearing his cries. She would have done anything to save him from that starving world.

On his first birthday, he got really sick—sleepy, and sick. Avenlie wasn't stupid; she knew he was dying. So, she left him with the town nana and climbed into the mountains with nothing but a knife. She stayed there for five days, drank from the rain, and ate what the gods provided her: small berries and stray acorns. She prayed. Day and night, every moment she was awake she prayed. She wanted him to smile at the sun and laugh with his love. Every plea was for her son's safety, a world he could thrive in. And then she took her knife and emptied every ounce of her own blood into that mountain. She looked to the gods, told them how much she loved her son, and proved it. She sacrificed herself for her son, and it wouldn't go to waste.

When the townspeople went to find Avenlie, they found a pool of crystal white, blood. After that day, the rain was plentiful, and the crops flourished. The people were happy and healthy for the first time in centuries. But there was another change too. Blood was no longer red but came in thousands of different shades. People quickly learned that there was a system, as described before, and we've been living by this ever since. There's no rule against dark blood, people just like to try and keep it light. One might not go to jail, but if someone sees you with a cut, and it's as dark as charcoal, that person might not be able to find a job. If it was dark enough, there would be no funeral when one died. Of course, black is different. The fact that you can only get blood that dark from murder means if they're found with it, they'll be executed.

•••

"Good morning, your majesty," Dakota announces as he slips into the room. God, how is he so awake all the time?

"You don't have to call me that, you know. You are my 'personal' guard after all. You should call me by my name."

"But there's another in the castle with the name Charlotte." *He's got to be kidding. I'm the queen, and he's worried about mixing me up with a maid?* "Do you have a nickname?

Oh, God. Nicknames. I've had hundreds, none of them that I like. They're always either something about burnt wood or boy names. *Charcoal, Chase, Carl, Charlie.* I hate them all. And they've only ever come from bullies.

"No, I don't have a nickname," I say as coldly as I can, hoping he gets the hint and drops it. But instead of dropping it, his face lights up like a little kid getting cake.

"Great, I can give you your first one!" I hate the idea, but... he's kind of cute when he smiles. I guess it won't be that bad. "How about Char?"

"Ugggggghhhhhhhhhhh. Fine. But I get to give you one too; it's only fair."

"Yeah, that makes sense. But my name doesn't have lots of options." I look at his face, trying to figure out what kind of person he is, what would fit with his personality.

"What about *Kota*?"

•••

Kota has been assigned to me for two months, and I've gotten to depend on his company. I know I'm supposed to hate having a personal guard, someone always in my business, but I've actually begun to really like it. It's like having a built-in friend. Every bad day starts with his warm smile and ends with him telling me goodnight. We're togeth-er all the time, not either of our choices, but it's not terrible. Our conversations are nice, and not covered in the sticky sucking up. It feels good, a breath of fresh air from everyone trying to kiss my ass.

Today is a beautiful fall day and the leaves are beginning to change to light orange, so I've decided we're going riding. I know Kota can ride a horse just fine, but I'm definitely better, and I like to be better than him at some things. Over the last few months, I've realized that even though he's not outright about it, Dakota is very proud. It's not very hard to spot once you're looking for it, but it's not necessarily a bad thing. He is quite good at most things. The first time I noticed it was during an archery lesson. He watched me shoot ONE time and decided he needed to fix my entire form. Like the knight in shining armor he is, he gladly twisted my shoulders and tweaked my hand placement for thirty minutes before letting me shoot again. I swear, by the end of it, I was holding the bow the same as before.

The stables are beginning to adopt the smell of crisp winter, even with it only being October. I go to get my saddle and tack but realize Artemis is already waiting for me. I guess Kota got here before me. Furthermore, I love Artemis; she's a beautifully spotted gray with smoky ears and has been with me for years, but she is one of my more calm and steady horses. Of course, he picked her. That's fine, though, I wasn't planning on racing anyone today. I honestly just want to enjoy the warmth of fall before winter sets its cold gaze on us. I lead Artemis out to the pasture and find Kota with his own horse, Jack; I know, what a dumb name for a horse. Jack is also more of a calm horse, but I think that's all Dakota can handle. Kicking myself over Artemis and into my saddle, I trot over to my guard and his light brown horse.

"Finally, I thought I'd be waiting till dinner," Kota teases. Kicking himself onto Jack, he asks where the destination is, and I simply tell him to keep up.

We reach an apple orchard after ten minutes of sweeping hills and a small stream filled with colorful rocks. It's the perfect place for a picnic. I lead Artemis to a small tree and jump down into the dry grass, tying her to a low branch. Jake and Kota trot in behind me, and he follows suit, leaving both our horses to munch on the late summer grass.

"I knew you'd be hungry, so I got you a picnic. Surprise!" I pull out the standard checkered blanket and begin setting up a spread of cheese and crackers, before realizing I forgot the fruit. A fall picnic is not right without fruit. Good thing we're in an apple orchard.

"Hey, Kota, can you help me. I need to pick a few apples. Just lift me up to that branch."

"How are you planning on staying up there, you have to balance of a drunk two-year-old."

"Ha-ha, very funny, now just help me." He pushes me up to the branches, but as I place my foot down, I feel it slip. Why is he always right? I feel gravity taking control, but just before hitting the ground, I'm caught. And then we're both falling.

Soft grass tickles my neck and his hands are on my waist. They're softer than I expected, but just as strong. A sweet breeze brushes past my cheek and I look up at Kota. It feels nice to be together. I feel saner. Looking into his emerald eyes, I can almost see a normal life for us. A small yellow house with three kids, a pleasant dog, and long summer nights on the porch. But, no matter how much I long to wake up to his face and have his lips on my own, I've always known I won't. Kota is my guard, and now that my parents are dead, it's even more important that if I marry, it's for power and stability. Not love. That being said, the heart is a naughty creature and always wants what it can't have. I've been sitting in his arms staring at him for way too long. I quickly contain myself and jump up, brushing off my dress.

"Ha-ha, sorry, I guess you were right," I blabber out. He looks a little sad but turns back to getting our picnic. The rest of our lunch goes smoothly, but I can't help but feel he's disappointed in me, for whatever reason.

•••

I think I've spent every minute I'm awake with him. Four months of constant flirting and teasing mixed with a deep understanding of my responsibility to our kingdom and the instability of our relationship have created a bond no one person could break. I've come to understand the day in the orchard could have been a kiss, but it was the start of something, nonetheless. Sir Benard found me the other night, sneaking out from a late night with Dakota. He wasn't happy, but not as a guard, as someone who loves me. I've always admired that about him. He didn't treat me as a spoiled and weak girl he had to protect; he treated me like a daughter. Like he wanted to keep me safe. And that includes not going after my guards, I guess. He can't do anything to stop me, I'm literally his boss, but he definitely gave me, "a talk." "Stay away from him", "you're going to get hurt", *blah blah blah*. He should know it's too late. Winter has moved in, and so has love for Kota in my heart.

•••

Young love is grown with secrecy
bottle-fed with hushed giggles
and gets fat on love poems signed by
   "your secret admirer"

his smile looks so much sweeter when
   it's hiding nights alone
sneaking around with only the moon to
   tell our story
wrapped in each other's arms and the
   lies we tell
tumbling through soft blankets and
   slipping through cracks in our stories

praying no one finds out
but hoping they wonder

a glance just for me
the touch of intimacy I feel from across
   the room
sly glances feel like slick fingers dragging down my skin
and I know we'll never be the same
   again

•••

It's late. Too late to be awake. But I am awake, and I can't fall back asleep. I had been woken from a terrible dream; a dream I have quite often. It's already spring, and the kingdom has moved on, but I'm stuck. Stuck on that night. It starts the same every time, sitting at breakfast with my parents, happy, but it has multiple different endings. They always end up dying, but it's the person that kills them that changes. Sometimes it's a guard; once in a while, it's Dakota; occasionally, a black splotch of a man with no face, and sometimes, most terrifyingly, it's me. A knife in my hand, sliding it across my own mother's wrist. Tonight, wasn't so bad, it had been one of the cooks that did them in. Either way, it hit a little too hard, and I couldn't bring myself to sleep.

Sitting up from my blankets, I throw on a light pink robe and head for the door. I don't know exactly where I was planning on going, but after an hour of wandering, I found myself in the guard's quarters. I'm not supposed to be in this section, but now that I'm queen, I technically can go anywhere. Stepping up to familiar room nine, I knock. He must have already been awake because he got to the door in less than a minute. And there he was. Hair messed up from his pillow, no shirt, and in boxers. He has a superb body. He must have seen my eye line to his chest because he promptly blushed and slammed the door. How rude. A few seconds later, the door opened again and there was a more awake Dakota standing before me. Sadly, he also had on more clothes.

"Hi, Char. Are you okay?"

"Yeah, I'm fine, just couldn't sleep."

"Yeah… me neither, actually," I know him so well. I ducked beneath his arm resting on the door and darted into his room. Before I could make it all the way in, though, he grabbed me by the waist like an over-excited kid being held back from candy. Again, how rude. I whipped my head around, planning on bitching him out, but instead, I'm caught in his eyes. I could feel my heart beating too fast, and before I could react, he kissed me. He kissed me and I think my heart exploded. It's everything I've dreamed it would be since the day in the orchard. Twisting my

hands up into his hair, I kissed him again. And again. I didn't want the moment to end, and I think we both realized this could be our only moment like this. I back into his room so he can close the door, but instead, bump into the bed. Unfortunately, he had been awake and was working out. Weights crash to the ground, indefinitely waiting for the entire barracks. I turn to find a place to hide, but a short knife covered in light gray blood catches my eye.

"Dakota, what is that?" My voice trembles as I ask him. I step back with fear in my eyes and within seconds I'm surrounded by guards. His hands are bound, and the guard turns to me for orders. As I'm opening my mouth, Sir Benard finally tumbles into the chaos. The scene is laid out before him, and his face darkens with realization.

"Charlotte, what do you want to do?" His voice is so dark. Pulled down with the loss of a friend and worry about me. The knife that killed my parents is lying on the floor. Shouldn't someone pick that up?

"Execute him."

•••

Guilt
Sitting in your bones and leaking into your heart
Poisoning thoughts
Why did you do it?
Did they cry?
Did it hurt?
Did it hurt you to hear them scream for mercy?

Guilt
Blood on your hands, trailing into your thoughts
Poising dreams
Thoughts
Did you think before you did it?
Slit their throats

They're guilty
I am not guilty
I am a savior
Saving us from them
From their dark blood

WE will be washed of our sins with their
  blood
Guilt

Maybe you're crazy
Maybe you're just guilty

•••

The sun kisses my face as I turn to the sky. A soft summer breeze brushes my cheek and the grass is warm. After six months of grieving and screaming for justice, they finally did it. They found him. The one guilty of their deaths. Dakota is crying, I can hear him calling out for me. We're in love, I know. It's not right, of course, but we are in love. I feel him coursing through my veins, his face lights up my heavy heart. But it's not right. The late nights and stolen kisses. Innocent glances drenched in remorse. Even on the site of my parents' death, he tries to defend himself. But it's too late for him. The people have called him guilty and no one can save him. No one but me.

My throne is waiting for me as I glide up the stairs in my heavy white dress. White again. It's the second and last time I will be wearing this symbolic color. The lace arms trailing down to the ground make me look shorter than I am, but the slender bodice fitted to my hips balances it out. A ball gown matched with a black veil over my crown. It's tradition for the monarch to wear black at an execution. I'm wearing mom's ruby earrings, elegant silver drops that create the whisper of the long-gone red blood of our ancestors. My hair is done, held up by a splash of silver twists made to match the earrings. I look beautiful; I look like my mom.

"*CHAR!*"

My nickname on his lips. It sounds as sweet as honey, rich like expensive wine. Something I hate so much is the epitome of elegance and young love coming from his mouth. My heart breaks when I turn to him, seeing the strong man I love crumbled on the floor.

"Please. Help me!"

Poor Kota. Suffering for the sins of the world.

My parents are dead, and they say he's guilty. How could I have fallen for someone I needed so badly to stay away from. It is all my fault, and now the one person I could love is being punished. Sweet memories are now smeared with guilt and rot. Rotting under the truth and the fact no one can ever know it.

A knife drenched in gray blood. Taunting me every day with what I'd done. Stashed under floorboards, it snuck into my dreams, seasoned my breakfast with sin, and coated my brain with remorse. I kept it in my room for months, debating what to do with it. I kicked out the maids so they wouldn't find it, but I knew I had to pick a target. I wasn't supposed to fall in love with Dakota. And I didn't think I would be able to go through with framing him. I don't know if I can. My kingdom needs me to be strong, but I can't. I need him. Please, God, no, I need him. I jump up from my throne, crashing through my guards. My dress is too heavy as I stumble down the stairs. My heels are too high. No, I can make it.

Thunk

Angelic white blood seeps onto the floor.

It's over. He's gone. Gone with my heart. My lungs don't want to work. My heart stopped beating. Everything is quiet for a second. The calm of pure dread in my soul. Gripping my heart are the cold fingers of a familiar friend. And then Chaos erupts in the square. Voices become a thrill in my ears and people shove to get to the ground. Everyone can see the white blood, but they still fight to get to the source. The man "responsible" for the deaths of the king and queen cannot have white blood; they got it wrong. The air is too heavy, and my head starts to spin. Things are getting fuzzy, I'm passing out. The ground is soft beneath me, sinking like quicksand, or maybe it's my bones; cracking and splintering as I try to stand. Stabbing my esophagus and making it impossible to breathe. Dirt in my hands. When's the last time I touched real dirt? The picnic. I grind it into my palms, desperate to turn my feelings back on and grasp a small piece of reality.

Small gasps
shallow breath
Quick thoughts
and a dead heart

A bleeding arm
split on the edge of a noble guard's sword
tumbling to get to my love
I didn't feel the slice
but I couldn't have ignored the blood
So different from his white
black
holding the sins of my world
and the crimes of his sentence

the angel is dead
and the devil is guilty

I could have taken responsibility
taken the guilt
I could have just not done it
stayed asleep that night
left the knife under the floorboards
and the hate in my heart

Maybe I shouldn't have killed them.
But maybe they shouldn't have made it so easy.

Heidi Helppi is a junior at Negaunee High School. She has loved reading all of her life and has recently gained a great interest in writing. She also runs track, at the High School. She participates in Business Professionals in America and is a class officer.

MARQUETTE FROM RIDGE STREET BLUFF.

Marquette from Ridge Street - circa 1860

Olive Branch

by Paige Griffin

◆❖◆

Nothing hurts more than realizing your child could be gone within months. They could be taken from you for good, in a way so unjustifiable. And you know there's hardly anything you can do.

My daughter Grace was diagnosed with leukemia about a year ago. She was only three. She didn't understand as I broke down there in the hospital, and—like the caring toddler she is—she squatted next to me and asked continuously, "What's wrong, mama?"

The drive home was silent, but I could tell Grace was beginning to get anxious. She occasionally would lift her head and look at the back of my seat expectantly. I tried to focus on the road before me, but it was a struggle.

When we arrived home, I mustered up the courage to try to explain carefully what was going on inside of her, taking small breaks to swallow the growing lump in my throat. "It's called cancer," I choked, "but it's nothing to be afraid of. We'll get through it."

The little girl looked at me. "Is that what makes me feel sick?"

I nodded. "But we'll get you to treatment and they'll make you all better. But if you start feeling sick, you have to let me know, okay, Honey?"

And she did a good job at it, too. Sometimes it would be unexpected waves, and others, it would slowly start.

I feel I've failed as a parent. I promised her she would be okay, but I wasn't exactly sure myself.

I looked out the window above the kitchen sink, scrubbing a plate with a sudsy washcloth. My daughter, now four, was looking at a picture book under the olive tree in our yard– her favorite place to be. My husband sat next to her, pointing to the pages with a smile. I could hear their voices faintly.

"What's that?" he asked.

"A kitty!" Grace gasped.

"It's a big kitty; a tiger."

"A tiger?"

"A tiger."

I smiled feebly. It wasn't fair that she had to deal with this disease. Kids and other adults would often look, or stare at her oddly, since we had to shave her head, until either she or I looked at them.

If I could, I would have it be me, rather than her.

I looked at the clock. It was almost three, the time Grace had to go in for her chemotherapy. I quickly dried off the dish in my hand, slipped my shoes on, and went outside.

My husband looked up, then looked back at our child and stood up. "Come on, Gracie."

Grace stood up and trotted to me.

"You ready to go?" I asked.

She nodded and grabbed my hand as we headed towards the car. I opened the door and helped her in, buckling her into the seat and circling to the driver seat. The car rumbled as the key plunged and twisted in the slot, and we took off to the hospital.

A few minutes passed by in silence until Grace began to fidget with her fingers. "I don't like going."

I looked at her in the mirror sympathetically. "I know, Sweetie, but it'll all be worth it in the end."

"But what if it doesn't work?" She said exactly what I had been thinking.

"It will," I responded dryly, and hopefully.

She didn't ask any more questions or say anything else. She stared blankly out the window at passing cars and children playing outside of their houses. I blinked threatening tears away and looked up to stop them from spilling.

•••

I didn't get it. Didn't those kids get sick, and tired sometimes too? Why was I special? I couldn't help but feel I was the one at fault for this, but I couldn't remember anything I did or said to deserve this.

I caught a glimpse of Mama in the seat diagonally from me. She was crying again. She did it a lot, and I never understood why. I once overheard her talking to Papa about how she couldn't bear the thought of losing me. I only giggled; it's not like I'd go anywhere. I always imagined how nice everything would be once I finished my chemo– whatever. Mama would

be happy, Papa would be happy—we'd all be happy and wouldn't have to listen to Mama cry all the time.

I think she's sad because of me. Is it because she hates the hospital like I do? Is she embarrassed? Because of me? I wouldn't think so. Mama tells me she loves me every chance she gets, and she or Papa have to stay with me at all times.

Life is just really confusing.

I looked at my arm, spotting a new bruise near my wrist.

Mama looked at me in the mirror. "Is that a new bruise?" she sniffed.

I nodded. *Where did this thing come from?* I normally would get the purple splotches if that part of my body got hit real hard, but sometimes they'd randomly show. Same thing with bumps.

"Okay, well, we're almost at the hospital, so I'll let your doctor know."

I don't know why bruises are such a big deal. I've seen everyone with at least one, but they're not rushed to some clinic.

A sudden wave of exhaustion flew over me, and my head started to droop sleepily until I snapped back up. Eventually, I let my eyes close, and I drifted off to sleep.

Mama woke me up, what felt like, a few minutes later. She unbuckled me from my seat and lifted me into her arms, propping me up so I was facing behind her. I twisted to face the other way, staring at the looming building that held a large blue cross above the doors.

As we entered, I noticed not as many people were there. Normally there were, like, a thousand humans buzzing about. But today there just wasn't as much. It seemed a bit empty.

Mama placed me gently on the floor next to her and gripped my hand, holding me there so I wouldn't wander. I let out a huff of annoyance and looked around. I saw a couple people sitting in chairs, staring at phones or at the ground, waiting to be told to follow a doctor into one of the scary rooms. One of the older boys looked at me and, with a slight smile, lifted his hand and waved. I only stared back, then huddled closer to Mama nervously.

After she was done talking to someone that hid from me behind a tall counter, we walked to an empty chair and sat. She lifted me onto her lap and cradled me against her chest as I nibbled on one of my fingers. "When are we going?" I asked impatiently; I wanted to leave.

"We have to wait for your doctor to come and get us." Mama looked down at me with a weak smile.

I looked at my right hand. The lady that did my treatment always had to stick a needle into the back of it, but it rarely hurt, and when it did it was just like a little pinch. But it was worth it, since I got to pick a piece of candy from the bucket after each session.

I began to grow impatient and kicked around with my legs out of sheer boredom. Mama pushed them down gently and said, "Just a few more minutes, Grace."

I hoped that was the case, but I also didn't. Chemo typically would last anywhere up to four hours, and sometimes overnight.

Finally, a tall familiar man poked around the corner. "Grace." He looked at me with a kind smile, and Mama stood up with me in her arms.

He led us down a dim hallway, past open rooms and closed rooms, and into the room he normally would take us into.

Mama positioned me on the bed, which wasn't even that comfortable, and stood beside me.

"So, anything new with her?" the doctor asked.

"Well, she has a new bruise, and has been sleeping more than usual. Slept on the way here." Mama stroked the top of my head.

The man adjusted his glasses and wrote something on his clipboard. "Alrighty. We can schedule another scan if you'd like. Just to see how the tumor is doing."

Tumor? What *is that*? I was told I just was sick with some cancer thing called Luke or something. Maybe the tumor's name is Luke.

"Sure," Mama replied.

"Okay. We can do that just before you guys leave here today." The doctor opened the door and winked at me. "The nurse will be right with you guys." The door shut behind him and his footsteps silenced down the hall.

The room was quiet. "Mama," I looked at her, "what's a tumor?"

"It's a mean lump that's growing on your brain, causing your leukemia." *Leukemia.* I'll never remember that.

"How did it get there?"

"I'm not sure. But your grandpa had one too."

"Grandpa Mike?" That was Papa's dad.

Mama shook her head. "No. My dad– your grandpa Tim."

"I don't know him. Have I seen him before?"

"No. He got really sick."

"Oh."

Mama looked sad again. I don't think she likes it when people are sick.

She began to tell me stories of when she was younger, and when they found out he had cancer. He sounded like fun, and I wish he was here so I could meet him.

After a few more minutes of a painful silence, the nurse entered. "Hi, Grace," she greeted cheerfully. I smiled at her, and not just because she was holding the treat bucket. "Are you ready to start?"

I nodded, even though I wasn't. Sometimes, you just have to lie. I wanted to get this over with, as fast as possible. Sometimes, we'd have to stay overnight. Not often, though.

But I didn't really mind it, if it stopped my sickness. It was a bit odd. I feel as if it gradually began to worsen. I'd been sleepier, more bruises and lumps showed on my skin, I felt sicker a lot more, migraines, fevers and random moments of coldness, and I even lost feeling in my hands and feet a few times. I thought this was supposed to stop all of that. But Mama told me it should get worse, then better. I don't get why, but I believe her.

The lady unraveled a small tube next to me and propped up the pillow on the bed. I squished myself against it, and laid my hand flat so she could put the tube in.

"Okay, you're going to feel a slight pinch," she said gently.

I winced as the needle-tip was inserted into the back of my hand, but the sudden pain diminished as quickly as it came. There was still a slight stinging sensation lingering, but it was bearable.

The nurse carefully dragged a stand that hung bags of liquid closer to me. I never understood what that was. Water? It was clear. I wonder if it tastes good. But the pipe that latched onto my hand was also attached to a machine and those bags, so it probably wasn't safe to drink.

The woman ripped a piece of tape off of a black dispenser and strapped it over the tube and onto my hand. She did that two more times until it was sturdy against my flesh.

Now for the boring part; waiting.

Normally I'd sleep through the whole thing, but I didn't exactly feel tired. I kinda ruined the feeling since I napped in the car.

Moments passed. Very slowly. The nurse had left, so only me and Mama remained in place. She didn't say a word, either. She stared blankly at the floor and picked around her thumbnail.

It took about thirty minutes for me to grow extremely bored and sleepy. I would rather feel sick every now and then than sit here for hours on end.

I began to doze off, my head bobbing every time I'd snap awake. I officially repositioned myself and fell asleep.

•••

A bright light dragged me awake. My eyes opened and I started to worry, since my vision was blurred. I sat up quickly, not sure where I was, which was a mistake. I got dizzy and sat there until my sight cleared.

Eventually it did, and I was relieved to know I was still in the hospital room. I looked around. Mama had also fallen asleep in a chair by the wall. I giggled. Somehow, it reminded me of the various times I'd fallen asleep against the olive tree in our yard. It was my favorite place to be.

I can't place why, though. I don't like olives. Maybe it's just magical? Majority of the time, when I feel sick or upset, I go sit by the tree and I feel better almost instantly.

The door opened, and the nurse quietly snuck in, assuming I was still sleeping. She straightened when she saw me up-

right and smiled as she closed the door and came closer to the bed. "All done," she chirped in a blissful tone. She lightly stripped the pieces of tape off of my hand, and slowly tugged the tube away. She wiped my hand off and clicked a button on the large machine. Then she picked up the bucket of sweets and displayed it before me.

Thrilled, I grabbed a large chocolate bar, and looked at it hungrily.

Mama woke, and after a few yawns, she stood and lifted me off of the bed. We made our way to the front, where Mama talked to the counter lady again, and left.

•••

Grace didn't say much during the car ride home; only when I asked her a question. I didn't mind the silence, since I was still being dragged by sleepiness, and was barely able to keep my eyes open. I almost didn't realize my daughter drooping forward. "Gracie," I called, trying not to startle her. But she started to startle me. "Grace." Her head lifted quickly, and a wave of relief flooded over me.

She looked at me with confusion, then put her head against the car door.

"Before you fall back asleep, what do you want to eat?" I yawned.

It took the girl a moment. "I'm not hungry."

Odd. She always had the same answer when I asked that question: spaghetti. "Not hungry?" I repeated aloud, astonished.

Grace shook her head. "I'm tired, Mommy."

"I know, Sweet Pea. But if you sleep now, you won't sleep tonight." Maybe she would. My daughter said nothing else, but her eyes would occasionally open, then close once more.

Once we finally arrived home, my husband greeted us and lifted our child out of the seat.

"What's for dinner?" he asked her with a grin.

"She's not hungry," I explained, exiting the car.

It took him a minute to fully process what I had told him. "Really?"

Grace nodded. She held her head up weakly and looked at the fence that caged our house. "Can I go sit by the tree?"

"Sure, Honey." Her father lowered her to the ground, and she quickly stumbled away with her little legs.

"Maybe it's just the chemo," I suggested. But that probably wasn't it. Chemotherapy effects took a while to appear.

"Hopefully."

We both walked inside, and I sat at the kitchen table. "Chemo is starting to get expensive," I sighed, pressing my hand to my cheek.

My husband looked at me. "Hasn't it always been kinda pricey?" "The cost has been going up."

"Well, I can get another job; one that'll pay decently."

"Then you'll be gone for almost an entire day. You already work eight to five. I don't want Grace to grow up only seeing her dad late at night on weekdays." I grew up hardly seeing my father. He worked all day. When he retired, I was already twenty. And then cancer overtook him.

"What are we supposed to do, then?" My husband asked, sitting across from me. "I don't know. Some type of fundraiser? Put up a GoFundMe page?" "We'll figure it out. Everything will be fine."

It better all be fine. The risk of losing our only daughter had risen within a year. I couldn't even imagine what I'd do if she lost this battle. I looked out the window. Grace was picking flowers that were shaded by the tree's branches and leaves. The sun behind her began to slip away slowly, and the sky was turning pink and purple. "I'll get started on dinner," I mumbled.

•••

I smiled at the cluster of flowers in my fist. Most of them were yellow, and the others were white and pink.

Papa came outside and walked up to me. "Those are such pretty flowers," he complimented. I handed them to him. "How about we put them in a water jar inside?"

I nodded, excited about the idea. Papa took my hand, and we went inside. In the kitchen, Mama was working over the stove. "What's that, Mama?" I asked quizzically.

"Pasta." Mama's tone sounded upset.

I loved pasta, but I wasn't hungry. I didn't want to make Mama even more upset, so I'd try to eat as much as I could.

Which only ended up behind a bit less than half of what was put on my plate.

"Can I be done?" I groaned.

My parents looked at my plate. "Not hungry?" Mama asked.

"Yeah."

"Okay, Honey. Go wash your hands and put your jammies on. Dad or I can help you brush your teeth when we're done."

I stretched one foot off of my chair and onto the ground, then the other. I quickly went into the bathroom, grabbing the white stool and dragging it by the sink. I turned both handles and stuck my hands under the water, rubbing soap on them and rinsing the suds down the drain.

After I finished and put the stool back, I went into my room. Pictures of me, Mama, and Papa lined the walls, along with drawings I had made throughout the years. A smaller-sized bed with pink and purple bedspread was pressed against the corner, with a closet containing toys and a dresser mirroring it. I walked across the white, fuzzy rug that was sprawled in the center of the room and pulled open a drawer from the wardrobe. My dog-speckled pajamas dropped onto the floor next to me, and I changed into them.

Before I could leave my bedroom, Mama walked in with my toothbrush in her hand, holding it horizontally so the toothpaste on top didn't drip onto the floor. She knelt down and started to brush my teeth.

When she finished, she gave me a kiss on the head and said the usual, "Goodnight." I heard Papa call it from down the hall, too.

"I love you," she cooed before standing up and turning on my nightlight.

I crawled into my bed and snuggled under the warm blankets, thankful, since I was beginning to get the chills.

Mama clicked the light switch off, and my room went dark, except for a dim glow that showed itself by the door.

I was so tired, yet I was having trouble sleeping. I felt sick. Not only that, I just felt awful in general. I felt weak and shaky, and my bones and joints felt sore. I closed my eyes and imagined a sheep leap over a fence. *Then another. Then another.* Soon I had counted up to twenty sheep and gave up. Suddenly, when my eyes opened again, I felt even worse. I felt as if I couldn't move. I was trembling so badly I was beginning to wear myself out. *It's probably just the chemo stuff working*, I told myself. I wasn't sure if that was it, but it felt good assuming that.

I closed my eyes again and imagined the olive tree outside. I imagined myself running outside and into the comfort of the tree, huddled under the branch that jutted out of the front. Then it started to feel real. Too real. I could feel the grass blades skimming across my feet.

I felt awful. The worst I'd ever felt before. As I squished myself against the tree, eyes jammed shut as I wished the feelings away, they immediately faltered. I didn't feel sick. I wasn't in pain. I felt amazing. I opened my eyes. I was outside, feeling the best I'd ever felt in my entire life. I turned to the tree and wrapped my arms around it in a hug. "Thank you!" I cried. It had once again saved me from the sicknesses.

I sat there for a while, staring up at the night sky. But when I tried to open my eyes again, to wake myself from this dream, it didn't do anything. They were open. And they were staring at the sky.

All of a sudden, a shrill scream echoed out from the house.

I stood up quickly and ran inside. I ran down the hall and to my room, where I saw Mama kneeling over my bed with her head pressed against something. A body. "Mama?" I went up to her, but she ignored me. I looked at the body. It was me. I giggled, even though I was confused. "Who's that?" Maybe Mama got me a twin, or some life-sized doll of me.

Mama ignored me again. Her sobs grew loud, and she screamed a few more times as she shook the limp frame. Papa darted into the room and sat beside her. Eventually, he began to cry, too.

"What's wrong?" I repeated, louder.

No response.

I grabbed Mama's hand. "Mama, I'm right here." She continued to ignore me. I started to cry. Mama was beginning to worry me. I'd never seen either of them so sad.

"Don't cry," an older, frail voice echoed behind me.

I turned around. An old man stood in the doorway. He had no hair, and glasses. I'd never seen him before. "Who are you?" I sniffed.

"I'm your grandpa Tim, Grace."

My crying had stopped. I thought he wasn't here?

The man's arm extended, outstretching his hand to me. "Come on. We're all waiting for you, little one."

•••

Months had passed. Many months. The house had grown quiet, and neither me nor my husband could make it even halfway down the hallway anymore.

Grace had left us for good; on a night where she seemed fine.

I felt numb. I knew I was never going to see her again, but part of me still had hope.

Hope that she wasn't dead, and she was still here. And maybe she really was still here.

Because sometimes I'd still see her.

Outside.

My daughter.

Sitting under the olive branch.

Paige Griffin is a fourteen-year-old from Lake Linden-Hubbell Middle School. She is a digital and traditional artist and writer. She has placed second in a school and district spelling bee. She isn't sure at the moment as to what she wants to do when she's older, but she knows it will be in the art field.

Help Sell
The U.P. Reader!

◆❖◆

The popularity of the *U.P. Reader* is growing, but we need it to grow more.

Help us sell the *U.P. Reader* by selling the Reader alongside your other books. The *U.P. Reader* at its wholesale price allows those who wish to carry it to make a nice profit on the sales. Bookstores and individuals can all benefit from helping the U.P. Reader grow.

If you have writing that has been published in the *U.P. Reader*, you should be selling copies of the Reader alongside your other work. This not only helps get exposure for your writing but for all the others that were accepted alongside yours. Part of the mission of the *U.P. Reader* is to get the many voices of the writers of the UPPAA in a single publication so that readers would have a place to find and sample the incredible talent that makes up the authors and poets of the Upper Peninsula.

Taking a few *Readers* to an event can make the difference in selling. Those who have been selling the U.P. Reader have seen good sales and considerable interest in the publication from readers and customers. Many customers ask the seller if they have a piece in the book to sign it. As the U.P. Reader is helping you as a writer, you can be helping the *U.P. Reader*.

Do you have local booksellers in your area? Encourage them to stock the *U.P. Reader*. Bookstores that are selling the Reader are seeing brisk sales. Many of the bookstores have restocked their issues several times and are saying how much they enjoy them. They are profitable and returnable. The *U.P. Reader* is a win-win situation for bookstores.

Take a copy of the *U.P. Reader* to your child's English or Language Arts teacher. The Dandelion Cottage Award is open to all children in U.P. schools and homeschool. There is never a fee to participate!

Back issues of the *U.P. Reader* are also still available. They can still be ordered right alongside the new issue and can be combined to sell as a set. There are many who still haven't discovered the *U.P. Reader* yet, and a package set is a nice way to introduce them to the joys of reading a *Reader*. These can still be purchased wholesale just like the current issue.

There are hardcover versions of the *U.P. Reader* as well. These are beautiful bound versions of the *U.P. Reader* that are a wonderful keepsake for the real *U.P. Reader* fan. Again, these can be ordered wholesale and sold right alongside the paperback versions.

To order, go to UPReader.org/publications on the web and put in your order. Contributing authors will be emailed a discount code and their orders will be discounted to the wholesale price (50% Off!).

Please help us, help you make the *U.P. Reader* a success!

Come join
UPPAA Online!

The UPPAA maintains an online presence on several websites and social media areas. To get the most out of your UPPAA membership, be sure to visit, "like," and share these destinations and posts whenever possible!

Web Sites
- **www.UPPAA.org**: learn about meetings, publicity opportunities, publicize your own author events, add your book to the catalog page, read newsletter archive.
- **www.UPReader.org**: complete details about deadlines, submission guidelines, how to place a print advertisement, where to buy U.P. Reader locally, and more.
- **www.UPNotable.com**: all the information about the U.P. Notable Book Club meetings
- **www.UPBookReview.com**: publishing 36 reviews of books by U.P. writers or about the U.P. every year!

Facebook Pages
- **UPPAA**: www.facebook.com/UPSISU/ —OR—type in **@UPSISU** into the Facebook "search" bar
- **UP Reader**: www.facebook.com/upreaders/ —OR— type in **@UPreader** into the Facebook "search" bar

Twitter

Twitter
- Message to **@UP_Authors** or visit https://twitter.com/UP_Authors

Comprehensive Index of U.P. Reader Volumes 1 through 6

CPSIA information can be obtained
at www.ICGtesting.com
Printed in the USA
JSHW010121270822
29664JS00001BA/2